USER-CENTERED
APPLICATION DESIGN
WITH VISUAL BASIC™

User-Centered Application Design with Visual Basic™

Peter D. Varhol

John Wiley & Sons, Inc.

New York • Chichester • Brisbane • Toronto • Singapore

Publisher: Katherine Schowalter
Editor: Philip Sutherland
Assistant Editor: Allison Roarty
Assistant Managing Editor: Angela Murphy
Text Design & Composition: Benchmark Productions

Library of Congress Cataloging-in-Publication Data:
Varhol, Peter.
    User-centered application design with Visual Basic / Peter Varhol.
        p.   cm.
    Includes index.
    ISBN 0-471-11522-3 (paper : alk. paper)
    1. BASIC (Computer program language) 2. Microsoft Visual BASIC.
3. Application software.   I. Title.
QA76.73.B3V37   1995
005.265--dc20   95-14640

Printed in the United States of America

10 9 8 7 6 5 4 3 2 1

CONTENTS

1

AN INTRODUCTION

TO VISUAL BASIC

Microsoft's Visual Basic is at the forefront of an emerging movement in software development—the use of graphical components as building blocks for applications that depend upon a great deal of user interaction in order to accomplish a task. The user interaction takes place at the level of the user interface, and frequently involves the use of graphics. Tools that make use of graphics in this way are often called visual languages. There are many different types of visual languages, but little agreement as to what constitutes a visual language. Microsoft's Visual Basic, one of the most popular of this class of languages, is a hybrid of visual components and a special implementation of the Basic programming language.

The typical Visual Basic application consists of one or more forms containing several graphical user controls. These controls may include buttons of various types, scroll bars, check boxes and text boxes, gauges, and plots. When the user manipulates one or more of these controls, the application performs a task in response. Most of the time the result is visible to the user in the form of a change to the control or to other parts of the interface, although there are times when it may not be. The result might be the displaying of a different form, or the opening of a dialog box, or the appearance of text or graphics in a window.

AN OBJECT-ORIENTED APPROACH TO SOFTWARE DEVELOPMENT

Visual Basic's approach to application development is related to the type of programming known as *object-oriented*. Object-oriented approaches to application development, which are beginning to move into the mainstream of software development, treat programs as if they were collections of interrelated modules, each communicating with one another. An object is an encapsulation of both code and data. These components both define what it means to be that particular type of object, and how that object behaves. For example, contained within a window object is the code that draws the window on the screen, as well as information pertaining to the type and size of the window.

There is often confusion between the terms *object, class,* and *instance.* The object itself is an abstraction, rather than an actual piece of code or a display graphic. The object is a template from which the user declares instances. An *instance* is the realization of that object template that can be directly manipulated by the programmer. For example, an icon on the display is an instance of the object that represents that icon.

A *class* is a collection of similar objects. In many object-oriented systems, classes are related to one another in a hierarchy. For example, at the top level of the hierarchy might be a single System Object class. At the next level of the hierarchy might be the Window class, which contains information on the variety of different windows that can be displayed on the screen. The next level deals with specific windows, such as the Resizable Window, Scroll Window, and Dialog Window.

The reason for the establishment of this hierarchy is to implement the object-oriented concept of *inheritance*. In most object-oriented systems, it is possible for classes at the lower levels of the hierarchy to inherit characteristics that *belong* to classes at a higher level. This hierarchy of object classes constitutes a library of constructs that can be utilized by the programmer to create new applications.

If the programmer using an object-oriented approach wants to use a window in an application, rather than writing the appropriate code from scratch, he or she can simply create another instance of the appropriate window class from the object hierarchy. This is a complete implementation of a window that can be used in an application as is, or modified to suit the particular needs of the application.

Many purists insist that only a product that has been designed and developed from the bottom up in an object-oriented manner, using all of the features associated with the technology, can be considered object-oriented. Others, especially those with a stake in existing products, can be much less exacting in their definitions.

Generally, there are a few guidelines in determining whether and to what extent a particular software application is object-oriented:

1. **Can it support the creation of new types of objects?** Many products come with several predefined objects. If these predefined objects can be modified and combined to create a new type with new behaviors,

it is much closer to the traditional definition of object-oriented. For example, an application development environment utilizing a library of seven or eight predefined object types does not allow these types to be combined to create an entirely new object type.

2. **Does it support inheritance of characteristics along a hierarchy of objects?** Inheritance is a critical characteristic of an object-oriented environment, because it enables definitions and procedures of more general objects to apply to more specific objects at lower levels of the hierarchy. This means an easier development effort and a more consistent application of object behaviors.

3. **Can the object structure encapsulate both the definition of the object itself and the procedures describing the permitted behaviors of the object?** For example, the C struct and the Pascal record both permit the definition of a structure that might be termed an object. However, it is not possible for this structure to contain the code that defines how the object might be manipulated. This is important from a software engineering standpoint, to be able to create objects that can be reused in other projects.

4. **Is the user presented with graphical screen objects that are patterned after real life constructs?** While the underlying program model may not be object-oriented, object-oriented displays have been shown to be highly useful for novice users and for the productivity of all users. In fact, a recent study by an independent market research group has indicated that users are more likely to make use of an application's more advanced and difficult-to-use features if the display is object-oriented.

VISUAL BASIC AND OBJECTS

Visual Basic satisfies two of the preceding four object criteria. It encapsulates both the code and data necessary to define its objects and their behaviors, and it lets the user manipulate graphical screen objects to create new applications. The graphical components within Visual Basic can be thought of as objects, in that they contain both data and the code necessary to manipulate that data. However, Visual Basic as it exists today is not strictly object-oriented, primarily because, except under special circumstances, it lacks the characteristic of inheritance and has only a very limited ability to create new types of objects. That is, new components can't easily be created and they can't inherit any of the characteristics or behaviors of existing components.

Figure 1.1 shows an example of Visual Basic components arranged on the computer screen. Each of the buttons, boxes, scroll bars, and labels contains the resources needed to accept events created by the user, along with a code editor for the application developer to write code to respond to the events. Visual Basic defines each of these components as an instance of the class of controls found available to use. Although this description is not strictly exact in object terminology, it is a useful way of picturing how Visual Basic components, or controls, as they are referred to in Visual Basic, are used.

The lack of inheritance in components, or the ability to easily create new components, does not seriously affect the ability of Visual Basic to produce highly sophisticated and useful applications. Many experienced software developers have turned to Visual Basic to easily create Windows-based graphical user interfaces, while many novices have been introduced to Windows programming with the Visual Basic approach.

THE EVOLUTION OF VISUAL BASIC

When Visual Basic first appeared on the market, it was considered by most to be too slow and too resource-intensive to be useful in commercial and custom application development. It also included only a small number of

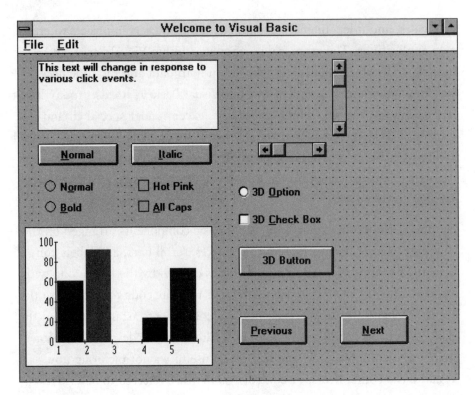

Figure 1.1 Samples of Visual Basic controls.

the control classes that are available for use today. However, with subsequent versions, Microsoft improved its performance and added features that made it a viable tool for the design of Windows-based applications. At the same time, the performance of the average desktop PC more than doubled, and large amounts of memory and hard disk space became standard equipment. All of these changes made Visual Basic a compelling alternative to traditional languages for all aspects of application development.

The result is that Visual Basic is increasingly being used in many different types of software development environments, and many applications produced with Visual Basic are considered of high enough quality, and fast enough, that they are virtually indistinguishable from applications created with traditional programming languages. Many commercial applications on the market today use Visual Basic for at least part of the application.

Visual Basic has become especially popular for the creation of graphical user interfaces. The underlying application may often be written in another language entirely, while the user sees only the graphical user interface developed in Visual Basic. This enables the application developers to modify the user interface quickly in response to customer needs, without changing the computational engine. However, the uses of Visual Basic go far beyond the development of graphical user interfaces, into entire applications and into self-contained components that can be used for a wide variety of purposes.

A User-Centered Approach

With traditional programming languages such as C or Pascal, there is rarely a direct relationship between the quality and quantity of the programmer's code and the appearance or usefulness of the resulting application. The code may be fast, or efficient, or even free of bugs, but this was not necessarily reflected in the quality of the application or its acceptance in the market. This is because the skills necessary to produce good code are not the same skills necessary to produce a good application.

These may seem like contradictory statements, but let us consider an obvious example: Microsoft's MS-DOS. As an operating system, it has achieved extraordinary popularity and continues to be considered a superb technical feat. Yet, most DOS users consider using the operating system a chore to be tolerated as the necessary route to the desired application. Some even use batch files to bypass it entirely so that they have to deal only with their application.

While in some ways the appearance of MS-DOS was the result of hardware limitations, it also reflected poor decisions by the developers about the information the product gave to the users, and resulted in a set of obscure commands and options that taxed users' memories and patience. (My personal favorite was the "Are you sure (Y/N)" message that was finally eliminated in DOS 5.0. Without even a clue as to what you were supposed to be sure of, this message intimidated many novice DOS users, or caused them to perform actions that they didn't want to.) This is not meant to criticize Microsoft or the original developers of MS-DOS; at the time, little was known about who would be using the operating system, or about the principles of good user interface design.

Visual Basic, on the other hand, is a language that puts less emphasis on the programming skills of the developer and more on the design skills and the resulting appearance and behavior of the application. Further, the requisite types of skills are not in program design or coding, but in user interface design. Programming skills are still important, since writing code is still required for virtually all applications, but you write less code, and less complicated code, with Visual Basic. The successful Visual Basic developer may be more adept in user interface design and layout than in programming. This means that application developers have to acquire an entirely different set of skills in order to make effective use of Visual Basic.

This characteristic means that there is a more direct relationship between the developer's new skills and the value of the resulting software product. If the developer can design an application's user interface that makes good use of Visual Basic's strengths, supplements the skills of the user, and accomplishes a worthwhile task, then it will probably be a popular application (of course, this does not take into account business factors, such as marketing, pricing, or advertising).

WHY USER-CENTERED APPLICATIONS?

Visual Basic is not an appropriate tool for every type of application. Given its heavy emphasis on graphics and user screens, it is not a good choice for many embedded systems or other types of applications that don't require user interaction. It is also not appropriate for applications that are computationally intensive or that have to manage memory or other system resources carefully. The Basic language has never been known for computational efficiency or for working close to the hardware, and Visual Basic continues in those traditions.

However, an increasing number of applications do require the user to be actively involved in performing a task. And the better an application is at helping the user, the more likely it is to be successful. This may not have been the case a few years ago, when the user community as a whole was relatively sophisticated, and only a few applications of any type were on the market. However, more recently, the commercial market for many types of applications has become very crowded, with dozens of selections possible for more widespread uses. Only the best ones have the chance to become a force in the market.

The user community is also much less patient with poorly designed software than it was in the past. Part of the reason is that there are so many more alternatives. More important, the user community is much larger, with a greater number of novices who are primarily interested in using the computer as a tool to do a job. This category of user is subsequently less computer-savvy than the typical user of the past. Today's users are less willing to spend a lot of time learning how to use computer software before they can even begin to apply it to their tasks. These people are not less intelligent or less motivated than users in the past; they are merely focused on their task, and less focused or motivated to acquiring general computer skills. They view the computer as a tool to serve their needs in other areas. The better the tool, the more likely they are to use it.

Further, Visual Basic and similar development tools are critical to the growth of the computer industry as a whole. Easy-to-use and compelling applications serve to sell computers, rather than the other way around. Users, especially novice users, rarely buy a computer and then decide what they want to do with it. Rather, users perceive the need to do a particular job, or perform a certain task, and purchase the computer and software that will serve that need.

This means that easy-to-use applications that assist users in doing a job have the potential to increase the overall number of computer users. This is good for the computer industry as a whole, and good for your application if it is truly useful to your users. Visual Basic can help us move one step closer to that ideal.

HOW VISUAL BASIC WORKS

Visual Basic works primarily as what is called an *event-driven system*. That is, when the user pushes a button or performs some other type of screen activity, Visual Basic generates an event, or a signal. This is where your Basic code comes in. You write a Basic subroutine to interpret the event and perform the action that the user intended. For example, pushing a button may cause a part of the display to change color, as shown in Figures 1.2a and b.

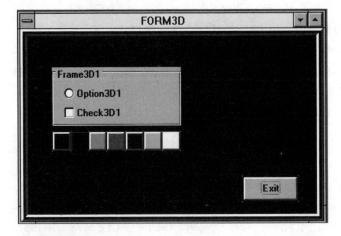

■■■■■■■■ **Figure 1.2a** Using buttons to change display characteristics.

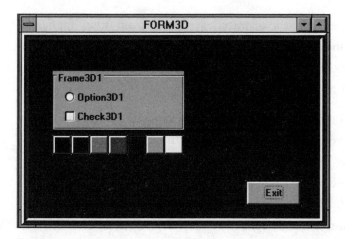

Figure 1.2b Using buttons to change display characteristics.

Each Visual Basic control includes a series of predefined events to which it will respond, such as a mouse click, a double mouse click, or a dragging operation. Each control also has a list of properties that describe and set a variety of characteristics for that control, such as its color, size, caption, and whether the control is visible.

All of this starts to give you an idea of how Visual Basic differs from a traditional programming language. Until the advent of sophisticated graphics and windowing systems, developers gave users a limited set of choices of tasks to perform, and gave them explicit (or sometimes not-so-explicit) instructions on how to perform those tasks. "Type the number of the task you wish to perform" was a common prompt in many applications. The application would wait for the user to type an appropriate character or characters, then interpret that character and go off and perform the task signified by that character. The program would literally stop running while it waited for the user to perform such an action.

Event-driven applications, on the other hand, are always running the program. They have to be, in order to update the position of the mouse pointer on the display as the mouse is moved by the user, and to accept and interpret messages from the operating system or from other applications. Such applications must allow for a much wider range of user actions, yet still be able to translate these actions into an appropriate and useful task for the application to perform.

The distinction between traditional methods of sequential, function-driven programming and event-driven programming can be one of the most difficult things for a new Visual Basic application developer to learn. In the event-driven style, the inside of an application can appear to be unorganized and disjointed. Much of the code is responsible for intercepting and processing events, and is mostly related to the screen objects. The nice thing about Visual Basic is that it performs most of the routine event processing for you. You don't, for example, have to worry about locating the mouse pointer, or determining whether the user clicked the mouse button once or twice.

Consider the following small Visual Basic application in Figures 1.3a and b that display text in a Visual Basic text box. The command button used to display the text in this application responds when you click on it.

Making these changes happen is simply a matter of changing the value of the properties for the various display components as a result of the different events. The events that a control can respond to are already defined as

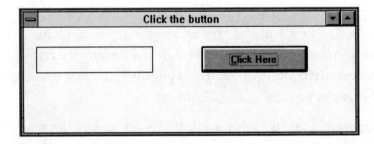

■■■■■■■ **Figure 1.3a** Using the mouse to create a Click event in a command button.

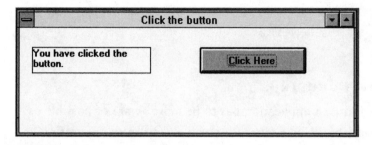

▬▬▬▬▬▬▬ **Figure 1.3b** Using the mouse to create a Click event in a command button.

a part of the control itself. Figure 1.4 shows an example of an event box within the command button control.

The only code that has to be written to accomplish these tasks is to change the value of the properties affected. This is done with a simple assignment statement in the subroutine that handles that particular event. The following code simply changes the FontBold property of the **lblTest** text box to True; in other words, it changes the font of the text in the box to boldface:

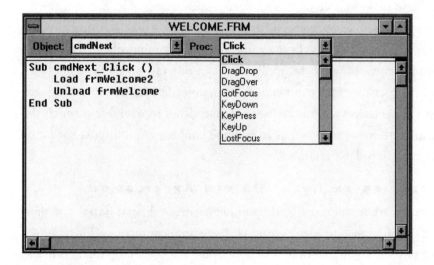

▬▬▬▬▬▬▬ **Figure 1.4** Events to which a command button can respond.

```
Sub optBold_Click ()
        lblTest.FontBold = True
End Sub
```

CUEING THE USER IN

Because an event-driven application has to be more aware of possible user actions, the design of the user interface on an event-driven application has to provide the user with a large amount of information on how the application works, and on what activity to perform next in order to accomplish a task. We can refer to this type of information as *cues,* since the application effectively cues the user on what to do next.

The ability to provide cues has led to increasing use of prompts, context-sensitive help, hypertext help, and balloon help (the different methods of providing online help are discussed in more detail in later chapters). But there is more to good user interface design than providing online instructions and assistance. The user interface itself has to point the way for the user to accomplish the task.

How does it do this? There are several ways. First, the interface can be designed to make simple tasks as unambiguous as possible. Second, the next step in a sequence required for a more complex task should be readily apparent. There should be little or no doubt in the mind of the user how to accomplish most of what the application can do, and a variety of cues within the user interface can make this possible. The user should be given enough information within the user interface itself to navigate through the application, but not so much as to become confusing. I'll discuss such cues in more detail in later chapters.

DEVELOPING AN EVENT-DRIVEN APPLICATION

However, there is still more to the unique nature of Visual Basic. The most important difference resides in how you, the applications developer, view the purpose of an application, and how you go about designing and implementing that application. Most software developers focus on the tasks that the application will perform, and secondarily on how the user can take advantage of the application to do a job.

Traditional programming languages supported this form of application development through the ease by which they can be used to code task-oriented algorithms. This resulted in applications that could do some amazing things if only the user could coax those things out of the chaff. And, in many cases, they were not helpful for tasks that had not been envisioned by their own developers.

Visual Basic, on the other hand, is at its best when used for laying out the user interface, letting developers focus on how the user will interact with the application. It is somewhat less good at task-oriented computational algorithms, but the combination of better-performing computers and the ability of Visual Basic to work with code written in other languages makes this deficiency less important than it was in the past.

Instead, Visual Basic is a true programming language for the 1990s. Its strengths include its user-centered approach to application development, a robust library of user interface components, and a programming language familiar to just about anyone with experience in software. The environment supports the rapid design and development of sophisticated applications that can meet a wide variety of needs.

THE VISUAL BASIC DEVELOPMENT ENVIRONMENT

Launching Visual Basic displays a worksheet, or form, in Visual Basic parlance. Figure 1.5 shows the opening display. The form, in the center of the display, is the background of the user's window when the completed application is running. Forms are usually used as a kind of storyboard to position other user interface components. Applications can consist of a single form, or they can be multiple forms, each with a different function.

The form, and every other user interface component, has a set of properties associated with it. In the case of the form, these properties are displayed in

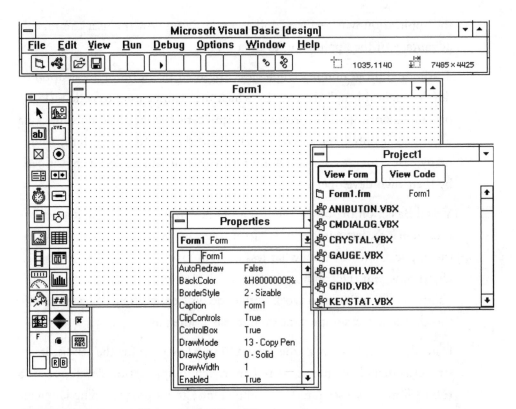

Figure 1.5 The opening Visual Basic screen.

a separate window. The properties vary, depending on the type of component; a form, for example, may have a particular execution state associated with it, whereas a radio button will not. If you have multiple components on a form, clicking on a particular component will display its properties in the Properties window (Figure 1.6).

The window on the left side of the display is the toolbox, which contains the set of user interface and other components that can be placed on the form. The buttons on the toolbox correspond to the type of component that will be painted on the form (Figure 1.7). These are the major building blocks for Visual Basic applications.

The last window available on the opening Visual Basic display is the Project window, which manages all of the files that comprise a Visual Basic

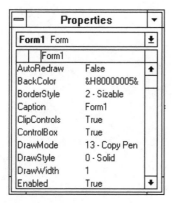

Figure 1.6 The Properties window.

application (Figure 1.8). These may include forms, Basic language code, and Visual Basic custom controls, or VBXs. This makes it easy to keep track of and work on the many different files that are used by a Visual Basic application.

Figure 1.7 The toolbox.

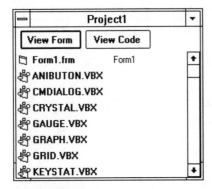

■■■■■■**Figure 1.8** The Project window.

Two other windows are not automatically opened when you launch Visual Basic, but are available through the Windows menu. The first is the Color Palette (Figure 1.9), which lets you change the color scheme on forms and components, or create your own color scheme. The second is the Menu Design window (Figure 1.10). This window provides a set of tools for the creation of pull-down menus on the top of a form.

All of these facilities will be used to help design and construct user-centered applications throughout this book.

A QUICK TOUR OF VISUAL BASIC FEATURES

The Toolbox

Visual Basic incorporates a wide variety of visual controls and components to make the development of sophisticated applications easy. Each of the

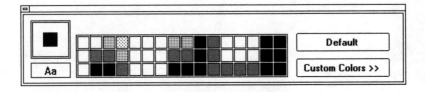

■■■■■■**Figure 1.9** The Color Palette window.

▬▬▬▬**Figure 1.10** The Menu Design window.

buttons in the toolbox provides a component that can be placed on a form and used as a part of any application. Among the most commonly used components are:

Command button. A command button is selected by the user to begin, interrupt, or end an activity being performed by the application. When chosen, a command button appears pushed in, and as a result is sometimes called a *pushbutton*.

Option button. An option button displays an option that can be turned on or off. Option buttons are usually used as part of an option group (defined by a Visual Basic Frame control) to display multiple choices from which the user can select only one.

Check box. A check box displays an X when selected; when selected again, the X disappears, clearing the box. Use this control to give the user a True/False or Yes/No option in an application. You can use check boxes in groups (defined by Frames) to display multiple choices from which the user can select one or more.

Text and Picture boxes. A text box control is sometimes called an *edit field* or *edit control*, and can display information entered by you at design time, entered by the user, or assigned to the control in your Basic code at run time. A picture box, in contrast, can display a graphic from a bitmap, icon, or Windows metafile. It displays only as much of the graphic as fits into the rectangle that you've drawn when creating the picture box on the form.

Scroll bar. Scroll bars provide easy navigation through a long list of items or a large amount of information in a text box or on a form. They also can provide a way of viewing the current position in the box or on the form. You can also use a scroll bar to input a value, or as an indicator of speed or quantity. For example, you can use it to set a quantitative value that is an input to another process.

Label. A label is a control that is normally used to display text that the user can't change while the application is running. You might want to use this to provide a user prompt, or to label a control.

The toolbox is customizable through the use of Visual Basic custom controls, or VBXs, which are discussed in more detail later in this book. VBXs can be loaded as parts of individual projects, as described below. Figure 1.11 shows a common toolbox configuration. This particular toolbox is the default when you load Visual Basic Professional.

If you are using Visual Basic custom controls, or VBXs (see Chapter 10 for a more complete description of VBXs and how to develop them), they will also mount on the toolbox when you open an application. You control what loads when you launch Visual Basic through an AUTOLOAD.MAK file. This is a simple text file that tells Visual Basic what components are loaded for each project. For your own projects,

Figure 1.11 A toolbox with several custom controls loaded.

Visual Basic will help you determine the contents of this file, depending on what files and components you create and use for a project, or you can change it manually by editing the file. In a sense, it is similar to a make file, commonly used by traditional programming languages to keep track of program files and to manage the application compilation process.

The Visual Basic Menu Bar

The File Menu

The primary method of managing the development of a Visual Basic application is through the project. The project consists of all files that make up an application. The files, whether they are forms or Basic modules, are stored separately on the hard disk. However, they are managed as a project, which is represented on disk as a .MAK file.

This is analogous to the make files used in the development of C language programs, except that this file is usually created automatically by Visual Basic and it contains none of the complicated control instructions of a C make file.

Several of the menu items in the File menu, shown in Figure 1.12, are for manipulating projects, letting you create a new project, open an existing project, or save a project. This menu lets you create new forms or add existing forms to a project, and import data from text files into the open project. It also keeps track of the last four open projects so that you can open one of these projects directly, rather than going through the File Open dialog box.

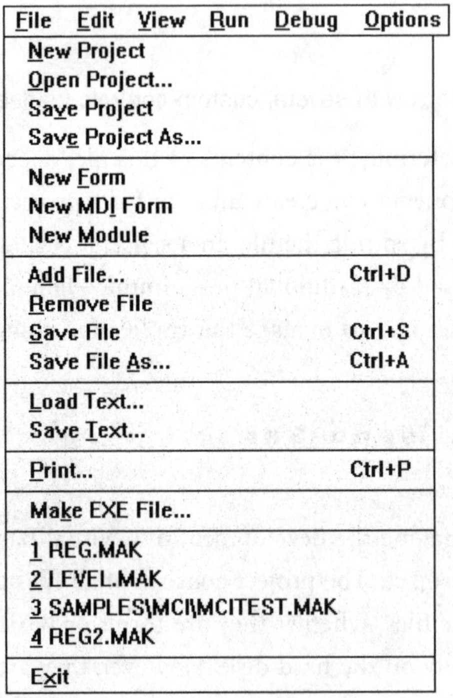

File	Edit	View	Run	Debug	Options

New Project	
Open Project...	
Save Project	
Save Project As...	
New Form	
New MDI Form	
New Module	
Add File...	Ctrl+D
Remove File	
Save File	Ctrl+S
Save File As...	Ctrl+A
Load Text...	
Save Text...	
Print...	Ctrl+P
Make EXE File...	
1 REG.MAK	
2 LEVEL.MAK	
3 SAMPLES\MCI\MCITEST.MAK	
4 REG2.MAK	
Exit	

■■■■■■■**Figure 1.12** The File menu.

The Edit Menu

The Edit menu, shown in Figure 1.13, works in much the same way as the Edit menus of other Windows applications. It includes the Cut, Copy, and Paste selections, which let you take code, display icons, and graphic images from one location and move or copy them to another. It also includes the Paste Link selection, which establishes a dynamic or *hot link* between data in a Visual Basic application and a separate application. A hot link, also known as a Dynamic Data Exchange (DDE), lets you paste data from one application file to another, and have that data updated across the link when it is changed in the original file.

There are also Edit menu items that work specifically in the code editors for screen objects and for Basic code modules. These include text find and replace facilities, and the Undo and Redo commands, which reverse and repeat the last action taken, respectively.

```
 Edit   View   Run   Debug
 Undo            Ctrl+Z
 Redo
 Cut             Ctrl+X
 Copy            Ctrl+C
 Paste           Ctrl+V
 Paste Link
 Delete          Del
 Find...         Ctrl+F
 Find Next       F3
 Find Previous   Shift+F3
 Replace...      Ctrl+R
 Bring to Front  Ctrl+=
 Send to Back    Ctrl+-
 Align to Grid
```

▬▬▬▬**Figure 1.13** The Edit menu.

The last set of commands in the Edit menu enables the developer to move windows and other objects to the front or back of the display. These are necessary because of the forms-based nature of Visual Basic; the many forms and windows that can be open at one time make it necessary to have a way to quickly jump from one to another.

The View Menu

The commands in the View menu, shown in Figure 1.14, help you navigate code that you write for your application. Since most of the Visual Basic code is associated with objects and events, it tends to be scattered in many different locations in an application. This makes it difficult to follow the logic in an application, to debug it, and to modify it. The View commands let you move easily between procedures, even if they are located in different objects, or designed to respond to different events. You can also view procedures that are called by other procedures, even if they're in different objects. For example, a procedure responding to a mouse click may also want to transfer the focus of the application to a particular form, so it may call the GotFocus to accomplish other event-driven activities.

Through the View menu, you can also turn on or off the toolbar. Many people prefer working entirely from the pull-down menus at the top of the screen, and removing the toolbar gives more screen space for designing an application. Whether you keep the toolbar turned on or off is a matter of personal preference.

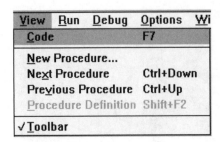

■■■■■■ **Figure 1.14** The View menu.

The Run Menu

Running your application within the Visual Basic development environment offers several advantages. You can run it at selected times during the development process to test a particular implementation, or to see how a particular component works. This also lets you show the application to users while you are still working on it, in order to solicit feedback. Unlike many traditional languages, you need not go through a Compile-Link-Load cycle in order to look at your application while it's running.

The Run menu, shown in Figure 1.15, offers three options: Start, End, and Restart. Start closes all of the open forms and files, and begins your application at its designated starting point. Once the application is running, this menu item turns into Break, which lets you interrupt execution at any point in time. End stops execution and closes the application, returning you to the development environment. Restart lets you continue to run an application that is already running but has been stopped by an error or a break. It will reset all of the application's variables to their initial values before continuing.

The Debug Menu

Through the Debug menu, shown in Figure 1.16, Visual Basic has a number of interactive facilities for identifying and locating errors in your application. These include statement and procedure steps, breakpoints, and watch commands.

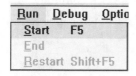

■■■■■■■■ **Figure 1.15** The Run menu.

Debug	Options	Window	Help
Add Watch...			
Instant Watch...		Shift+F9	
Edit Watch...		Ctrl+W	
Calls...		Ctrl+L	
Single Step		F8	
Procedure Step		Shift+F8	
Toggle Breakpoint		F9	
Clear All Breakpoints			
Set Next Statement			
Show Next Statement			

■■■ **Figure 1.16** The Debug menu.

All of these commands enable you to examine Visual Basic code a line or a procedure at a time, or even at locations that you define yourself through the use of breakpoints. At every break or step, you can also examine the values of any or all variables that have relevance at that point in the application execution. The values and any error messages appear in a separate debug window available from the Windows menu.

The Options Menu

The Options menu, shown in Figure 1.17, gives you two types of options: *environment options* and *project options*. The environment options describe a number of characteristics you can use to customize your development environment. This is a large collection of attributes, including the font style and size, tab size, colors of different types of text and background, and characteristics of the grid used to position objects on a form.

There are only three project options. The first lets you specify command-line options that are included as a part of the executable file in the properties

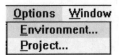

■■■ **Figure 1.17** The Options menu.

selection when the application is configured as a Windows icon. The second specifies the first form that appears whenever the user launches the executable application. The third identifies the name of the Help file that accompanies the executable application.

The environment options refer only to the environment you see as the application developer, and enable you to set up Visual Basic so that you can make the most effective use of it. The project options are for the convenience of the user; you set these up to assist the user in running your application.

The Windows Menu

As mentioned previously, the Windows menu, shown in Figure 1.18, provides menu access to all of the various windows that make up the Visual Basic development environment. These include the Project window, the Properties window, the Color Palette, the Debug window, and the Menu Design window. Selecting one of these commands will bring that window to the front of the display.

The Help Menu

The Help menu, shown in Figure 1.19, is similar to the user-oriented Help menus found in most Windows applications. It consists of a Contents command, a Search command, a set of Visual Basic tutorials, and an About Microsoft Visual Basic . . . box. The Help commands can be useful in

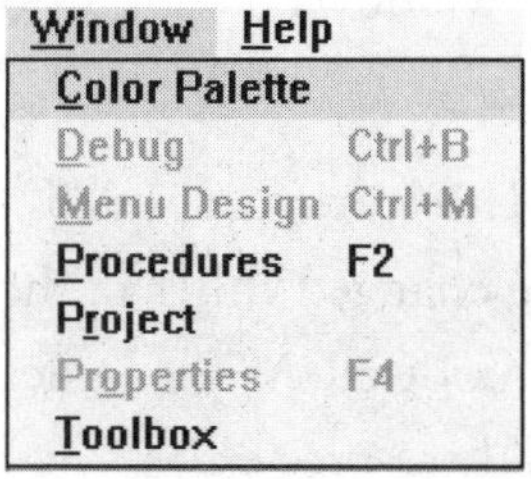

Window	Help
Color Palette	
Debug	Ctrl+B
Menu Design	Ctrl+M
Procedures	F2
Project	
Properties	F4
Toolbox	

Figure 1.18 The Windows menu.

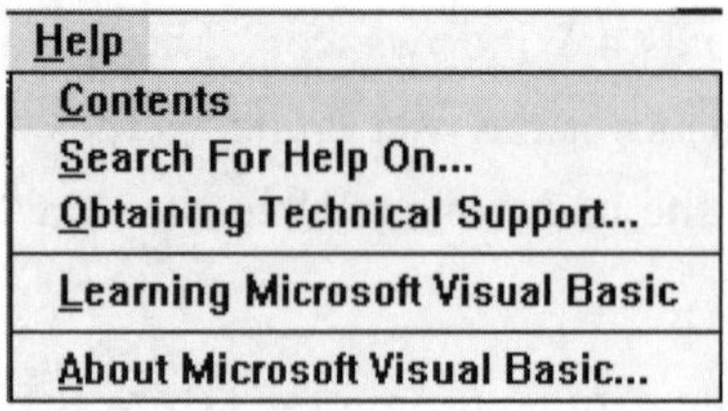

Help
<u>C</u>ontents
<u>S</u>earch For Help On...
<u>O</u>btaining Technical Support...
<u>L</u>earning Microsoft Visual Basic
<u>A</u>bout Microsoft Visual Basic...

■■■■■■■■■ **Figure 1.19** The Help menu.

looking up the function of a particular command, or to reference one or more Visual Basic concepts. This set of tutorials can be useful in introducing a novice user to Visual Basic, but do not take a user beyond a brief introduction to the development environment.

Overall, Visual Basic has one of the most comprehensive and useful Help facilities available for any application. Many of the Help topics also include code examples that you can cut out of the Help file and paste directly into your application. You will have to refer to the paper manuals only for specialized information or for certain custom controls.

ASSEMBLING A VISUAL BASIC APPLICATION

All Visual Basic applications start out with a form. Some applications may have multiple forms, but all have at least one form. In a running application, the form presents the active window to the user. In multiform applications, you may have multiple windows that individually become active while the application is being used, or you may have windows nested inside one another.

Each form has certain properties associated with it. These properties define the appearance and behavior of the form, and can be changed either in the development environment or in the running application itself. While building your application, you can set or change many of these properties through the Properties window. Depending on the particular property, you

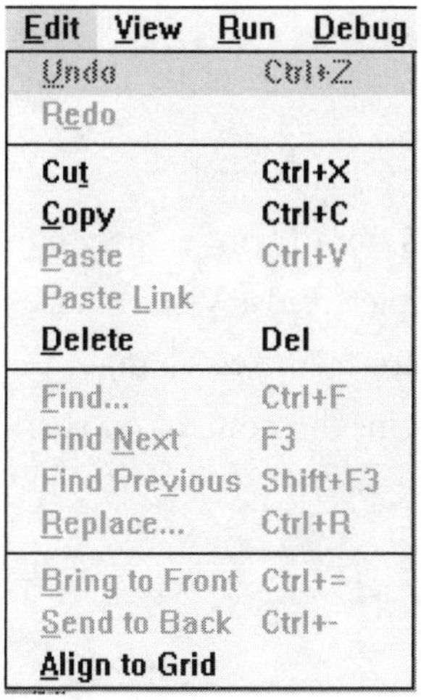

```
 Edit   View   Run   Debug
  Undo              Ctrl+Z
  Redo

  Cut               Ctrl+X
  Copy              Ctrl+C
  Paste             Ctrl+V
  Paste Link
  Delete            Del

  Find...           Ctrl+F
  Find Next         F3
  Find Previous     Shift+F3
  Replace...        Ctrl+R

  Bring to Front    Ctrl+=
  Send to Back      Ctrl+-
  Align to Grid
```

■■■■■■**Figure 1.20** Grayed-out menu items that cannot currently be used.

can either click on it to bring up the options available, or simply type in a new value. In the case of colors, the property is expressed in a hexadecimal value so that each of the many colors available does not have to be identified by a separate name.

Alternatively, you can define or change a property while the application is running, in response to some user action. This represents a powerful way of communicating information to the user, and to make the application more user-centered. For example, you can change a color or a font size or style to send the user a message. In Figure 1.20, actions that make no sense within the context of a particular use are grayed out, prohibiting the user from taking those actions. In this case, the user cannot paste an object onto the screen until there is something to be pasted.

The method of changing a property within a form, or of any other screen object, from within the running application is to reference the screen object, then the property, and assign it a new value. It is a simple Basic assignment statement that refers to the appropriate components and properties. It takes the general form:

```
object.property = value
```

For example:

```
Form1.FontItalic = True
```

This will italicize the font in any text found on the form Form1. Frequently, you reference the properties of controls on a form, rather than the form's properties themselves. If you have multiple forms, Visual Basic may not know which control on which form you are trying to change. When this is the case, you have to reference the form, the control on the form, and then the property:

```
form.object.property = value
```

For example:

```
Form1.Command1.FontItalic = True
```

will italicize the font in the text found on the Command1 command button on Form1.

WHERE TO PUT THE CODE

Visual Basic has several places in which to insert code. Each screen object, including a form, includes its own special procedures, or subprograms, that respond to events, such as mouse clicks, on that object. Each form also has a general section that provides definitions and procedures available to any object residing on that form. Last, Visual Basic also includes modules, or separate groups of code, that apply across all objects in the application.

The code sections of screen objects are accessible through the object itself, by double-clicking on it. You are presented with a window for editing, along with two pull-down menus. The first gives you access to any object on the current form, and the second shows you a list of the events that the object will respond to. If you select one of these events, a code shell will appear in the editor window, letting you write Basic code to perform an action in response to that event. The code window associated with a screen object is shown in Figure 1.21.

Where you place your code depends on what you want it to do. Code such as the **Form1.FontItalic = True** in the previous section will likely be associated with an event occurring in an object on Form1, such as a mouse click on an Italics button. Code placed in the general section of a form, or in a module (represented with a .BAS extension in a Visual Basic project), will probably not be designed to respond to events, since it would not be clear which screen object the event applies to. This code is usually global in nature, in that it can be referenced from all objects on a form, or from all objects across the application. This code is likely to be called from multiple controls as a subroutine to perform the same task from many different locations.

Events are the key to writing Visual Basic applications. This book will not exhaustively describe all of the events that every Visual Basic application will respond to, and all the properties in all of the controls. Rather, it will describe some of the more commonly used events and describe how many of the event handling procedures work when discussing individual development techniques.

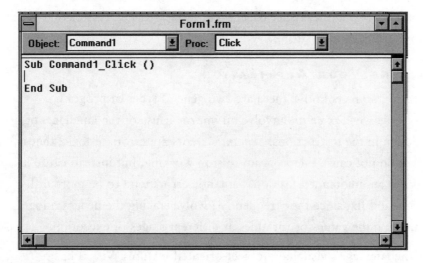

▌▌▌**Figure 1.21** The Edit window.

ADDING OTHER SCREEN OBJECTS

Most of the other objects available in the Visual Basic toolbox are designed to be placed on the forms. These include command buttons, radio buttons, check boxes, text and picture boxes, scroll bars, and a variety of others. Each of these objects has properties associated with it, although the properties and their values may be different between different types of objects. Each object also has a list of events associated with it, enabling you to write event-handling subprograms customized to each object.

Therefore, to run the code in the preceding Italics example, you would move a command button onto the form Form1. You probably also want to change the Name property of the button from Command1 to Italics. Next, you open the button's code window and select the Click subprogram. Then you simply insert the line of code into the shell provided, as follows:

```
Sub Form_Click ()
        Form1.FontItalic = True
End Sub
```

Anytime the user clicks this button, the text in the form will change to italics. You probably also want other buttons to change the text in other ways. Once you understand the Visual Basic event model, it is as easy as that to make your application perform.

DEBUGGING YOUR APPLICATION

As most programmers know, there are two general types of program errors, or bugs: *Syntax errors* involve an improper use of the language, or a contradiction in the instructions. *Semantic errors* are errors of logic; that is, errors that do not cause the program to stop working, but instead cause it to behave in an unintended fashion. Semantic errors tend to be more difficult to find and fix, since they frequently involve tracing the program logic and examining the values of variables at different stages of execution.

Despite the language's visual and object-oriented features, Visual Basic applications are still susceptible to both of these types of errors. The Visual

Basic debugging facilities let the developer address both through the use of its Step and Watch functions, described earlier. The idea behind both of these debugging tools is simple. Step lets you execute one statement of code at a time, so you can identify the particular line that is causing a problem. Watch lets you view the value of any variable during a particular stage of execution. The combination of these two commands enables you to run a Visual Basic application one line at a time, and to look at the values of any or all variables at each step along the way. Virtually any error should be able to be identified and fixed with these commands.

Other debugging calls include the Calls command, which displays a list of the currently active procedures; Set Next statement, which lets you control the order of execution of program statements; Show Next statement, which displays the next statement in the sequence to be executed; and Procedure Step, which steps through a program one procedure at a time. Like many source code debuggers for traditional languages, Visual Basic also lets you set breakpoints, which instruct program execution to stop at specific points. Errors and any of the values for any watches you set will appear in the Debug window while the application is running. Figure 1.22 shows the Debug window as it appears in a running application.

What the debugger lacks is the ability to step through portions of code that were developed outside of the Visual Basic environment. Since this code is probably already compiled into a library or other type of executable file, you would need a debugger that could examine it in compiled form, rather than source form. Since sometimes there could be an error in such library files, you may have to leave Visual Basic and investigate these problems in the language in which they were developed.

PREPARING AN EXECUTABLE FILE

Visual Basic lets you compile an application into an executable file so that it can be distributed on computers that are not running Visual Basic itself. The process is very simple: Select the Make EXE File from the File menu. This will open a dialog box asking you for the drive and directory location

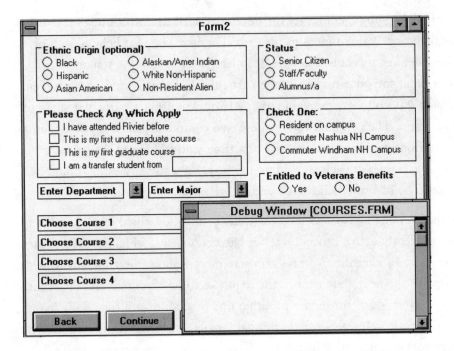

Figure 1.22 The Debug window.

of the application files, the name of the target application, and the icon to be used to represent that application in Windows.

Clicking on OK will create that application as an executable file. The amount of time taken by the compilation process depends upon the size of the files and the speed of the computer, but it doesn't generally take more than a few seconds. The size of the executable file varies, but is generally smaller than the source files that make up the application. If you've debugged your application successfully from within the Visual Basic environment, this step should be virtually automatic.

However, even in compiled form, the application won't run along. You have to include the file VBRUN300.DLL with the executable in order for it to work. This dynamic link library, or DLL, joins with the executable file when you launch it, and provides a set of definitions and instructions for the Visual Basic components.

For more complicated applications, Visual Basic includes an Application Setup Wizard. This Wizard automatically determines which files your application needs in order to run as a stand-alone application, outside of the Visual Basic environment, and the directories in which they have to reside. The Wizard will then automatically copy those files onto a diskette, and include an Install routine that will copy them properly onto other computers.

PREPARING USER DOCUMENTATION FOR VISUAL BASIC APPLICATIONS

The user-centered style of application development encouraged by Visual Basic also provides a roadmap for preparing user documentation. Like the application design and development process itself, the documentation can take an outside-in approach to describing the application and how the user will accomplish program tasks.

This means that you can pattern the user's documentation after the problem that the application was intended to address, and be confident that you are also approaching the description in the same way that the user will approach the problem. User-centered design also offers clues on how to use hypertext, to dynamically link different terms and concepts within the Help files. Applying the Help guidance as the user performs activities in the application should assist in addressing a particular problem in the same way that the user is approaching that problem.

Visual Basic also makes use of the Microsoft Help Compiler, a tool for creating and incorporating Windows-based Help files into your applications. The Help Compiler takes files formatted in Microsoft Word or other word processor, and prepares them to be called as online Help. These files can be configured so that the resulting online Help can include the ability to *jump* between different Help topics, incorporate graphics into Help topics, link in other Help files, and a variety of other things that can make online Help a dynamic and useful tool for learning how to use your application.

WHERE VISUAL BASIC LEADS

The initial version of Visual Basic provided little more than an adequate range of user interface-building tools, along with the ability to make user interface components perform common actions. Through the efforts of independent software developers, Microsoft programmers, and enthusiastic users, Visual Basic has gained many of the characteristics of a sophisticated application development environment, with the capability of attacking a wide variety of different, yet relevant and valuable, problems in information systems.

Today, you can use Visual Basic to develop all manner of applications. It is possible to encapsulate existing code into a Windows Dynamic Link Library (DLL), and write a Visual Basic user interface on top of it. You can produce components that are transferable across different applications, delivering on the promise of code reusability. You can develop sophisticated custom controls, or VBXs, that can be added to the Visual Basic development environment to give you still better development tools. Several of the buttons in the toolbox in the Professional Version of Visual Basic are actually VBXs.

In terms of applications, Visual Basic can be applied to the development of databases, multimedia presentations, information managers, graphical front ends, and a wide variety of other applications. One of this author's colleagues is using it to write networked applications utilizing the TCP/IP communications protocols, something normally associated with low-level C or assembly languages. All of these examples illustrate the enormous power and flexibility of the Visual Basic language and development environment.

VISUAL BASIC FOR APPLICATIONS

One of the extensions Microsoft developed is a set of adaptations to Visual Basic to turn it into a scripting language for its suite of desktop productivity applications. Present or future versions of Excel, Word for Windows, PowerPoint, and others include Visual Basic, with a dialog editor replacing the forms editor, as a powerful scripting language for customizing these applications.

Some of the tasks you can do include automatically accessing a database file and preparing form letters, filtering electronic mail, and preparing complex financial analyses. Using the same language across an entire suite of applications lets you reuse code from one to the other, and lets you use the same skills and techniques for making your applications smarter and more responsive to your needs.

THE PRINCIPLES OF USER-CENTERED DESIGN

WHAT IS USER-CENTERED DESIGN?

As implied in Chapter 1, an application developer using Visual Basic has to view design and development of an application differently than when using a traditional language. This is because of the user-centric nature of all program activities in a Visual Basic application. The entire application revolves around what the user sees and the actions taken, which the application itself refers to as events. There is no excuse not to have a user-friendly Visual Basic application, since the developer works with the exact application view that the user does. However, developers who are used to working primarily with traditional programming languages may not be used to this view of an application.

This raises the question of what are the steps necessary to design and develop a user-centered application, and what makes an application user-centered in the first place. This chapter addresses both of those questions.

THE TRADITIONAL DEVELOPMENT CYCLE

In the past, most application developers followed a series of steps to start with a user's problem and end up with an application addressing that problem. The most widely followed development strategy is the Waterfall model, so called because each step is designed to be substantially completed before moving on to the next step. While there are many variations on the basic technique, the steps could be summarized as follows:

1. **Requirements statement.** The users describe their needs to the application developers, using the terminology of their business.

2. **Functional design.** The application developers respond with a description of software that they believe addresses the users' problem. This is usually in the terminology of application software.

3. **Detailed design.** The application developers prepare a detailed description of how the application would work, what data would be used and how it would be used, how the different states of the program and flow of control would occur, and even what variables would be used for specific purposes.

4. **Coding.** The application developers implement the software, usually in a traditional programming language such as C or Pascal. Individual programmers would be responsible for the correctness of their portions of the code.

5. **Testing.** The developers assemble the application and test it against the requirements. They identify both bugs and areas where the application fails to meet the requirements.

6. **Delivery.** The software is packaged, user manuals are prepared, disks are copied, software is shipped, and, if applicable, the software is installed and integrated with the customer's computing environment.

7. **Maintenance.** After delivery, maintenance is concerned with fixing any problems found in the field, and with implementing new features in subsequent versions.

This methodical approach to application development has worked well over the years, but it has a number of failings. First, and most important to this book, it is not user-centered. Typically, the user's input into the process ends with the acceptance of the functional specification. This means that if the needs change, or have not been expressed or understood properly, then the resulting software may not meet those needs. There is usually a mechanism for changing the scope of a project, but it is usually cumbersome, expensive, and despised by all parties.

Further, since the functional specification is written in the terminology of the developers, the user may not even have a good understanding of what the developer is proposing. Frequently, the user cannot completely identify requirements without first viewing examples of the application itself. The potential for miscommunication is high at every step in this process.

In general, the traditional software development process is too rigid to take into account rapid changes in user needs, computing technology, and organizational changes. Further, it usually results in poor communications between users and developers, and misunderstood needs. The resulting application usually needs a period of maintenance before it becomes useful to the users. This makes some sense when you're using a traditional programming language, because all of the parts of the program tend to be tied together. Changing the way the user interface works, for example, may also require changes in how results are computed and displayed. Letting the users initiate changes in the interface, or in the operation of the application, frequently results in massive rework that delays the application and drives up the cost of development.

APPLICATIONS DEVELOPMENT
WITH VISUAL BASIC

Visual Basic supports development processes that address many of these failings. A component-based visual language tends to produce more modularized applications than a traditional language. This means that discrete parts can be more easily changed without affecting the whole application. The components also make it possible to assemble large parts of an application in a short period of time, while writing only little pieces of code.

For example, Visual Basic can be used in rapid prototyping, a technique whereby essential features of an application are quickly implemented so that users can gain an understanding of what the application will look like and how it will work. The users can then feed back their impressions and correct any misunderstandings, which can then be integrated into the application as it grows and takes shape.

The purpose of rapid prototyping is to get a working application into the hands of users as fast as possible, and then to refine that application in response to user feedback. Visual Basic does this in two important ways. First, it provides a collection of reusable components that enable a developer to quickly lay out a wide variety of screen designs. These components include the user interface objects included in the standard Visual Basic package. They also include a wide variety of third-party VBXs, Visual Basic custom controls, that can be integrated into the toolbox in the Visual Basic development environment and used just like the other components. These VBXs need not be simply user interface objects; they can include data access or computational components that can also be used to build the back end of an application.

Second, the Basic language behind the components is powerful enough to produce a workable application usually with only a few lines of code. In part, this is because there is no need to write user interface code, which frequently takes up as much as 50 percent of the code written for a program written in a traditional language. Second, the Basic language for Visual Basic has been enhanced to enable it to manipulate user interface components and their properties.

RAPID PROTOTYPING AND JAD/RAD

Visual Basic can also be used to support Joint Application Design/Rapid Application Development (JAD/RAD), an emerging software development methodology that lets users play very specific roles in determining application requirements, and to participate in the actual application development. This process, popularized by systems-analysis guru James Martin, is useful in quickly identifying and resolving conflicting requirements. It also lets applications be rapidly assembled according to the requirements developed as a result of JAD. Sometimes, prototyping is done while the JAD team is watching so that feedback can be immediate.

Both rapid prototyping and JAD/RAD will be discussed and applied to Visual Basic programming in Chapter 6.

STARTING WITH THE USER INTERFACE

How does Visual Basic differ from traditional languages and traditional approaches to application development? Visual Basic forces the application developer to address user interface issues as the first priority of the application. The developer is presented with a blank form to be filled out with graphical user interface components. It is not physically possible to write code until at least some aspects of the user interface design are worked out. An experienced Visual Basic application developer will actually lay out most, if not all, of the user interface of the application before writing a single line of code.

As mentioned earlier, Visual Basic also makes it possible to greatly reduce the amount of work required to produce a user interface by providing virtually all of the Windows user interface constructs as Visual Basic components. The dozen or so user interface components provided by the Standard Version of the Visual Basic package lets the application developer construct a surprisingly wide range of different user interfaces. The Professional Version, which includes a number of VBXs, is capable of producing virtually any type of look and feel possible in a Windows application.

What Does It Mean to Be Easy to Use?

Unlike the very explicit rules governing traditional programming practices, there are few hard and fast rules for designing an application to be easy to use. Much of the conventional wisdom depends on the purpose of the application and the type of computer on which it will run. Most users cannot even state with any certainty what makes some applications easier to use than others. What they can frequently do, however, is identify poorly designed applications. They are quite capable of complaining long and loud on the shortcomings of a user interface, and even refusing to use an application that does not sufficiently ease the burden of their tasks.

This means that the burden of understanding what makes an application user-centered, and implementing user-centered characteristics, is the primary responsibility of the application developer. The developer must understand the principles of user-centered design, know the needs of the intended user, and be able to use the software development tool to make all of these principles come together.

The admission that software application usability is an inexact or hard-to-define science doesn't mean that developing an easy-to-use application is a hopeless prospect. Nor does it mean that you have to be born with a good sense of design. Mostly, it means two things: first, that you recognize that you may not be the prototypical user of your application, so you might not be the best judge of the best approach to a task; and second, that feedback from others on your initial user interface designs may be your most important source of expertise, even if others may not be able to explain their reasoning. Such feedback, along with your own impressions, will help you directly with an application today, and will help you form more general principles that you can apply in the future.

You may have a perfectly good understanding of how your application works, but then, you designed it, and you've been working with it intimately for weeks or months. Another person, more expert in the task domain than yourself, or with a different view of the problem, may find your user interface to be confusing, unclear, or just plain difficult to navigate. This person, and others, have a lot to contribute to your application development effort.

To take advantage of user impressions, an increasing number of large software developers have outfitted comprehensive user interface laboratories as an integral part of their development facilities. These facilities are usually controlled laboratory environments equipped with computers of all types, with sophisticated ways of recording users' movement through the features of a software package, their responses to system messages, and even their specific keystrokes and mouse movements. This data can be analyzed to determine where users became lost or confused, why they tried to perform an activity in a particular way, and how they reacted to system responses.

These laboratories are superb tools for improving the ability of applications to be responsive to users. However, they are expensive to build and maintain, and are frequently out of the economic reach of small software development organizations and individual developers. They also add to the usually lengthy period of time needed to field even the most straightforward application. One of the goals of user-centered design is to get user-friendly applications into the hands of users as quickly as possible, and the usability test lab does not contribute to this goal.

Also, smaller application development groups, or smaller applications, cannot reasonably take advantage of these expensive facilities. They are more dependent upon a combination of design sense, intuition, understanding of their users, and the incorporation of a few general principles of user-centered design in order to produce worthwhile applications.

COLLECTING AND INCORPORATING USER FEEDBACK

Many of the existing rules in designing user-centered applications can be learned from watching how people accomplish a particular task that you would like to automate. This was the original impetus behind the spreadsheet, which faithfully modeled the way bookkeepers worked, while automating the computational aspects of the work. The computations were the part of the task that was difficult for people to do quickly and well, but were those that computers were quite good at. The combination of the simplicity of the user interface with the ability to do things that people themselves were not designed to do make the spreadsheet among the most spectacular software successes to date.

Users are still the best source for specific user interface design suggestions and recommendations. One way of collecting information on desirable user interfaces is through the use of questionnaires. Several software human-factor textbooks include questions that enable the developer to distinguish just what user interface characteristics are important to the target user audience. Based on the results to these and similar surveys, the application developer can devise a user interface strategy that responds to user needs and concerns.

However, survey questions are a poor substitute for direct feedback to a prototype user interface. As a rule, people provide higher-quality and more specific responses when they can see and explore the construct or display they're critiquing. This is for two reasons: First, they don't have to form an imperfect image of the construct in their minds; the reality is in front of them. Second, the construct is constant from person to person. There is no variability in what they are critiquing, as there would be with mental images. Perhaps most important, it takes time to develop and disseminate a questionnaire, and to collect, analyze, and interpret the responses. This is time that can be better spent in prototyping, and in gradually refining an application in response to the feedback.

While surveys and labs and user feedback all help in developing an effective user-centered application, recognizing and understanding some of the physical and psychological characteristics of people can give you a head start. You can learn to make the connections between your user interface components, the nature and behavior of your application, and human perception and cognition.

WHAT PEOPLE DO BEST

In order to understand what design considerations are important, it is first necessary to gain an insight into how people think and perceive the world around them. While some of these insights will seem to be abstract, with some reflection they can all be easily related to some solid recommendations in user-centered design.

These insights are expressed as broad generalizations of how people think and react. For the more analytical readers (I normally fall into this category), they can be almost maddeningly vague and subjective. However, once you recognize and understand the principle, applying it to your development effort is simply a matter of mentally making the connection between the abstract and the concrete, something people do every day in their lives. This chapter provides some of these broad generalizations, and this and the next two chapters describe how to apply them using Visual Basic controls and development techniques.

PERCEIVING THE APPLICATION ENVIRONMENT

People are good at forming overall perceptions, rather than dealing with details. They can quickly grasp the essential meaning of a display, but tend to ignore the details or to put off the understanding of the details until later, when they have to know them to make progress. Even then, they pay attention to only those details that are immediately necessary for them to understand a situation or accomplish a task. This characteristic has long been a human survival trait and may be thought of as becoming even more so in an era of information overload; we automatically filter out the nonessential information so that we may focus on the characteristics that are immediately relevant.

This principle has several implications to software developers. A display should not have any extraneous text or objects that do not contribute to the meaning of the display. It should be as simple as possible to communicate the necessary information. None of the essential components of the software or how to accomplish a particular task should be hidden in the details of a display. Many developers add graphical decorations to an application, thinking, wrongly, that decorations alone can make the application seem more attractive or easier to use. Nothing can be further from the truth. Any display design without a specific function is simply a useless distraction to the end user.

This does not mean to say that display designs should not be attractive or graphical; simply that each part of the design should contribute to the user's understanding of how the application works, and how to use it. This is a relatively easy design test—does the flowery border, for example, serve to highlight important information for the user, or is it just there because you could do it easily?

This principle can even be applied to software documentation. A complex and detailed user's manual will usually only sit in the box unused unless the user absolutely needs it for a specific task. The simple and direct manual, on the other hand, will act as an extension to the application, and likely spend its time sitting right beside the computer. This principle has prompted many different approaches to documentation, such as quick reference guides, simplified "read this first" pamphlets, and detailed reference volumes organized by task.

Consider the following Visual Basic forms, designated Figure 2.1 and Figure 2.2. Both forms provide an interface for entering some information on the user, and moving on in the application. The first is a straightforward user interface that gets the job done with no flair or extraneous designs. The second uses the drawing tools and control properties to make the user interface look fancier, but without adding any additional functionality or enhancing the ability of the user to understand the form or its purpose.

The second form may be more eye-catching, but it can actually hinder the ability of the user to understand the purpose of the form and to respond properly without confusion. That is because it presents information without purpose, which requires that the user sort through unnecessary data in order to make use of the form.

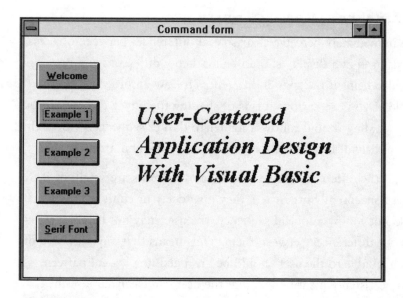

■■■■■■■■**Figure 2.1** A simple screen.

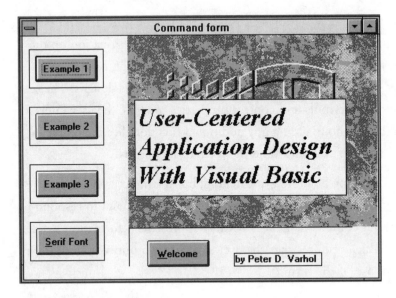

Figure 2.2 A complex screen.

ORGANIZING FOR USER CLARITY

People can immediately perceive clear spatial differences between objects. Any patterns used in a display should be markedly different from one another. It also helps if the spatial differences follow an orderly pattern. For example, if you use various forms of shading to convey different information, the shading should follow a lighter to darker sequence, with each stage being clearly distinguished from the ones before and after.

Conversely, if the differences between sizes and patterns are small, or if they are not conceptually organized, they may delay or confuse the user. If shadings do not follow a logical sequence, the user may not be able to easily identify the differences between them. This means that any sequence of operations available to the user should be arranged in a logical pattern, and should be visually identified so that the user can easily choose the desired operation.

▮▮▮▮▮ **Figure 2.3** A gradation of color patterns.

Distinguishing between components and their resulting tasks can be accomplished by arranging the components in a logical order, distinguished by different sequences of shadings or by gradually increasing or decreasing sizes. Figure 2.3 shows a series of Visual Basic picture boxes, each shaded with a pattern of gradually higher density. This serves to illustrate a sequence of events or different levels of the same information. A user can more easily distinguish between different levels of information, or even between completely different types of information, when the accompanying visual patterns follow a logical sequence.

SIMPLE AND COMPLICATED TASKS

The type of task the user is performing determines the design approach of the user interface. It might be appropriate to classify tasks as routine and repetitious on the one hand, or unique and creative on the other. Routine tasks, such as opening a file or scrolling a window, should be readily apparent and easy to accomplish, with few movements or operations necessary. The user need not think about the task, but only carry it out as rapidly as possible. The action may, in time, become almost reflexive.

The unique tasks, like laying out formatted text and graphics on a page, can be less straightforward and more time-consuming. These tasks can be more complicated from the standpoint of the software, especially if they require the user to think about how to best carry out the task. In other words, the software can give the user time to contemplate the activity and to be creative. This type of activity will probably never become second nature to the user; it will always require some thought.

This distinction and the design decisions it leads to require an understanding of which tasks are simple and which are complex. In general, simple tasks are those that are applicable across different applications, and that are essential in order to perform any activities with the application. These may include opening, saving, and closing files; printing documents; entering and formatting data; and cutting, copying, and pasting. These types of tasks should require few keystrokes or mouse movements, and should be apparent to the user at a glance.

Visual Basic, along with other applications, puts many such tasks into a toolbar of some type. The toolbar lets the user carry out a simple task with a quick movement of the mouse and a click of the mouse button. Figure 2.4 illustrates the Visual Basic toolbar, as an example of how to organize simple tasks into a readily recognizable and quick-to-use software component. The toolbar uses small icons to represent tasks, and groups these icons into a logical order so that the user won't have to hunt around for the proper button. Some applications will even let the user select the tasks for the icon bar, and arrange them to suit individual needs. This lets the user decide which simple tasks to make readily accessible.

Another common way of simplifying a repetitive task is through the use of shortcut keys. Most applications today let the more experienced user bypass the menus or toolbars, and complete an action directly from the keyboard, usually by pressing some combination of two or more keys. Keystroke combinations, which require the use of recall rather than recognition memory, have a steeper learning curve than the menus, and are usually used by those more familiar with the application and its tasks.

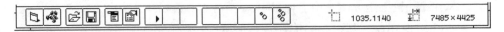

Figure 2.4 The Visual Basic toolbar.

While this seems like a step backward in usability, because it involves using the old-fashioned keyboard, it actually takes advantage of the fact that the experienced users can accomplish a task more quickly if their fingers don't have to leave the keyboard. In the time it takes to grasp a mouse, move the pointer to the menu bar, and make a selection, this type of user can accomplish three or four similar actions from the keyboard. For common or repetitive tasks, it is always a good idea to provide a shortcut keystroke combination.

The shortcuts in an application should always be consistent and should provide the user with a mnemonic, or memory hint, between the shortcut and the task. You should not use the same keystroke combination to mean different things in different places in the application. The mnemonic used is often the first letter of the equivalent menu command, or the first letter of the description of the action. One popular mnemonic used in virtually every Windows application (and in applications written for other operating systems) is Control-C for copying file text or graphics.

Similar to shortcut keys are speed keys. These let you quickly navigate the application's menu to select a particular option, but not to automatically execute it. To execute your selection, you have to press the Enter key. The speed key is identified by the underlined letter for both the menu item on the menu bar and the individual selection. The speed keys let you quickly move to a menu selection without removing your fingers from the keyboard, just like the shortcut keys, but let you pause before executing the selection.

In Visual Basic, the Menu Design selection from the Window menu gives you the option of assigning a shortcut and/or a speed key to any menu selection you design. The distinction between simple and complex tasks should assist you in determining which menu selections you should consider assigning a shortcut key. In general, menu selections that are multilevel or that require user input should not have a shortcut key. For example, many productivity applications use a shortcut key to save an

```
New...
Open...                    ^O
Close

Save                       ^S
Save As...

Import Picture...
Doc Info...
File Management...

Master Document...
Merge...
Print Envelope...
Print...                   ^P
Printer Setup...

Exit
```

■■■■■■■■ **Figure 2.5** File menu with Save shortcut key.

existing document, but not to save a new one. Figure 2.5 shows the File menu from the Ami Pro word processor, which does just this.

More complicated but still repetitive tasks can be accomplished by the use of macros, which provide a way to record multiple tasks and play them back again with a simple keystroke combination. However, note that macros deal with multiple but simple tasks, rather than more complicated tasks, even though the macro itself may be quite complicated. A macro is more of a series of reflexive tasks, rather than a single reflective one. This sequence of tasks should not require any thought, since the sequence will execute automatically.

COMPLEXITY REQUIRES TIME FOR THOUGHT

Complicated tasks, on the other hand, involve using the application in order to produce an end product. They usually involve entering data of some type, manipulating that data, and creating something new. These tasks may involve a complicated series of decisions and actions that may not be replicated in the same way every time. Further, the results of one action may prompt a decision and action that might not normally be a part of the accepted sequence. In other words, circumstances may determine actions. The sequence of actions probably won't be repeated very often, if at all.

These tasks, incidentally, are where menus and mouse movements are an advantage. Accessing a pull-down menu with a mouse is slower than using a shortcut key, but moving the mouse and making a menu selection gives the user the opportunity to pause and think about the activity. This is yet another reason to not assign a shortcut key to a complex, reflective activity. The users may act in haste or become confused, when they should be taking their time. To return to the previous example, saving a new document requires a user to think of a file name, which is clearly a reflective act.

There should be no shortcut to this type of activity. Some applications assign a default file name to a Save command so that the user can simply OK the default name and continue working. The problem with default file names is that they make it difficult for users to remember what a file was for, and can force them to open and examine multiple files before finding the one they want. Another problem is that some applications overwrite default file names when users expect that a new file will be created, or create new files when users expect an overwrite.

CUSTOMIZING THE USER INTERFACE

Different people work in different ways. This is why many of the attempts in an organization to standardize on a single application for a particular type of work do not succeed very well. It is difficult to explain why this is so. In some cases, the first application used by individuals dictates their preferences in all subsequent applications. In other cases, learning experiences earlier in life determine the approach that works best for a person. Given this uncertainty on the one *best* way of organizing an application, it seems to make sense to offer several different alternatives and to leave the choice up to the individual user.

Much of the debate within the computer industry concerning which user interface features are easiest to use are based on all people working in pretty much the same way. The fact of the matter is that, due to past experience, different thought processes, or simply out of personal preference, users prefer setting up an application to match the way they want to work. For example, I feel most comfortable working in multiple documents, and even multiple applications, at the same time. Before Windows, I was unproductive on PCs because the single-tasking nature of DOS was not conducive to my preferred way of working.

After years of having to work in a single way, more and more application developers are giving the end users the opportunity to set up and use applications in individualized ways. While the overall paradigm can rarely be changed in an application, users can often change the functions of keystrokes, write macros, create and modify toolbars, and give their preferences on a wide variety of screen appearances and application functions. Any or all of these alternatives let users feel more comfortable in an application, and enable them to work better.

USING COLOR AND FONTS

Color and font style are both useful in displaying information and catching the user's attention. Color should be used mainly as an enhancer of information, rather than a unique identifier. In this way, it can still accommodate those who use black-and-white monitors, or those who are color-blind. Soft colors are easier on the eyes and are more restful, although bold colors should be used to help identify important information, or to make a critical event or activity stand out. When using bold colors, they should still follow the same color pattern as the overall display.

The issue of fonts can be a difficult one. Because the computer screen frequently does not have the resolution of the printed page, larger fonts are more readable than smaller fonts, and simple fonts are more preferable to complicated ones. Microsoft uses a sans serif font as its system font. Sans serif fonts, such as Helvetica, are those that lack flourishes on the letters. Serif fonts, on the other hand, have flourishes on the letter. This book is laid out with a serif font. Figures 2.6a and b show a common serif font (Times New Roman) and a common sans serif font (the MS Windows System font) as a label on a Visual Basic command button.

The primary problem with computer-generated fonts is that, while sans serif fonts display better on the computer, serif fonts such as Times Roman are easier to read, especially for more than just a sentence or two. Publishers have known this fact for decades, which is why virtually all books and magazines today use a serif font. With the higher-resolution computer displays that are commonly used today (640 by 480 pixels or better on the screen), it is possible to display serif fonts that are very readable under most circumstances, and you should not hesitate to use such fonts where appropriate.

For buttons or other controls that you expect the user to identify immediately, use a sans serif font. For consistency with other Windows applications, the MS Windows system font or the MS Sans Serif are the best choices. For longer text, such as Help files or prompts, consider using a serif font. This will hold the user's attention longer, and make it more likely that the text successfully conveys the meaning that you intended.

■■■■■■■■ **Figure 2.6a** Example of a sans serif font in Visual Basic.

Times New Roman Font

■■■■■ **Figure 2.6b** Example of a serif font in Visual Basic.

Fonts can also take on other characteristics, the most common of which are boldface and italics. Both are used for emphasis of text. Most commonly, boldface is used to catch the user's attention, often in stand-alone text such as found on a menu bar or command button. It is also used for section and document headings in text so that users can immediately read the heading and determine if they want to continue to read the following text. Italics are often used within normal text to emphasize a particular word or phrase, without necessarily making it stand out in the text. Underlining is used for a similar purpose as italics. It often catches the user's attention without making the underlined text stand out from the accompanying text. Figure 2.7 illustrates all of these types of font characteristics in a typical Visual Basic Help topic.

CONSISTENCY OF USER INTERFACE DESIGN

Within all of these principles lies the underlying assumption that the user interface, whatever it may do, presents the user with a consistent framework of how it operates. Keystrokes and menu selections should not work one way in one part of an application, and another way elsewhere in the same application. While you may think you have good reasons to break this assumption, you almost always do so at the expense of the user.

At a high level, this is one of the primary reasons behind design guidelines such as IBM's Common User Access, or CUA. CUA attempts to enforce a level of consistency, both within applications and between

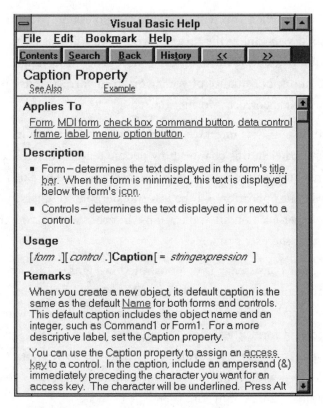

Figure 2.7 The use of different font characteristics in a Visual Basic Help topic.

applications, that makes it possible for users to easily learn one application, then transfer much of that knowledge to others. However, CUA and other design guidelines usually do not address consistency of meaning within an application. This is up to you. Keystrokes and menu selections should do the same thing throughout your application. Words and concepts should keep the same meaning, and hopefully many of those concepts can be applied to other applications.

A lack of consistency in the user interface has several implications. First, and possibly most important, it increases the likelihood that the user will make a mistake. If you as the user anticipate that an action will accomplish one task, because it did so earlier, and it actually accomplishes another, then you will probably do something you did not intend. Even if you caught the mistake, you have still wasted your time. If you did not catch the mistake, the consequences can range from a perception of poor quality of your work to incorrect decisions made on the basis of incorrect information.

Second, an inconsistent user interface will take more time to navigate (remember from earlier in this chapter how people tend to generalize their perceptions) and may make the user less productive. The skills the user learned in your application will be less transferable to others, requiring more experience on all applications. In other words, you are once again wasting the user's time.

An example of poor consistency is demonstrated in Figures 2.8a and b. On the first form, command buttons labeled Previous and Next in boldface text are used to move between the prior and following windows. On the second form, the command buttons use italicized text labeled Before and After. If these forms are used in the same application, the user is faced with a shift of appearance and terminology that will almost certainly cause confusion.

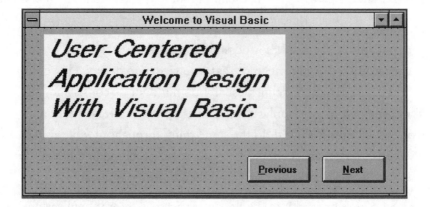

■■■■■■■■■ **Figure 2.8a** Poor consistency between forms.

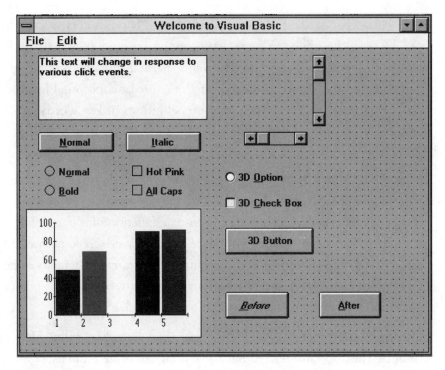

Figure 2.8b Poor consistency between forms.

GUIDE THE USER

Many of us (including myself) hate reading computer software manuals. Even the very best of them seem to waste your time when all you need is one specific piece of information. We want to get down to work, and the manual seems to get in the way more than it helps. Remember that your user has a job to do, and that job probably doesn't involve reading a software manual. Only the best of the manuals or manuals for the most complicated of applications are heavily used. Therefore, both the software and manual design have to be done in parallel to complement one another. The manual should emphasize reflective and complex activities, while providing primarily a reference on the simple tasks.

Well, that's what online Help is for. And online Help has greatly improved over the years, becoming in some ways context-sensitive (you get help for only the task you need help on), utilizing hypertext (the ability to jump from one part of Help to another through the use of conceptual links between information), and short, pop-up definitions of key words and concepts. Most online Help today also offers the ability to access help information in different ways, including by contents, word or concept search, and menu item.

Some software packages today also offer context-sensitive prompts. A prompt is a brief statement on the purpose or function of a particular screen item that displays when you place the cursor or screen pointer on that item. On applications that use prompts, this statement usually appears in a narrow status bar across the bottom of the active window. Prompts can be useful reminders of the purpose of a particular item.

However, there is more to guiding the user than providing online Help or prompts. The application itself has to be designed to help the user get through its tasks. How many times have you used an application where, part way through a complex task, the next step was not clear? An example is the word processor I use, Ami Pro. In trying to format a document recently, I suddenly came across the inability to figure out how to modify a style to change the spacing between lines. The solution I finally hit upon, after considerable delay, was probably not the ideal one, and resulted in a less-than-perfect document.

The key here is to plan out the steps for all tasks before even starting the implementation. At each step, determine the possible user actions and whether all of these actions are readily apparent to the user. Last, of course, is to show your solution to several prototypical users to see if they agree.

GRACE UNDER FIRE

Most successful applications end up being used in ways that were not imagined by their developers. Lotus 1-2-3, for example, which was originally introduced as an electronic aid to accountants and bookkeepers, became an indispensable tool for quantitative analysis and modeling of all kinds. Many people began using it as a database to store numerical data, and a few enterprising souls even used it as a word processor. This flexibility added to the value of the product, but it also made it necessary for the developers to handle a very wide range of user activities and enable it to respond appropriately.

The truly user-friendly application should let the user determine how to make best use of the application. The best use for an individual user may not be what the developer has envisioned. If the application has limits (as all do), it should be able to inform the user of these limits in an informative and noncondescending way (the response "Error Code #1171—Call Technical Support," for example, does not qualify). If a user makes a mistake, the application should be able to recover gracefully; that is, with a minimum of effort and a minimum loss of data to the user. An application that crashes with no warning, loses or corrupts data, or uses uninformative error messages is intimidating to many users, making it difficult to use the application effectively.

One example of poor "grace under fire" is Windows itself. Few of us have never encountered the messages "Unrecoverable Application Error" or "General Protection Fault," which effectively result in the involuntary closing of an application, the loss of any unsaved data from that application, and usually the inability to do anything else in Windows until it is closed and restarted. The problem may not have been the fault of Windows, but Windows should have been made capable enough to deal with the problem in a less-threatening fashion.

The reverse side of this is that it should be difficult for a user to make a mistake in the first place. This can be accomplished in one of two ways. The first way is by limiting the actions that the user can perform. This was often used with DOS software, where the only user input was with keystrokes, but is more difficult to do with graphical software under Windows. The second way is to give the user far more options and features, so that it is less likely that the user will try to perform an unintended action. This requires more and better quality code, more user testing, and a more robust software design, but is the better approach in the long run.

For obvious reasons, I won't provide an example of a Visual Basic application that reacts poorly when mishandled. What I will do, however, is give an example of error messages that don't insult the user, while also providing information on how not to make the same mistake again. For example:

> The file cannot be saved because the disk is full. Delete some files and try again.

> There is insufficient memory to open this file. Try closing some other files or applications first.

> There is no file by that name. Do you want to create a new one?

All three of these messages tell the user what is wrong, and suggest a way to fix the problem. The language used is clear and not condescending to the user. Writing error messages such as these is no more trouble than writing cryptic error messages, and will make any application easier and less frustrating to use.

Many Windows applications also use a stop sign icon or an exclamation point icon in the error message dialog box to send further information to the user. The stop sign icon is frequently used to tell the user that a particular user action cannot be understood or carried out. The exclamation point icon, on the other hand, is often used when the problem is not with a user action, but rather with an application task.

THE USER'S LANGUAGE

Many of the above generalizations of how people think and respond can be summarized as "speaking the user's language." This means that the application uses terms, appearances, and behaviors to which the user is accustomed. The spreadsheet is once again a good example of this. The user interface, a seemingly simplistic data grid, is very similar to the paper spreadsheets used by the green-shade generation of accountants. As a result, spreadsheet users immediately find themselves in a familiar and friendly environment. In other specialized fields, it becomes even more important to use the language and other aspects of that field in the software.

However, the user's language means more than just the right words and phrases. It also means a particular way of looking at a problem that makes the user feel at home. There is no one look that works for all users or for all applications, so it all comes down to understanding the problem from the user's perspective.

The best way of doing this is by designing the software so that it can be easily changed, and by showing the software under development to prospective users. As users suggest modifications of ordering, style, the placement of controls, and the names of options and features, you can quickly change the appearance of your application in response to their feedback. This approach to user-centered application development will be explored in more detail in Chapter 6.

WINDOWS VISUAL DESIGN GUIDE

Microsoft includes a basic online guide to Windows user interface design concepts as a part of Visual Basic. While this design guide is short and focused on the appearance and external behavior of Windows constructs, such as buttons, windows, and menus, it is a worthwhile introduction to the visual aspect of Windows applications.

Windows applications follow a style, originally developed by IBM as a part of its System Application Architecture, called the Common User Access, or CUA. While IBM never developed the CUA on all of its platforms, Windows and Windows applications make use of many of the design features described by CUA. The CUA guidelines define such things as the look and the behavior of individual windows, how the pull-down menus work, and the type of icons that appear in the display. Visual Basic already incorporates the major aspects of the CUA guidelines into its user interface components, although the application developer still determines how these components are used in an individual application.

CONSTRAINING THE DESIGN WITH VISUAL BASIC

Visual Basic provides graphical application construction tools and components that take much of the detailed design decisions out of your hands. For example, except for their sizes, all of the button controls have the same appearance, and behave in the same way to the user. You do not have an infinite number of application building blocks to use, and you can use them in only a limited number of different ways.

For the most part, this consistency is a good thing, since without this help, Windows applications created with Visual Basic could be wildly different in look and feel. While some will turn out acceptable to the user, and a few will be superior, many will be unsatisfactory in look and feel in one way or another. For the most part, the unsatisfactory applications are a result of a greater focus on the programming structures than on interacting with the user. Visual Basic forces the application developer to pay as much or more attention to the user interface as to the rest of the application, and gives him or her the development tools necessary to do at least a credible job of interface design.

Further, consistency between applications also helps the users, who will probably be using several Windows applications on their computers. Having a similar look and feel between these applications makes it possible to move easily between them, leveraging the knowledge and skills gained from one application to others. It also helps the developer, who can turn to other existing applications for design guidance, and can count on user skills on existing applications making it easier to learn their application.

The controls, properties, and events provided by Visual Basic offer more than enough flexibility to develop a wide range of different applications. The next chapter describes some of the ways you can use these tools to implement the design guidelines discussed here. Even though some application developers prefer not to be constrained, the potential complexities involved in writing applications for Windows, and the need to deliver usability and consistency to the users, makes using Visual Basic a good trade-off for both you and your users.

3

APPLYING DESIGN

GUIDELINES TO VISUAL

BASIC APPLICATIONS

As you consider building a Visual Basic application, one of the things that you'll notice is that you will make hundreds or even thousands of design decisions during the course of the development. Many of these decisions you may not even be consciously aware of, but you will be making them anyway, by default. These may include the color and shape of a border, the size of a button, or the font in a dialog box.

This is true of any software program, but the user-centered nature of a Visual Basic application makes the results of these decisions readily and sometimes painfully evident to the end user. Since much of the Visual Basic code is geared toward responding to user events, virtually all of the application layout and the accompanying code will affect the look and feel of the application. Even more directly, all of the screen designs that make up the heart of most Visual Basic applications are the bridge between the user and everything else underneath.

There are no hard and fast rules for many of the design decisions you can make, and you are not likely to stop and consciously think about the size or placement of every button and check box in your application. However, you should be aware that you are making such decisions at every step along the way so that you don't have to be locked in to letting Visual Basic make many of the decisions for you, and so that you are open to new ways of doing things.

Visual Basic itself makes many of your design decisions by providing a particular look to a form, a button, or other prepackaged component, and by supplying default values for properties of a component. In a larger sense, the form-based paradigm of Visual Basic largely dictates the overall look and feel of your application. That is, virtually every Visual Basic application uses forms, buttons, menus, and scroll bars, with the appearance and behavior defined by the appearances and behaviors that already exist as a part of Visual Basic. It is much easier to make use of the design paradigm presented to you than to come up with your own, which may make many Visual Basic applications look very similar.

The default appearances or properties are satisfactory in many circumstances. Microsoft has invested far more effort in studying good user interface design than you possibly could, and the defaults in Visual Basic reflect the results of its investigations and corporate expertise. However, in other cases the default design decisions made by Microsoft may not fully utilize the potential of your application, and may not sufficiently distinguish your application from others. Therefore, this chapter describes how to get the most out of the tools that Visual Basic provides, along with some general guidelines of when to break the rules and strike out on your own.

You can apply the design guidelines and user's considerations discussed in Chapter 2 at all stages during the building of a Visual Basic application. The principles inherent in good user-centered design can be implemented in a Visual Basic application to ensure that the application meets all of the needs of the users.

Ways of Informing the User

One of the biggest challenges for any software developer is understanding when to present the user with what kind of information and direction. Many end up presenting as much as they can at one time, resulting in applications that look much more complicated than they actually are. It is also possible to provide the user with too little information at one time. The skill here is often not so much in knowing when to present information, but knowing when to leave it out.

One way that Visual Basic lets you present the user with only the information essential to the next task is by letting you *gray out* menu and button selections that are not relevant at a particular time. If you prevent the user from having these options, then that is less information that the user has to be concerned with at any time while using the application. As an added benefit, it also provides the user with context cues on what can and cannot be done in a particular situation. A context cue directs the user on how to accomplish a more complex task. By turning on or off a button or other control, you can give the user signals as to the sequence of steps involved in completing that task.

Graying out the text in both buttons and menu selections is easy in Visual Basic. One of the properties in most Visual Basic components is the Enabled property. When set to True, the component works as it was designed to in response to events. When set to False, the encapsulated code is disabled so that the component will not respond normally. Setting this property to False also grays out the name of the component, signifying to the user that the component is disabled. For example, the statement:

```
Command1.Enabled = False
```

in your code will disable the ability of that command button to respond to a user activity, and will also gray out the text label in the button.

You can also set the Enabled property for a menu selection or other control while you are designing your application. However, it makes more sense to initialize it to one or the other value when the application starts running, then change it, depending upon what the user is doing in the application at a particular time.

It is up to you to determine if and when the Enabled property should be set to True or False. The general rule of thumb is that it should be set to True only when using it will have the intended effect. However, this may not always be the case. At times, you may want to keep it enabled as a cue to the user that a particular activity is possible at all times, although it may not be necessary at the current time. In most Windows applications, the Save command is available at all times, even though the file may have just been saved, and nothing has been changed. After all, it never hurts to save your work, even if there is nothing new to be saved.

Consider the form in Figure 3.1. This form asks for the user's name and address, then closes. This information may be used by your application as a key into a database containing more information about the user, or it may be used as a login prompt to another application. Without the necessary information, the user can't close the form and continue. You often see similar behavior in the Save As . . . dialog box in many applications. In

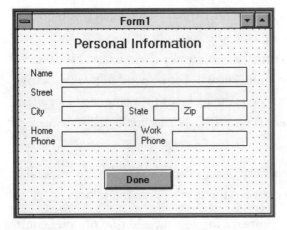

■■■■■■■■■ **Figure 3.1** A form that requires user information before closing.

other words, a file can't be saved without a name. You may want a command button labeled Done to display only when the user fills in some information in a text box. Therefore, your code may test to see if there is text in the text box before you set the command button to Enabled.

The code to do this simply checks the text property in the text box, and toggles the Enabled property on the Done button if any text exists. It looks like this:

```
If NameText.Text < > ' ' Then
        DoneCommand.Enabled = True
```

This says that if the Text field in the NameText text property is not blank, then set the Enabled property on the DoneCommand button to True. You also have to worry about where in your application to put this code, something that we will discuss in the next two chapters.

If the form in Figure 3.1 is used as a login prompt, you may want to take the next step of comparing the user's input to a list or database of legal logins, and let the person continue only if their input matches a legal one. I will discuss creating and modifying files and databases in later chapters. If you do this, you will also have to prompt the user if the input is incorrect. You can use either another text box or a label for this. If the user's input did not compare to one in the list, you can write a message to the text field of the text box or label to that effect, like this:

```
if LegalInput = False then
        Text1.Text =  "Incorrect User ID"
```

where LegalInput is a Boolean flag that is assigned the value of either True or False, depending on whether there is a match between the input and the list. Note that it is also possible to count the number of incorrect inputs with a second, integer variable in case you want to lock the user out after a set number of attempts.

You also have to be careful about stopping the user unless the input is correct. The user may want to exit from the application without completing the process, and to return to it later. You must let the user exit at any time, so you may want to prompt them that their input is incomplete, but then let them exit anyway if they desire. A common way of doing this is with a dialog box. I talk about the use of modal forms as dialog boxes in the next chapter.

USER CUES WITH DIFFERENT FONT TYPES

Using the component properties in Visual Basic, there are other ways of sending cues to the user on when and how to perform certain steps. It is possible to make changes to the font on different components in response to user events, including displaying a *strike-through* font when a particular step should not be taken, and changing it to a *bold-faced* font when that step is appropriate.

Figures 3.2a and b show a command button starting off with a line through its name when it is inactive. When that control becomes active, the line disappears and the font becomes bold. You can also change the font type, although unless the two fonts have drastic differences, it is less likely that the user will notice the change as a cue.

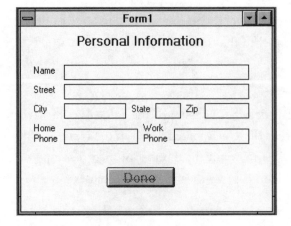

■■■■■■ **Figure 3.2a** Using font changes with a command button.

▰▰▰▰▰ **Figure 3.2b** Using font changes with a command button.

This type of technique should be used with care, since most users are familiar with the grayed-out control to refer to an inactive activity. However, there may be good reasons for using this technique, or even for combining the two. Many users still often attempt to select a grayed-out control in a Windows application, and become frustrated when it doesn't work. A line through the control label is an unambiguous message that that particular function is not available at that time.

ONE FORM AT A TIME

Another way of controlling the flow of information to the user is through the judicious use of forms. The best way of ensuring that the right amount of information is given in order to guide the user to the successful completion of a task is by breaking the task down into multiple steps, each of which could be accomplished by a simple activity on the part of the user. This activity might be a mouse click, or a scroll, or the insertion of text.

Rather than displaying all possible user input boxes on a single form, you may want to break up the inputs into multiple forms, each of which serves to complete a well-defined portion of the problem. This saves users from information overload, and also allows them to mentally break up the

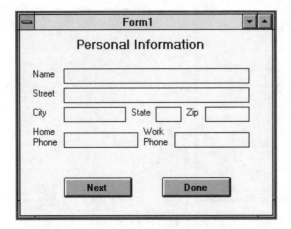

Figure 3.3a Using forms to control the presentation of information.

problem in the same way the application does, making the process clearer and easier to understand.

Figures 3.3a and b show an application that consists of two forms. These forms are not too crowded, and the user learns to expect to give personal

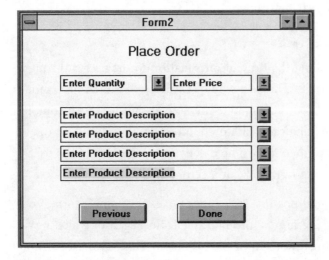

Figure 3.3b Using forms to control the presentation of information.

information on the first form and to order information on the second. It is possible to display one form without the other so that the user need not see both at the same time. Command buttons are used to switch between forms or to exit the application. In this case, the forms are meant to be shown in sequence, and the two command buttons controlling the sequence are labeled Previous and Next. I will discuss how to program these buttons in the next chapter. Note that it is also possible to gain the same effect with a scrolling form, with the added advantage of letting the user control what portion of the information input he or she sees.

Last, entire components can be hidden on a single form until their use makes sense from within the context of the application. Virtually every component in the Visual Basic toolbox has a Visible property. When set to True, the component is visible to the user while the application is running. When set to False, the component is hidden from the user. I'll discuss some ways to hide and show controls in Chapter 12.

Like other Visual Basic components, the Visible property can be changed while the application is running. As described in Chapter 1, you can do this simply by referencing the component name, followed by a dot, followed by the property name, such as:

```
Picture1.Visible = True
```

As when changing the properties of other Visual Basic controls, you will probably do this in response to an action on this control or on another control. Rather than checking the value of the control's property, however, we may write a Basic subroutine to perform the action as a part of an event.

For example, consider Figures 3.4a and b. The window hides a graphic until the user clicks on a check box, then displays it. In this case, the Visible property of the picture box is changed as a result of manipulating the check box. The ability to change the behavior of one control from within the code is another one of the strengths of Visual Basic.

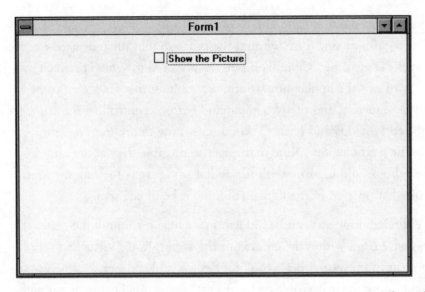

Figure 3.4a Using one control to change the property of another.

Visual Basic provides the template and supporting structures for necessary event-handling routines. All you have to do is tell it what you want it to do. In this case, the graphic will appear when the user clicks on the ShowPicture check boxes:

```
Sub ShowPicture_Click ()
        Picture1.Visible = True
End Sub
```

You may also want to hide the graphic in the picture box when the check box is unchecked. This would require a test of the check box's Visible property:

```
Sub ShowPicture_Click ()
        If Picture.Value = 1 Then
                Picture1.Visible = True
        ElseIf Check1.Value = 0 Then
                Picture1.Visible = False
        EndIf
End Sub
```

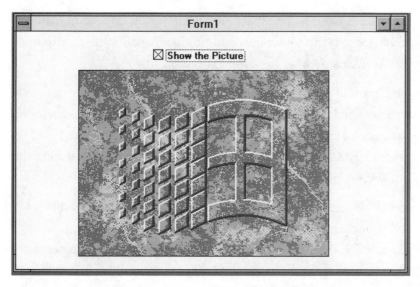

Figure 3.4b Using one control to change the property of another.

We'll demonstrate just where this Basic code fits into the application in Chapter 5.

This hiding technique should also be used with care, since it is also possible to present the user with too little information at one time. This is related to the next principle, giving the user enough information to develop a mental model of how the application works, which is discussed shortly. Note that in some instances, such as when using command buttons and check boxes, it would probably be better to use the graying-out technique instead, because the grayed-out button cues the user that there is another step to perform before the task is completed; that is, clicking on the suddenly darkened and enabled button.

FORMING A MENTAL MODEL

The ability of people to form overall impressions rather than dealing in details also means that it should be possible for software users to immediately see how to begin an activity in the software, and they should have confidence that the solution or end product is within reach, even if they're not sure exactly how they will get there.

This is an important principle to understand in laying out a user interface, because people tend to form mental models to understand new situations, such as navigating software applications. They use these mental models as a guide to understanding how to use the application, especially during the learning phase.

Once again, this can be accomplished through the careful use of multiple forms. By grouping information logically on multiple forms, you can enable the users to mentally group what tasks have to be done on each form, and you can let them comprehend where the application is taking them. The three forms in Figures 3.5a, b, c, and d, for example, gradually expand the application to include more controls and more information for the user to comprehend. The forms move from the simple to the more complex, and lead the user into more and more of the application's features.

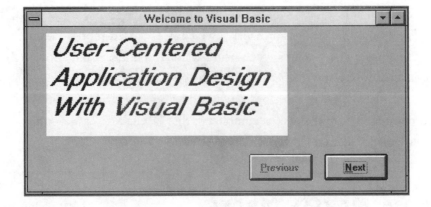

■■■■■■■■■ **Figure 3.5a** A sequence of forms containing gradually more and different controls.

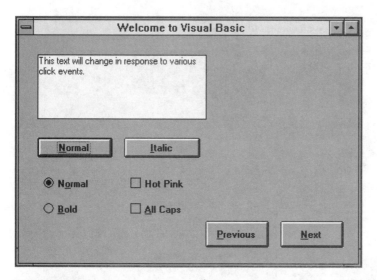

Figure 3.5b A sequence of forms containing gradually more and different controls.

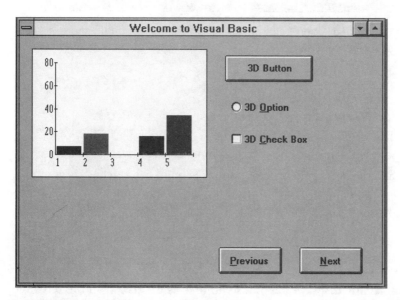

Figure 3.5c A sequence of forms containing gradually more and different controls.

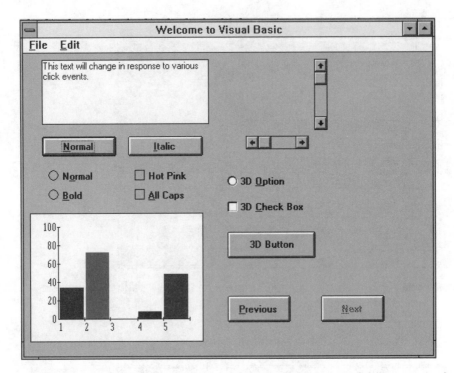

■■■■■■■ **Figure 3.5d** A sequence of forms containing gradually more and different controls.

USING THE MOUSE POINTER AS A CUE

There is one visual cue that the user has some control over—the mouse pointer. The user moves the mouse pointer around the screen by moving the mouse or trackball, and performs a large amount of exploration in an application through the use of the mouse. It is possible for an application to send the user information about the state of the application, or about what to do next, through the mouse pointer as the user manipulates it.

Windows normally displays the mouse pointer as an arrow on the screen. Visual Basic gives you the opportunity to change the shape of the pointer at different points and different times in the application. Probably the most common alternate mouse pointer is the hourglass, which displays whenever the application is performing an activity that requires the user to wait. However, there are a number of other alternate pointer icons that you can use to send the user information on what to do next.

The shape of the mouse pointer is controlled by a Visual Basic property contained within individual forms, and within controls and boxes on the form. The MousePointer property determines the type of mouse pointer displayed when the mouse is over a particular part of a form or control at run time.

The MousePointer property settings are:

0	**Default**	The pointer shape is determined by the control. It is usually an arrow.
1	**Arrow**	This is the normal shape of the cursor when moving through an application.
2	**Cross**	This is a cross-hair pointer, which is often used when drawing a shape in a drawing application.
3	**I-Beam**	The I-beam is the normal cursor when inserting text into a document or text box.
4	**Icon**	This value will display a small iconic square within a square.
5	**Size**	This is a four-pointed arrow pointing north, south, east, and west.
6	**Size NE SW**	This is a double arrow pointing northeast and southwest.
7	**Size N S**	This is a double arrow pointing north and south.
8	**Size NW SE**	This is a double arrow pointing northwest and southeast.
9	**Size W E**	This is a double arrow pointing west and east.

10	**Up Arrow**	This is an arrow pointing straight up to the top of the display.
11	**Hourglass**	The hourglass signifies that the application is perform ing an operation that requires the user to wait.
12	**No Drop**	This is the circle with the diagonal line through it, indicating that a component being dragged by the mouse can't be dropped in a particular location.

The MousePointer property controls the shape of the mouse pointer. This property is useful when you want to indicate changes in functionality as the mouse pointer passes over controls on a form or dialog box. The Hourglass setting (number 11) is useful for indicating that the user should wait for the process or operation to finish before continuing to interact with the application.

When it is set for the Screen object:

```
Screen.MousePointer = Value,
```

the MousePointer property changes across the entire screen. This means that it overrides all of the MousePointer settings for other objects and other applications. This is useful if, under some circumstances, you want a consistent mouse pointer shape across your entire application. Setting **Screen.MousePointer** to 0, the default, restores the previous behavior.

One thing you might want to do with the mouse pointer in an application is to show the hourglass and disable the form until whatever action the application is performing is completed:

```
Form1.Enabled = False
```

Disabling the form is a safety mechanism; it prevents the user from doing anything with the form until the action has been completed. Otherwise, the user can still use the mouse pointer, even in the hourglass form, to per- form screen actions that the system is not in a position to respond to.

This is very easy to do by manipulating the properties of the form. If you want to show that the form is waiting for something, you disable the form, using the syntax in the preceding paragraph, and change the mouse pointer (**Screen.MousePointer = 11**). You have to change the mouse pointer back to whatever it was and enable the form when you are done. You can also change the mouse pointer to a variety of other shapes, as described earlier. These shapes help the user determine what to do at different points in your application.

INCORPORATING THE MOUSEPOINTER INTO A SUBROUTINE

Following is an example of how to change the pointer to an hourglass while circles are drawn across your screen, and then change the hourglass back to a pointer at the end of the procedure (the text beginning with an apostrophe (') contains comments to the code):

```
Sub Form_Click ()
      Dim I
      Screen.MousePointer = 11           ' Change the mouse pointer to
                                             the hourglass shape.
      Call server(param, InV, OutV)      'Call a subroutine from an external
                                            program
                                         'and wait for it to complete execution.
      Screen.MousePointer = 0            ' Return the mouse pointer to
                                             normal.
End Sub
```

PRESENTING INFORMATION CLEARLY

Visual Basic provides a wide variety of ways for the application developer to present information and visual cues to the user. In addition to the standard user interface components on the toolbar, many of these techniques are provided through the use of VBXs, or Visual Basic Custom Controls.

Many of the VBXs included in the Visual Basic Professional Edition, or available from third-party vendors, serve to enhance the user interface facilities of the basic package. Some of the available controls, such as picture boxes, serve to display different types of information. Others, such as three-dimensional frames and panels, group information in different ways.

The ability of your application to inform the user about how the application works, and what to do next, depends on how you use the controls available in Visual Basic. You can use virtually any of the properties available for the commonly used display controls to send information to the user, including different fonts and font styles, color, making a control hidden or visible, or changing the mouse pointer in response to user actions.

Frequently, it is useful to make use of combinations of the techniques described here. For example, combining of the changing of the mouse pointer to the I-beam, while highlighting the text box in which it is located, serves to reinforce the user's understanding of that control.

USING A FRAME TO
SET APART RELATED OPERATIONS

One way of cueing the user about a set of related operations is to use the Visual Basic concept of the frame. A frame is an identifiable grouping of controls that are set aside and outlined by a box on the screen. Like all Visual Basic controls, the box need not be visible. If it is not visual, then some of the effect is often lost, even if it is apparent on the display that a set of controls is grouped together. Nevertheless, if the controls are set off from other operations on a form, or grouped in an obvious manner, the user understands immediately that the controls complement each other in some way.

A frame is useful functionally as well as visually. First, it lets you move a group of controls around on a form without having to first select them individually. This aids you in constructing the application. However, all of the controls to be included within a frame have to be created in that frame.

If you draw a control outside the frame and then try to move it inside, the control will be on top of the frame and you'll have to move the frame and controls separately.

Second, it serves to group option controls so that only one can be selected at a time. If you have three option buttons all grouped in a frame, only one of the options can be selected at a time. In addition to being functional, it is also useful to the user, who knows by looking that the three options are related and that only one is possible at a time.

Like any Visual Basic screen object, the frame can be distinguished in other ways as well. Its foreground and background colors can be changed, or the cursor can change its shape whenever it's within the frame, or the the caption can be changed, or any of the text labels inside the frame can use different fonts.

Following is an example of a frame with option buttons. Just by creating the buttons within the frame, they are considered *grouped* so that only one button will remain depressed at a time. This particular example italicizes the button's caption when it is selected, and returns the caption to normal when another button is selected. This is done simply by setting the FontItalic property of each option button to True or False:

```
Sub Option1_Click ()
        If Option1.Value = False Then
                Option1.Value = True
                Option1.FontItalic = True
        ElseIf Option1.Value = True Then
                Option1.Value = False
                Option1.FontItalic = False
    End Sub
```

The two different states produced by this code are shown in Figures 3.6a, b, and c.

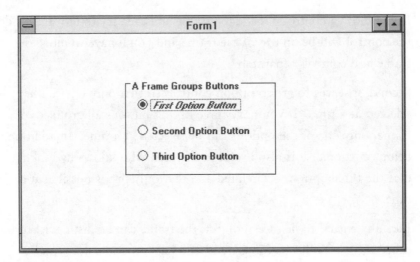

Figure 3.6a Changing the font of an option button based on the button's value.

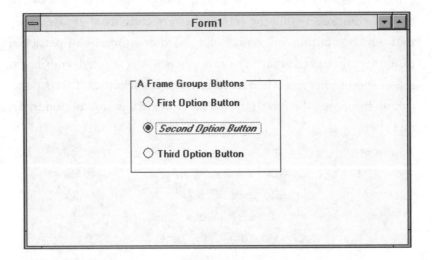

Figure 3.6b Changing the font of an option button based on the button's value.

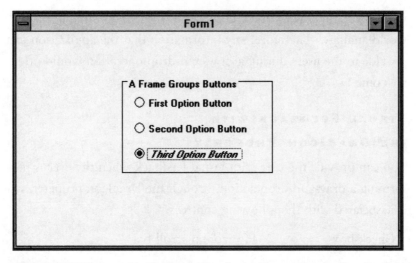

■■■■■ **Figure 3.6c** Changing the font of an option button based on the button's value.

If you don't want to perform any action other than change the value property of the button, the Option button in a group will do that by default. You should also know that Visual Basic will set one option button on every form to True by default. If you don't want this behavior, you have to manually set the value of each button on the form to False. The best time to do this is when each form is loaded:

```
Sub Form_Load ()
      Option1.Value = False
End Sub
```

COMMUNICATING WITH THE USER DURING DRAG-AND-DROP OPERATIONS

One of the most common activities that a user performs in a graphical application is dragging and dropping objects on the screen. This is a common way of moving or copying files between different locations, for example. However, this seemingly straightforward operation is difficult for many novice users, because for most it doesn't have a real-world analogy. Therefore, any information that the application can provide to the users during a drag-and-drop operation would often be welcome.

VISUAL FEEDBACK WITH THE DRAGICON PROPERTY

You can provide the user with visual feedback when the user is performing a drag-and-drop action through the DragIcon property, which is associated with the following controls:

Check box	Horizontal scroll bar
Combo box	Image
Command button	Label
Data control	List box
Directory list box	OLE control
Drive list box	Option button
File list box	Picture box
Frame	Text box
Grid	Vertical scroll bar

The DragIcon property determines the icon to be displayed as the pointer in a drag-and-drop operation. The default value is None, meaning that Visual Basic will continue displaying the arrow pointer during a drag-and-drop operation. Alternatively, you can associate a custom mouse pointer icon with the pointer during this operation. You specify the icon by loading it using the Properties window when you are designing your application. You can also use the LoadPicture function at run time in order to change the icon, depending on what the user is dragging. The file you load must have the .ICO file name extension and use that graphic file format.

Dragging an object across the screen can be difficult for many users, especially those who have not completely mastered the use of the mouse. Associating the DragIcon property with the drag operation can provide these users with visual feedback on the progress and success of their action. It is also useful when the drag operation is an especially critical or important one. A good time to make use of it is when dragging an object and setting it on top of another will cause your application to do something. A common example is when you can drag a file icon and deposit it on the printer icon, causing that file to be printed.

From an application development standpoint, you usually set DragIcon as part of a MouseDown or DragOver event procedure. Whenever the user clicks the mouse button down on an object, or drags that object, the mouse pointer will change shape correspondingly. At run time, the DragIcon property can be set to any control's DragIcon or Icon property, or you can assign it an icon returned by the LoadPicture function.

As an example, consider the form in Figures 3.7a and b. When you drag the icon loaded into a picture box, it changes the icon to a different

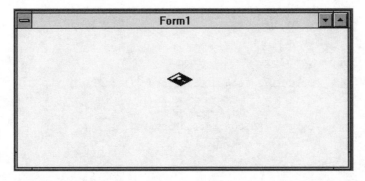

Figure 3.7a Using an icon with the DragIcon property.

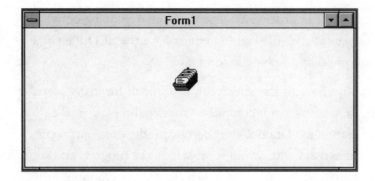

Figure 3.7b Using an icon with the DragIcon property.

one during the drag process. When the drag process is completed, the icon returns to its original state.

The code works from the DragDrop event handler associated with the form. Move is a predefined Visual Basic subroutine, or method, that controls the movement of a form or control while the application is running. When the picture box (declared as a Control type in the event handler) that you're moving on the form is moved, Visual Basic loads the icon file CHANGE.ICO and substitutes it for the given icon. When the drag operation is completed, the CHANGE.ICO file is unloaded again and the original icon is restored.

```
Sub Form_DragDrop (Source As Control, X As Single, Y As Single)
      Dim IconFile
      Source.Move X, Y
      Pic = "icons\change.ico"
      If Source.DragIcon = False Then
            Source.DragIcon = LoadPicture(IconFile)
      Else
            Source.DragIcon = LoadPicture()
      End If
End Sub
```

DragIcon can be used with the DragMode property, which is associated with the same Visual Basic components. DragMode determines manual or automatic dragging mode for a drag-and-drop operation. For most dragging operations, the user has to click and hold the mouse button while dragging. However, it is also possible to structure an activity that lets the user drag simply by clicking on the object and moving the mouse, without holding down the mouse button. Usually, you should use the manual DragMode, unless dragging is the primary or the only action that can occur with that object. The values that DragMode can take are:

0	Manual	This value requires using the Drag method to initiate dragging on the source control. This is the default value and the most commonly used type of drag-and-drop.
1	Automatic	With this value, clicking the source control automatically initiates dragging.

When DragMode is set to 1 on a Visual Basic control, that control does not respond as usual to mouse messages. You can use the 0 setting to determine when dragging begins or ends; this is useful for initiating dragging in response to a keyboard or menu command, or for allowing a source control to recognize a MouseDown event prior to dragging. Clicking while the mouse pointer is over a target control or form during a drag operation generates a DragDrop event for the target object, which ends the dragging operation.

While a component is being dragged, it cannot recognize other user-initiated mouse or keyboard events, such as KeyDown, KeyPress or KeyUp, MouseDown, MouseMove, or MouseUp. However, the component can receive events initiated by code or by a DDE link, since it is identified and recognized by name rather than by location.

USING DragMode WITH A VISUAL BASIC COMPONENT

Like other Visual Basic properties, DragMode can be changed while your application is running. The following example enables and disables the ability to drag a command button each time the button is clicked.

```
Sub Command_Click ()
        If NextCommand.DragMode = 0 Then
                NextCommand.DragMode = 1
        Else
                NextCommand.DragMode = 0
        End If
End Sub
```

USING COLORS IN VISUAL BASIC

Colors in Visual Basic are controlled by the Color Palette window. The Palette gives you up to 48 colors to work with at one time, and the ability to create millions more. The Custom Colors selection provides you with the ability to minutely control the amount of red, green, and blue in a color combination, as well as adjust the hue, saturation, and luminescence. Using this facility, you can get precisely the color you want for any use.

However, I recommend using the default colors unless you have a specific need for another color combination. Unless you are, or you are working with, a trained graphic artist, frequently you can do more harm than good with custom color combinations. Your application can become an eye-hurting and inappropriate combination of colors that sends confusing visual signals to your user. When working with custom colors, getting expert advice is your best bet.

Colors are represented as a hexadecimal value in the range of 0 to 16,777,215 (&HFFFFFF). The high byte of a number in this range equals 0 for a custom color, while the lower three bytes, from right to left, determine the amount of red, green, and blue, respectively. The red, green, and blue components are each represented by a number between 0 and 255 (&HFF). If the high byte is not 0, Visual Basic uses the default system colors for the color you choose.

Unless you are used to working with hexadecimal values, or have to do so because of the requirements of your application, I recommend working as little as possible with these values. It is easy to make a typing mistake or a mistake in mapping the hexadecimal value to the appropriate color. When you have to do so, double check the resulting color to make sure it is the one you intended.

CONTROLLING THE COLORS

You control colors in your application through the properties associated with each of the user interface components. There are three properties in most of the Properties windows relating to color: BackColor, ForeColor, and FillColor.

The ForeColor represents the color of the text or graphic displayed in a Visual Basic object. The color you use here should make the text or graphic stand out in the object, and maybe even on the form, if it is sufficiently important. The intent of using color on a forground object is that you want the color to help communicate the purpose of that object to the user, so using a soft or subtle color can hinder or confuse the user.

BackColor defines the background color of an object. The background is the area of the object upon which a text or graphic rests. In general, the background color should be subdued and should not clash with the other colors in the object. If you are using text in the object, the background color you choose should be a solid one, since otherwise the text would be difficult or even impossible to read.

FillColor is the property used to fill in shapes within Visual Basic controls, or to fill in circles and boxes created with the Visual Basic drawing tools. These types of objects usually don't have a need to stand out within your applications, so they are not usually strong or bold colors. In fact, they are most often softer colors, or even cross-hatch or other broken colors, as shown in Figure 3.8:

ForeColor = &H000000FF&

BackColor = &H00C0C0C0&

FillColor = &H00000000&

Note that the colors in the Properties window are represented as hexadecimal values representing the combination of red, green, and blue shades that make up the color, rather than as color names. This is because the number of possible colors in the palette can be as many as 2.7 million, which are far too many to name using conventional color names. You can fill them in with the actual hexadecimal values, as just described, or you can double-click on the appropriate color field in the Properties window to increment the color value. This is a much easier way to adjust the color during application design time.

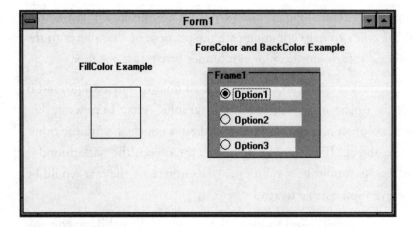

■■■■■■■ **Figure 3.8** Examples of the use of ForeColor, BackColor, and FillColor.

Unfortunately, if you want to change a color during run time, it is not so simple. The use of hexadecimal values for colors can make it difficult to manipulate colors while the application is running. For this reason, and to avoid too much confusion on the part of the user as colors change as a result of user action, you should keep color changes during run time to a minumum.

QBColor and Other Versions of Basic

Visual Basic can also make use of color codes used in other implementations of Basic, such as Visual Basic for DOS. This is done using the QBColor function call. You can also use this in place of the hexadecimal values previously described. There are considerably fewer colors available using this method, but they are easier to use. The QBColor argument is an integer in the range 0 to 15, so you have 16 colors with which to work. Starting with the least significant byte, the value specifies the red, green, and blue values used to set the appropriate color in the RGB color system used by Visual Basic.

Table 3.1 shows the possible settings for QBColor: Using QBColor is a good way of making use of colors without having to worry about using the hexadecimal values. The following code shows how you can paint an object, in this case a form, with a color using one of the QBValues. This simple function will paint the entire form light green when it is loaded:

```
Sub Form_Load ()
    QBColor(10)
End Sub
```

▬▬▬ **Table 3.1** QBColor Settings

Number	Color	Number	Color
0	Black	8	Gray
1	Blue	9	Light Blue
2	Green	10	Light Green

Continued

Table 3.1 Continued

Number	Color	Number	Color
3	Cyan	11	Light Cyan
4	Red	12	Light Red
5	Magenta	13	Light Magenta
6	Yellow	14	Light Yellow
7	White	15	Bright White

As mentioned in Chapter 2, colors should be used to supplement or high-light information, rather than stand on their own in delivering information to the user. This is because many users may still be using black-and-white displays and will not be able to readily discern a color change. Others may be colorblind, physically preventing them from perceiving the use of one or more shades of color. As much as five percent of the population may fall into this category. Nevertheless, colors serve an important role in communicating information to the user.

CHOOSING AND CHANGING FONTS

Using some of the properties associated with fonts can be an effective way of giving the user visual cues, and making text more readable under different circumstances. Manipulating fonts in Visual Basic is done through the Properties window. You have the following font properties to use and modify:

FontName

FontBold (True/False)

FontItalic (True/False)

FontSize

FontStrikethru (True/False)

FontTransparent (True/False)

FontUnderline (True/False)

Many of these properties are easy to understand and use. FontBold, FontItalic, FontStrikethru, and FontUnderline are all available as a part of the font options on virtually all Windows applications, and are Boolean in nature; that is, they carry the value of True or False. FontName designates the style of the font used on a form or component, and FontSize the size of the font in points. The size of the font is usually dependent upon what you are using it for, and the default values in Visual Basic are usually appropriate for that particular control.

FontTransparent determines whether background text or graphics are included with the characters in a particular font, and applies only to forms, picture boxes, and the Printer object. Setting FontTransparent to True permits background graphics or text to show through the characters in a font. Setting FontTransparent to False masks out existing background graphics or text.

These can be set and modified just as other properties are, by changing the value in the Properties menu for that object. When designing your application, you can toggle through the possible alternatives by double-clicking on the field name in the Properties window. Some, like FontBold and FontItalic, toggle only between True and False. FontName, on the other hand, will toggle through all of the fonts on your system.

You can also modify these values in code so that changes take effect while the application is running, as a result of user actions. The font properties have different behaviors during run time, depending upon which type of object you are referring to. For forms, picture boxes, and the Printer object, setting these properties from Basic code in a running application does not affect graphics or print output already drawn to a form, picture box, or Printer object. For all other controls, such as text boxes and command buttons, font changes take effect on the screen immediately.

The obvious property to manipulate while you're designing your application is FontName, which designates the style of the font used. Chapter 2 discussed the readability of different types of fonts, and you can easily implement these concepts in your application.

WHERE TO CHANGE FONT CHARACTERISTICS

Changing the style of a font while an application is running is a risky thing to do. If you're trying to signal or cue the user, it may not be noticed, or it may cause confusion if it is (except if the user initiates the change action, as might occur in a word processor). Therefore, the best thing to do is to select a set of font styles for use in different aspects of the application, based on the principles described in Chapter 2, and leave them alone while the application is running.

Other characteristics of a font may be used to inform the user while the application is running, especially if it is used along with other cues. For example, a strikethrough can clearly indicate that a particular option is not available, while changing a font to boldface can signify that the option it labels is active or has been selected, or that the user should pay particular attention to that text.

However, cues like this should rarely be used alone, especially if the information they convey is important. While the changes may be readily apparent, it is not always apparent what such changes mean, since they are not often used across a wide range of applications. Also, they may not be noticed by users unless used properly. For example, Figure 3.9 shows a sequence of command buttons that change the font in different ways when selected. They include Boldface, Italics, Underline, and Strikethrough.

Font-related properties can be set only to values for which actual fonts exist. This limits your ability to use fonts as mechanisms for sending information to the user. The variety of fonts that you have on your system may not correspond to the font libraries of your users, especially outside of the custom software market.

In Visual Basic, you should change the FontName property before you set size and style attributes with the FontSize, FontBold, FontItalic, FontStrikethru, FontTransparent, and FontUnderline properties. However, when you set TrueType fonts to smaller than 8 points, you should set the point size with the FontSize property, then set the FontName property, and then set the size again with the FontSize property. The Windows environment uses a different font for TrueType fonts that are smaller than 8 points.

Assisting the User through Online Help

A comprehensive online Help is a necessity to any Windows application. Many users prefer not to spend their time looking through manuals, but are more than willing to check out a specific feature, or try to determine how to perform a particular action, through the online Help.

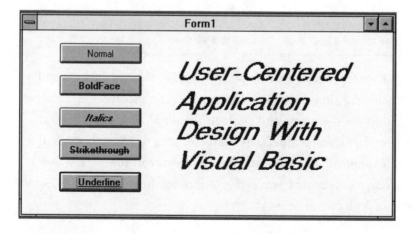

Figure 3.9 Using Command buttons to change font characteristics.

Online Help has advanced significantly since the use of Windows applications has become widespread. One important reason for this is the use of hypertext, a method of linking together related concepts. In Windows Help, certain key concepts, as determined by the Help developer, are highlighted in green and underlined with a solid green line. Clicking on one of these words changes the context of the Help screen to the description or explanation of that concept. This lets you quickly move between related concepts without having to return to a table of contents or index.

A related concept is the pop-up capsule definition. Certain Help concepts are highlighted in green and underlined with a dashed green line. Clicking on one of these words displays a pop-up box with a brief definition of that word.

Another reason for the growing sophistication of Windows Help systems is the availability of Help compilers. These tools enable you to prepare a Help file from a word processing document and incorporate many of the features that have become common in online Help, such as hypertext, graphics, and different ways to navigate the file. The components of a Help file, and how to develop a Help file, are discussed in detail in the next chapter.

PUTTING THE PIECES TOGETHER

Your Visual Basic application will typically consist of several forms and a number of controls, along with a Help file. You can incorporate different colors and fonts for the forms and controls, load and use graphics, and provide facilities to change the visual characteristics of controls while the application is running. You can set a group of controls together if they logically belong together, and you can group controls to make them work in conjunction with one another.

All of these capabilities give you a large number of tools and enormous flexibility in creating and testing your graphical user interfaces. There are many possible combinations, so it is important not to focus on one particular way of doing things in your applications. What works for one group of users may not work for another. Take advantage of the flexibility of user interface construction tools to experiment with the best ways of presenting information, taking into account the characteristics of your users.

DESIGNING AND LAYING

OUT THE USER INTERFACE

In developing an application using Visual Basic, the user interface is the beginning point of the process, and in many cases the primary part of the application. Sometimes, an application may have little or no code beyond that required to implement the user interface. Therefore, designing an application in Visual Basic should begin with its appearance to the user. This chapter will examine how to start the applications development process by focusing on the user interface. Subsequent chapters will discuss how to look behind the user interface design to implementing the action behind the scenes.

THE BEGINNING OF THE APPLICATION DEVELOPMENT PROCESS

Designing a Visual Basic application is an unusual process for a programmer used to working in a traditional language. With Pascal or C, for example, the programmer may not actually see on the screen what the application looks like until it is mostly or completely finished. The programmer codes one piece at a time, and integrates it together through the compilation process. In many ways, it requires a stretch of the imagination to see what the user will see at the very end of the process.

In Visual Basic, on the other hand, the application developer looks at the user interface from the beginning of the development process, and, in fact, rarely looks at anything else. Programming in the traditional way is usually the last step in user-centered application development with Visual Basic. This puts the application developer and end user much closer together in their goals than with a traditional language.

Therefore, the first step in the Visual Basic programming model is designing and laying out the user interface. In order to begin this process, it is important to understand the components available to build user interfaces, and how these components work.

BEGINNING WITH THE FORM

The basis of a Visual Basic application is the form. The form is a combination drawing board, place mat, application window, and even dialog box. Initially, you can treat it as a kind of sketch pad, where you lay out the components of your user interface, and rapidly change it in order to incorporate new ideas or requirements. It gives you enormous flexibility to lay out, modify, and adjust the details of your user interface.

An application can have more than one form. Consider the form as being comparable to a window in a running application. It is not unusual for applications to have multiple windows, depending on their complexity and purpose. One of the windows must then act as the startup form, which displays initially every time a user launches the application. By default, an application will start up with the first form that you created, which is the one at the top of the Project window.

However, if your application has more than one form, it does not have to start up with the first form in the project. Rather, you can start your application with any form in your project, or with a Sub Main procedure in a module (discussed in the next chapter). To specify a startup form other than the first one, choose the Project item in the Options menu. Visual Basic will display a dialog box, shown in Figure 4.1. From this dialog box, you select the Set Startup Form item. You can select any form in the project with which to start your application.

MODELESS VERSUS MODAL FORMS

Forms can behave in two separate ways in an application. With most general-purpose forms, the user can iconize the form or send it into the background. This type of form is known as *modeless*. Modeless forms enable the user to determine the ordering of activities in an application,

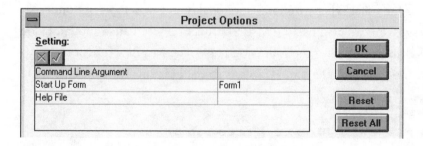

Figure 4.1 Selecting the initial form from the Project Options menu.

and are the preferred way of implementing a form, because they give the user greater control over the application. When the application is running, this is a normal user interface window.

Modal forms, on the other hand, prevent the user from doing anything else in the application until the form is closed. This is useful when there is just one activity that the user has to perform before the application can continue. Modal forms are used primarily for dialog boxes, where the user has to make a response before the application can continue. This type of form exerts control over the user, rather than the other way around, and should be used sparingly.

One caution when using modal forms is that although other forms in your application are disabled when a modal form is displayed, other applications are not. This means that the user will be able to switch to another application, even if the current application is stopped. If your application is exchanging data or interacting with other open applications in some way, this could cause a problem. While this is a characteristic of Windows applications in general and you can't eliminate this problem entirely, you can minimize its potential by carefully considering when and how to use modal forms, and using them only when absolutely necessary.

Distinguishing between modeless and modal forms involves the use of the Show method, discussed in the following section. You designate the form as one or the other when you load and display it (the default option is modeless). You can also use the MsgBox function to create a modal dialog box, as demonstrated on the following page. The MsgBox function is usually used for creating alerts or warnings to the user toward a specific user action.

EXAMPLE OF A MODAL DIALOG BOX

The following subroutine uses MsgBox to display a modal dialog box with a Yes button and a No button, with No as the default response. The

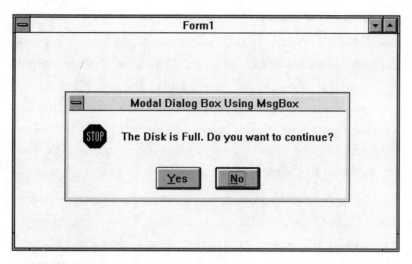

■■■■■■■■■ **Figure 4.2** A Modal dialog box using the MsgBox function.

MsgBox function returns a value based on the button chosen by the user. The MsgBox statement uses that value to display a message that indicates which button was chosen. The resulting dialog box is shown in Figure 4.2.

The code that generated this box looks like this:

```
Sub Form_Click ()
        Dim DgDef, Msg, Response, Title
        Title = "Modal Dialog Box Using MsgBox"
        Msg = "The disk is full."
        Msg = Msg & " Do you want to continue?"
        DgDef = 4 + 16 + 256        'Codes for different messages
        Response = MsgBox(Msg, DgDef, Title)
        If Response = 6 Then
                Msg = "You chose Yes."
        Else
                Msg = "You chose No or pressed Enter."
        End If
        MsgBox Msg, 0
End Sub
```

LOADING OTHER FORMS

There are several ways of working with forms in an application with more than one form. It is possible to have more than one form displayed on the screen at a time, and simply shift the focus between the multiple windows using the GotFocus and LostFocus events. However, it is probably more common to have only a single form open in an application at a time. The question then becomes one of how to manipulate forms so that the correct one is being displayed to the user.

This can be done with two Visual Basic predefined subroutines, or methods: Show and Hide. Show and Hide do exactly what their names imply: displaying forms and hiding them. They are used in appropriate places in a Visual Basic subroutine to display or close a form in response to an event. Their syntax is as follows:

```
FormName.Show
FormName.Hide
```

Show takes two parameters:

1. The name of the form to show. If you don't specify a name, Visual Basic will show the form associated with the module that contains Show.

2. An integer value that determines if the form is modal or modeless. If style is 0, the form is modeless; if style is 1, the form is modal. If this value is left out, Visual Basic assumes that the form is modeless.

Visual Basic makes a distinction between loading a form (with the Load method) and displaying it (using Show). It is possible to load a form without displaying it. Although this does not directly affect the user immediately when using Load, it may display forms faster once they are called.

If the form is not loaded when the module calls the Show method, Visual Basic automatically loads it from disk. When a modeless form is displayed, Visual Basic code that occurs after the Show method is executed as it is encountered. When a modal form is displayed, no Visual Basic code after the Show method is executed until the form is hidden or unloaded.

Show behaves in different ways, depending on whether you specify the form as modeless (the default) or modal. If it's a modeless form, Show will enable the application to continue executing other code if necessary. If, for example, the user wants to shift the focus of the application to another form, or even to close the application altogether, using Show with a modeless form will let that happen. However, if you specify a modal form, Show will suspend execution of all other code in the application until that form is closed. This produces the behavior that we expect of a dialog box.

Hide, on the other hand, takes only the name of the form as a parameter. When a form is hidden, it is removed from the screen and its Visible property is set to False. A hidden form's controls are not accessible to the user, but they are available to the running Visual Basic application itself, to other processes that may be communicating with the application through dynamic data exchange (DDE), and to timer events. When a form is hidden, control does not return to the user until all code in the event procedure that caused the form to be hidden has finished executing. If the form is not loaded when the Hide method is invoked, it is loaded but not shown.

Like Show and Load, Visual Basic also makes a distinction between Hide and Unload. Hide removes the form from the display, but still keeps it loaded in memory. Unload, on the other hand, removes the form both from the display and from memory.

Using the Show and Hide Methods

This example uses the Show method to show a new instance of a form. It creates a number of new instances of a form called **F(i)**, based on a user input elsewhere in the application, and then uses Show to load and display as many new instances as are necessary. Figure 4.3 shows the resulting forms.

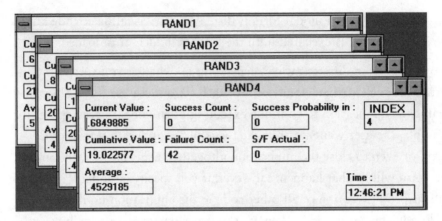

Figure 4.3 Cascading form instances.

```
Sub Form_Click ()
        For i = 1 To GBLRCNT
                F(i).Caption = Trim$("RAND" + Trim$(Str$(i)))
                F(i).LinkTopic = F(i).Caption
                F(i).Text9.Text = i
                F(i).Text6.Text = GBLPROB
                F(i).Show                 ' Load and display new instance
```

This part of the subroutine moves each of the newly created form instances
to a location on the screen that cascades them across the display. It uses
the Move method and a calculation based on the location of the previously
created form. The following line also gives each form a background color
with the Visual Basic predefined RGB function, which lets you specify the
combination of red, green, and blue for the Background property. Using
the RGB function is an easier way to generate a color when the application
is running than worrying about working with hexadecimal values directly.
In this case, the function generates a set of random colors using the random number generator **Rnd**.

```
        F(i).Move Left + (i * 400) + (Width \ 10), Top + (i * 400) + (Height \ 10)
        F.BackColor = RGB(Rnd * 256, Rnd * 256, Rnd * 256)
    End Sub
```

The following subroutine uses the Hide method to hide a form that is currently being displayed. Show and Hide give you enormous flexibility to display and hide both forms and controls as needed to control how much information your application shows the user at any one time. Depending on what the user is doing, your application can display different combinations of forms, controls, and prompts.

```
Sub Form_Click ()
        Form1.Hide
End Sub
```

FORMS AND FOCUS

An important aspect of using forms involves the focus of the application. Focus refers to the window that is not wholly or partially covered by other windows, and is the window in which the user is currently working. In Windows, this is the only window that can accept mouse clicks or other user-generated events. In an application with multiple open windows, focus refers to the window on the top of the stack. In a single-form application, the concept of focus is not quite as important, but is still used to distinguish between multiple running applications.

The reason the concept of focus is important is that windows and controls on those windows often have different behavior, depending on whether or not they are in focus. The active window is said to *have the focus*, and lets the user accomplish a wider range of activities. For example, you may want your application to display a short, descriptive prompt to the user, indicating the purpose of a particular form whenever that form has the focus, and hide the prompt otherwise.

The concept of focus is important on many controls as well as forms. If a user has the cursor in a text box, for example, that text box has the focus. When the cursor is moved away, the text box has lost the focus. The GotFocus and LostFocus events, which can be used to execute event-handling code in Visual Basic, are predefined events for the following components:

Form (though not an MDI form)	Horizontal scroll bar
Check box	List box
Combo box	OLE control
Command button	Option button
Directory list box	Picture box
Drive list box	Text box
File list box	Vertical scroll bar
Grid	

Focus is identified and controlled by both the GotFocus and LostFocus events, as well as by the ActiveForm, ActiveControl, and Enabled properties. You may want to use these events and properties to gray out or hide forms or controls that don't have a use at a particular point in an application, and display them prominently when they do. This provides important visual cues to the user about what can and cannot be done at a given time in the application. Using these events and properties to accomplish these things will be discussed in detail in the next chapter.

MULTIPLE DOCUMENT INTERFACE (MDI) FORMS

A multiple document interface (MDI) form is a form that serves as a background window for an application. The MDI form might be thought of as the main form or window of your application, since all other forms will appear on top of it. Other forms in your application are considered to be children to the MDI form. You tell other forms that you are using an MDI form through the MDIChild property on the form:

```
Form1.MDIChild = True
```

Using an MDI form provides several advantages to your application. For example, forms that are inside an MDI form can be resized or maximized only to the size of the MDI form, giving you a set amount of display space to work in if you so desire. Second, menu bars that you design for specific forms will appear on the MDI form when the application is running. This allows you to provide your application with multiple menu bars that change as the active window changes.

Visual Basic provides a separate form, selectable under the File menu, for use as an MDI form. It has only a few properties and can respond to only a few events, because of its nature. In particular, it does not respond to GotFocus and LostFocus events, since the MDI window should never receive the focus in the first place. The MDI form looks like the one in Figure 4.4.

Many commercial applications make use of the appearance provided by the MDI form. Word processors, for example, let you work with multiple document windows within the application window. The MS Windows Program Manager itself is, in effect, an MDI form. You should strongly

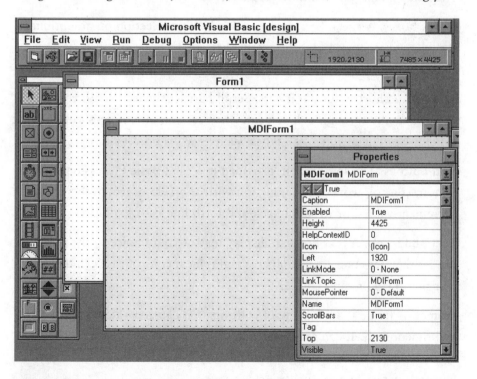

■■■■■■■■■ **Figure 4.4** The MDI form.

consider using an MDI form if you plan on permitting more than one window open at a time in your application.

PLACING OBJECTS ON THE FORM

Once you have selected a form or forms to use, Visual Basic includes a number of user interface components that can be placed onto a form to make it look like a Windows application. These include:

Command buttons. A command button lets a user begin, pause, or end an application task. You often see it used in dialog boxes, for example, to Save or Not Save a file.

Option buttons. An option button lets a user turn on and off an option or set of options. You can see an example of option buttons used in many Print dialog boxes in Windows applications.

Check boxes. A check box gives a user a Yes/No selection on an option. It is similar to an option button, except that option buttons can be grouped so that only one option at a time can be selected.

Vertical and horizontal scroll bars. Scroll bars let the user scroll vertically or horizontally through a document. They are common in applications that make use of documents of all types, such as word processors.

Spin buttons. The spin button, provided in Visual Basic Professional as a custom control, works in conjunction with another control to increment or decrement values, or to scroll back and forth in a list of choices.

Text and labels. A text box can display text of your choice to the user, or can let the user enter text. A label is a graphical control that can display text that the user can't edit.

Frames. A frame is a grouping of controls that can separate both visually and functionally. It can set apart controls on a form so that the user can identify them as performing complementary tasks, and it can make option buttons operate in a mutually exclusive way.

To use these controls, you simply select the control from the toolbox and place it onto a form (though not an MDI form, which can take only other forms, picture boxes, menus, and certain types of custom controls). They take on the appearance of Windows controls, and can be positioned and sized almost infinitely.

These controls can make a Visual Basic application every bit as attractive and functional as one that traditional programmers write in more conventional languages. The difference is that with Visual Basic it can be done faster, and it can be done with more attention to the needs of the end user. In many cases, users can actually assist in the placement and operation of these controls, leaving to the developer the task of producing the desired behaviors.

This places a powerful tool into the hands of both the developer and the user. The user has certain expectations that cannot often be expressed in concrete form, while the developer can give them that form, but cannot read the user's mind. In the hands of the user, Visual Basic can bring an abstract idea to a surface reality, and in the hands of the developer, that surface reality can be brought to life.

An added benefit is that each of these controls contains a minimum of default behaviors. While these are not enough to provide all of the functions needed for a complete application, they are frequently enough to demonstrate to the user how the control will appear to function. Using the default behaviors will often change the appearance of the control or even the entire display, but will not do anything else without the intervention of the developer.

For example, running a form with the check box will automatically display an X in the box when clicked on by the user. Option buttons will display a filled-in circle when selected. While this is only visible behavior, it is very important to the user during the application design process.

DESIGNING MENUS

Virtually all Windows applications make use of pull-down menus. Pull-down menus appear at the top of a window, and clicking on one of the menu titles displayed across the menu bar brings up a list of menu selections underneath that title. Figure 4.5 shows a typical menu bar in a Windows application, such as Visual Basic.

Microsoft has design conventions for menus and their contents to be used with applications running under Windows. These conventions ensure consistency between Windows applications, lowering the overall learning curve once Windows itself is mastered. Fortunately, Visual Basic enforces many of these conventions in its Menu Design feature. Menu Design, selectable from the Window menu, lets you lay out a functional pull-down menu structure in just a few steps.

The blank Menu Design window is shown in Figure 4.6. Although this tool can make a wide variety of different menus, even the most basic menus can be created with only a few simple operations. First, all menu titles remain unindented in the display window. For example, the File title will stay flush left in the window, since it is a menu title.

Second, menu selections under that title will be indented one space. Submenus under individual menu selections will be indented two spaces, and so forth. Submenus created in this way are communicated to the user by solid arrows on the right edge of the higher-level menu item, as shown in Figure 4.7.

■■■■■■ **Figure 4.5** The Visual Basic menu bar.

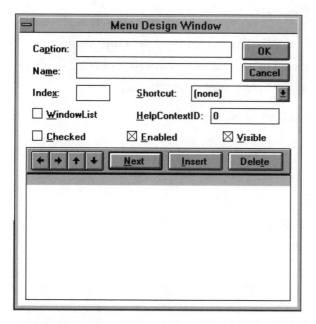

▬▬▬▬▬ **Figure 4.6** The Visual Basic Menu Design window.

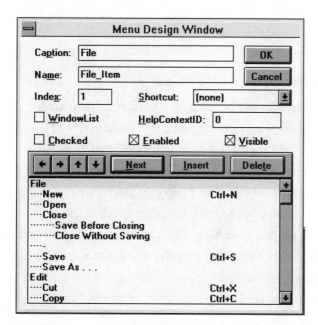

▬▬▬▬▬▬ **Figure 4.7** Adding menu items and selections to a menu bar.

Third, placing a hyphen (-) in the caption field of the menu item places a separator bar between groups of menu items under the same menu title. The separator bar is often used in application menus to group menu selections that provide similar or complementary operations.

The effect in the Menu Design window looks like this:

```
File

        New

        Open

        Close

                    Save Before Closing

                    Close Without Saving

        -

        Save

        Save As

Edit

        Cut

        Copy

        Paste
```

BUILDING MORE FUNCTIONAL MENUS

The operations with the Menu Design window are sufficient to create a basic menu, but there are several ways to enhance this structure. For example, you can assign HelpContextID, which determines an associated context number for an object. It is used to provide context-sensitive Help for the menu selection. For context-sensitive Help to a menu item, you must assign the same context number to both the object and to the associated Help topic when you compile your Help file. If you've created a Help file for the menu item and set its HelpFile property, when a user presses the F1 key, Visual Basic automatically calls Help and requests the topic identified by the current context number. The current context number is the value of HelpContextID for the object that has the focus.

The checked control lets you display a check mark by a menu item to show that is has been selected. You often see this selecting a font size, or choosing among menu options that mutually exclude one another. Visual Basic itself uses the checked menu item to indicate whether the toolbar is displayed.

ALTERNATE ACCESS TO MENU COMMANDS

Some users prefer not to use a mouse or other pointing device to access menu commands. Using the mouse can be a time-consuming process, and experienced typists know that they lose precious seconds every time their fingers leave the keyboard. Other users may have learned on a command-line interface such as MS DOS, and feel more comfortable navigating an application from the keyboard. Still others may not be very coordinated with the mouse, which can be difficult to use for some. For all of these users, it makes sense to provide other ways of using menu commands.

There are two ways to provide users with alternate access to the menu bar. The first is with access keys. An access key lets the user select a menu item without using the mouse pointer, by moving to the appropriate menu title, then to the desired item. Access keys work in conjunction with the Alt key; by pressing the Alt key and a key code, you can pass control to the desired menu item. The key code is designated by the underlined letter on both the menu title and menu item.

The second way of accessing menu items is with shortcut keys. The shortcut key lets the user perform a menu action with a single keystroke combination. The difference between the shortcut key and an access key is that the access key actually traverses the menu, but does not perform the action until the user presses the Enter key.

The WindowList box activates the WindowList property, which specifies whether a menu maintains a list of the current Multiple Document Interface (MDI) child windows in an MDI form. The WindowList property is read-only at run time, and its settings can be set to True or False. When True, the menu maintains a list of open windows and displays a check mark next to the currently active window. Users can click a window name to activate that window. When false, the menu does not maintain a list of open windows. This is the default value.

Many MDI applications have a Window menu containing a list of open MDI child windows. This property enables you to add this functionality to your application. Only one menu control on a form can have a WindowList. When you set WindowList to True on a menu control, the WindowList menu structure is appended to the menu items indented below it.

Last, you can choose whether a particular menu item is enabled and visible at the time the application is launched. A menu item that is not enabled is grayed out so that it cannot be selected. A menu item that is not visible simply doesn't appear on the menu at all. The advantages of graying out a menu item, or hiding it, are clear. As discussed earlier, graying-out cues the user immediately that the item is not available. Making an item invisible shields the user from extraneous information. In the next chapter, I'll discuss how these properties can be changed while the application is running.

USER INTERFACES IN THREE DIMENSIONS

One useful technique for prototyping a user-centered design is to make use of the three-dimensional controls included with the Visual Basic Professional version. While they are not truly in three dimensions, since the display is only in two dimensions, the three-dimensional controls are a relatively recent and worthwhile design strategy.

3D controls are displayed so that they appear to extend out from the display, and to change position of the control when it is manipulated by the user. For example, a button can appear to be extending outward from the screen. When clicked by the user, it can appear to depress into the display. Other controls, such as check boxes and radio buttons, can work in a similar way.

These controls are useful because they are better models of real life than flat, or two-dimensional, controls. Users are better able to tell when they've selected an option, and what that option is supposed to do within the application, if they can actually see the control move and remember the position of the control when working with the application. It is a way of providing another visual cue to the user on the state of the application. The 3D control also stands out on a form so that the user can easily recognize it as a selectable operation within the application. In general, such controls improve communication between the application and the user.

The following sample application demonstrates some simple ways to make use of 3D controls. It uses many of the 3D components available in Visual Basic, which are described in the following. It was loaded with the make file shown, which is similar to that provided as the default autoload file with Visual Basic Professional.

```
SIMPLE.FRM
C:\WINDOWS\SYSTEM\GRID.VBX
C:\WINDOWS\SYSTEM\MSOLE2.VBX
C:\WINDOWS\SYSTEM\ANIBUTON.VBX
C:\WINDOWS\SYSTEM\CMDIALOG.VBX
C:\WINDOWS\SYSTEM\CRYSTAL.VBX
C:\WINDOWS\SYSTEM\GAUGE.VBX
C:\WINDOWS\SYSTEM\GRAPH.VBX
C:\WINDOWS\SYSTEM\KEYSTAT.VBX
C:\WINDOWS\SYSTEM\MSCOMM.VBX
C:\WINDOWS\SYSTEM\MSMASKED.VBX
C:\WINDOWS\SYSTEM\MSOUTLIN.VBX
C:\WINDOWS\SYSTEM\PICCLIP.VBX
```

```
C:\WINDOWS\SYSTEM\SPIN.VBX
C:\WINDOWS\SYSTEM\THREED.VBX
FORM3D.FRM
ProjWinSize=152,402,248,215
ProjWinShow=2
```

The VBX required in order to mount 3D controls in the toolbox is THREED.VBX. This VBX provides the ability to use the following 3D controls:

3D check box. This control lets you display a sunken check box, with the ability to click and display a check that appears recessed in the box.

3D command button. This control lets you display a raised push button and include an icon or bitmap on the face of the button.

3D frame. The 3D frame lets you group a set of controls so that they appear to stand out from the rest of the application, and to perform similar operations.

3D group pushbutton. The 3D group pushbutton changes its state when clicked, and can be grouped together in a manner similar to the toolbar in Visual Basic or other Windows applications.

3D option button. This control can display an option that can be turned on and off. This can be used within a frame to group option buttons that present mutually exclusive options.

3D panel. The 3D panel is a raised surface that can be used as a place setting for other types of controls to set them apart from other user interface features or to emphasize a particular label or control.

A typical set of three-dimensional controls is shown in Figure 4.8. This example opens with a set of buttons that visually show the difference between a 3D control panel, a flat button, and a simple text label.

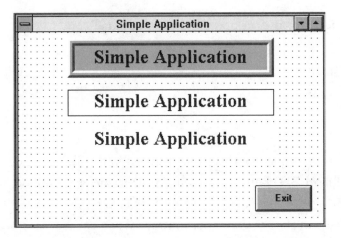

Figure 4.8 The difference between a 3D control panel, a flat button, and a simple text label.

Each can be coded with an operation, but note that the 3D button is much more easily recognizable as a control than the alternatives.

Clicking on the 3D button (or either of the others) opens yet another form with some other three-dimensional controls, shown in Figure 4.9.

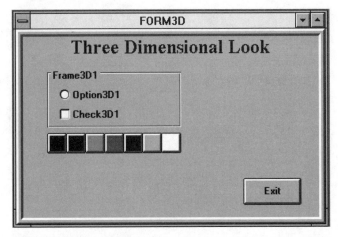

Figure 4.9 Other three-dimensional controls.

The code that performs that operation uses the panel's Sub Click event handler:

```
Sub Panel3D1_Click ()
        form3d.Show
        simple.Hide
    End Sub
```

The second form, called from the code included in the 3D panel, contains several more 3D controls, including a 3D frame, a 3D option button, and a 3D check box. The colored buttons below this control group make use of the 3D group pushbutton. When clicked, each of these buttons changes the background color of the form on which they reside. The code for doing so in a typical group pushbutton follows:

```
Sub GroupPush3D1_Click (index As Integer, value As Integer)
    If value < > 0 Then
        Select Case index
            Case 0
                Panel3d1.BackColor = &H0
            Case 1
                Panel3d1.BackColor = &HFF
            Case 2
                Panel3d1.BackColor = &HFFFF&
            Case 3
                Panel3d1.BackColor = &HFF00&
            Case 4
                Panel3d1.BackColor = &HFF0000
            Case 5
                Panel3d1.BackColor = &HC0C0C0
            Case 6
                Panel3d1.BackColor = &HFFFFFF
            Case Else
                Panel3d1.BackColor = &HFFFFFF
```

```
        End Select
          Else
        Panel3d1.BackColor = &HC0C0C0
    End If
  End Sub
```

Note that when a button is pushed, any other button that is depressed will pop back up so that only one button is depressed at a time. By setting the GroupAllowAllUp property for each of the buttons to True, you can start out with none of the buttons depressed, or you can raise all of the buttons (and choose a default background color for the form) based on another user action, such as clicking on a Reset button.

EXPERIMENTING WITH THE USER INTERFACE

In creating your application, you should already have a good idea of approximately how many screens or windows it will have. This doesn't mean that you have to have the user interface designed to the last detail, since Visual Basic encourages experimenting with different layouts. However, you must have some plan as to what controls you will need, how they will work, and how multiple forms, if necessary, will interact.

A good approach is to decide on the primary task of each form. By thinking of most modeless forms as application windows, it should be possible to visualize how you want to lay it out based on what you want the user to do with that form. If you plan on displaying multiple windows at the same time, use an MDI form as your background and build other forms on top of it.

You can then add controls to forms. Since controls have some default behaviors, it is not necessary to begin programming at this point. You can lay out sample configurations of controls, and evaluate them yourself or show them to prospective users. You can determine all of the controls you need, how to best group and arrange them on the form, and how many forms you will need in your application.

Once you have a layout for a form, you can look at it just as it will appear in a completed application simply by running it. While you won't be able to do a lot with this application shell, you are looking at exactly what the user will see when the application is running. Before giving a great deal of thought to the sequence of operations in your applications, create all of the forms so that you can see what each individual operation or task will look like. Only after you have the look and feel approximately correct should you worry about the programming details to make the application work properly.

The Visual Basic programming model is discussed in detail in the next chapter.

PUTTING IT ALL TOGETHER: THE MAKE FILE

As mentioned in earlier chapters, you can control the controls and files that are loaded into Visual Basic through the make file, which is represented with the file extension .MAK. The make file contains all of the custom controls (which have the file extension .VBX), forms (with the extension .FRM), and general procedures (with the extension .BAS).

The make file is created automatically when you save the project for an application. However, the make file is a text file, and you can also edit it manually, using any text editor. You may want to do this to control which files, particularly VBX files, are loaded for a particular project. By default, all of the custom control files included with the Visual Basic Professional version are included in any application you build. These take time and memory to load, and you may not need them for your application. You can prevent them from being loaded simply by editing them out of your .MAK file.

CREATING VISUAL BASIC HELP FILES

One of the most important considerations in the process of user-centered application design is the Help file. Help files are important because they provide guidance on how to navigate your application, and give the user immediate information on features, controls, and menu selections. A well-written Help file can provide virtually all of the information a user may need to understand and effectively use your application.

The same design guidelines for applications in general also apply to the look and feel of Help systems. Limiting the amount of information presented to the user at any one time is probably the most important principle to follow.

The one aspect of Help systems that is different from most applications is that Help systems can be navigated randomly, whereas in applications users usually follow a limited number of possible paths. This means that it is more difficult to break down Help screens into discrete steps, since each screen has to be able to stand on its own in addition to supporting the entire Help process.

MICROSOFT'S HELP COMPILER

Microsoft and other language vendors include a special compiler for creating Help files that are accessible from Windows applications. This Help Compiler enables you to combine bitmaps, Windows metafiles, hyper-graphics, and text files into a single Help file comparable to those found in commercial Windows applications. This tool is run from the DOS command line and works like most command-line compilers—you invoke the compiler, tell it what files you want to work with, and tell it the desired result.

Creating an application Help file using the Windows Help Compiler included with the Professional version of Visual Basic is not difficult, but it does require a number of steps. The possible components of a Help file are:

Project file. The project file is similar to the .MAK file for a Visual Basic project.

Topic files. Topic files are the actual text containing the help information. The topic files, which use the .RTF extension (for Rich Text Format), also include the links that tell the help compiler which topics are to be linked together and how. It is important to use a word processor that supports the .RTF format, because its hidden text facility is used to incorporate some of the Help Compiler instructions.

Graphics files. A Help file can include several different types of graphics files.

The Project file names all of the component files that will go into your Help file. The other types of files comprise the Help text, reference material, descriptions, and any graphics file that may improve your application's Help facility.

A Help File Example

In Chapter 6, I develop a rapid prototype to enable college students to register for courses electronically. This application, while it accurately emulates the appearance of the old manual registration process, still requires a Help file for several reasons. Students don't require help on filling out the form, but they do require help in understanding the registration process itself, in explanations of some course topics, and in knowing where to go to get personalized assistance. As I describe how to conceptualize, set up, and write a Help file, I'll be making reference back to this example.

WRITING A HELP FILE

Writing a Help file is not as simple as just taking the application's user's manual, or a feature reference, and placing it in an on-screen window. A Help file has to be planned out just as carefully and just as rigorously as the application itself. The many possible components of the Help file have to fit together into an integrated whole that satisfies the users' needs for assistance.

Some people claim that the Help file (and other documentation) should be written before beginning the actual development of the application itself. The rationale is that if you can't describe it exactly, you can't properly code it. While there is some validity to this approach, the user-centered development process necessitates changing an application rapidly in response to user requirements and feedback.

A Windows Help file is a combination of text, highlighted (bold-faced, underlined, or italicized) information, graphics, examples, cross-references, and links between different but related topics. This makes for a complex document that takes a great deal of thought to develop so that it provides users with the information they need to successfully navigate your application.

The first step in developing a Help file is to identify the user of the application. You should know the overall skill level of your typical user, and whether users will have diverse skill levels. These skills should be in computers in general and also in the tasks that your application will perform. For example, your users may be computer veterans but may not be familiar with the activities of your software. In this case, there should be less Help on the mechanics of using the application, and more on the process of getting something useful out of it, complete with example uses.

In the case of my example, the users will be college students, most of whom are computer-literate. Most of them have also used the manual paper-based registration process at least once, so they are not attempting an entirely new task. Further, the task itself is a relatively simple one, and the application consists of just three forms with requests for personal and course schedule information, so the first thought might be that little or no Help is needed.

In a sense, this may be true. Educated and computer-literate college students should not require a great deal of help in working out the mechanics of the application. Where they may benefit, however, is with help on the registration process itself, and on the course selections they should make.

This does not mean that the Help file should choose courses for them. Rather, it can provide descriptions for selected courses, and list prerequisites for all courses. It can also provide information on billing and financial aid, whom to contact for more information, and even qualifications of instructors.

What Should Help Contain?

Given knowledgeable computer users, most of whom are familiar with the task to be done, the Help files should consist of a minimum of assistance with the mechanics of using the computer or the application (such as how to operate the mouse, or how to make a menu selection). However, there will be prerequisites listed for all courses, and course descriptions for all elective courses. It should also have a step-by-step description of how the registration process works, information of special interest (like billing or class attendance policies), and where to go to get more information.

An online Help usually consists of several components, or access points. To be consistent with other Windows applications, Help menus should include at least these items:

Help (the menu bar label)

Contents. This is analogous to a Table of Contents, listing in logical order the topics covered in the Help file. Contents lets the user access Help much as though it were a traditional user's manual. It often follows the same form as the application's user's manual, although it frequently uses hypertext to cross-reference key items or concepts. Once in the Contents screen, the user can read through chapter by chapter or *browse* any topics or features of interest.

Using Help. This is a roadmap to the Help file, showing the users what kind of Help information is available and how to get access to it.

Reference. The Reference section lists and describes all of the menu items and features, usually in the same order as the items appear on the menu bar. The descriptions are usually short and to the point.

About <your application>. The About section normally lists the name of the application and its developer, along with any copyrights. It may also list the name of the registered user. I also like to give a brief description of the application here so that users can immediately determine if the application can meet their immediate needs. The About box is usually a single dialog box, often with its own access into the mainstream Help files.

There are several other Help menu items that your users may also need, depending on the purpose of the application and the skill level of the users. Other Help menu items often seen in applications include registration information, where and how to get technical support, and information on any upgrades or enhancements:

Search. This is a personal favorite of mine. It lets the user search the Help file contents by a key word or phrase, and go directly to help for that item.

Index. The Index is similar to the Search item, except that it is frequently more limited and lists topics in alphabetical order.

For More Information. This is a catch-all section that can list telephone numbers for technical support, sales literature, electronic bulletin boards, or other places that can provide information beyond the Help file.

How Do I? This section describes commonly performed tasks and how to go about accomplishing them. This is often a good place to include examples.

These lists of Help menu items are a good starting place, but by no means comprehensive. You can select other topics that may serve to present information about your application effectively to its users. Unless you have to give the users a number of different ways of navigating the Help file, the Help menu should contain no more than seven different selections. This makes it easier for you to construct the Help file, and less confusing for the users.

Once you have developed the menu structure, it can be used to help you organize the topics underneath. For example, the Contents, Reference, For More Information, and How Do I? can be high-level items with several separate topics organized under them.

Context-Sensitive Help

Context-sensitive Help automatically displays Help for the selected component in the application. If, for example, the user highlights a particular control and presses the F1 key (traditionally the Help key on PCs), the Help window would pop up with Help on that control, if it exists.

Context-sensitive Help is very useful on a complicated application, or if users are computer or application novices. It usually provides a description or explanation of a particular control or feature, rather than on how to accomplish a task. The WinHelp function, which is a part of the Windows API, includes the ability to produce context-sensitive Help files. This function can be called from Visual Basic, so it is possible to provide your Visual Basic applications with this feature.

Designing and Creating Help Topics

A Help topic is a text description that is generally small enough to fit onto a single Help screen without scrolling. While scrolling in a Help topic is not prohibited, anything much longer is often too complicated for the user to comprehend as a single topic. Topics should be as short and to the point as possible. A Help file for a moderately complex application may contain several dozen Help topics.

A Help topic has to include a title, which can be up to 128 characters. The title goes to the right of the context string, described in the following. You have to include a dollar sign ($) just before the title. A typical title might look like this:

```
$ How to Register
```

One of the common characteristics of a Windows application Help file is the ability to jump between different but related topics. This is identified within the Help file by an underlined and green highlighted word or phrase, called a *keyword*. When you mouse click on the highlighted text, the topic *jumps* to the topic identified by the highlighted word.

Within your Topic file, you designate keywords used for jumps with *strikethrough* (or double-underlined) text. After formatting the keyword in this style, you type a string representing the destination topic of the jump. This string, called the *context string*, is simply a word or word combination (without spaces) at the top of the file that uniquely identifies that topic. The context string can be up to 255 characters, and is not case-sensitive. You designate the context string at the very top left-hand corner of the topic file, like this:

```
# CS_DESCRIPTIONS
```

You can also set up keywords for a Help search facility. Since searching is often the fastest way of accessing Help on a particular word or feature, you should add search keywords to all of your Topic files. Each Topic file can be configured with multiple keywords so that you can jump to the same file from several different routes. You set up a keyword list in the following format:

```
K computer; registration; business; courses
```

There are several other things you can add to a Help file, such as browse sequences, secondary Help windows, and bitmaps or other graphics files. These can make your application's Help more useful, a richer source of information, and easier to navigate. An increasingly popular Help feature is the pop-up window. The pop-up window is usually associated with a particular word or phrase, and is represented in green highlight with a dashed underline. Clicking on a pop-up term will display a small modal window with a brief definition or explanation. Developers are using the pop-up window to define unfamiliar words or to provide brief prompts for terms or features that do not need their own Topic file.

You create the pop-up window in much the same way you would perform a jump. The only difference is that, rather than identifying the keyword or phrase with strikethrough or double-underlined text, you identify it with single-underlined text. The context string still goes immediately after the keyword in hidden text.

While you have a great many facilities available to you in creating a comprehensive Help file, it is best to begin in a simple and straightforward manner. Too many graphics or access methods to a Help file may be confusing or difficult for you to produce, and may not be helpful to users. It is best to start with relatively simple Help files, with a few Topic files for major features, and some jumps between related topics. Using the rapid prototyping methodology described in Chapter 6, users of the application will have the opportunity to provide feedback and influence the continued development of your Help file.

Given a gradual approach to the development of the application's Help facility, the basic configuration of a Help Topic file would look like this:

```
# CS_DESCRIPTIONS        $ SPECIAL TOPIC COURSE OFFERINGS
Spring 1995
    CS 690B,C, &D        Farley, J.                    W:  7:45 - 9:45
        690B        Fundamentals of Desktop Operating Systems <double-underline>
```

```
                                                    First 5 weeks (Jan. 18 -
Feb. 15)

        This course will be an in-depth introduction to the architecture
and features of common PC operating systems.  It will include an analysis
of DOS, along with a detailed architectural comparison of Windows and
OS/2, with an analysis of the advantages and limitations of each.

        690C       Fundamentals of Windows Programming

                                                    Second 5 weeks (Mar.
1 - Mar. 29)

        This course will introduce some of the concepts essential to
understanding how to design and develop an application in MS Windows.
It will include an overview of the Windows architecture, Windows memory
management, and the components of a Windows application. Prerequisite: C
or Pascal <double-underline>.

        690D       Database Management Using MS Access <single-underline>

                                                    Third 5 weeks (Apr. 5 -
May 3)

        This course will introduce the concept of designing relational
databases through the use of Microsoft Access. It will include a discus-
sion of relational concepts, setting up database tables, and writing
queries.
```

Organizing Help

As much time should be put into planning the Help file as goes into developing it. This is because it can't be presented in any old way and still be
effective. You should start at the top level—the names of the Help menu
selections—and work down from there. You may find that drawing a tree
diagram of the menu selections down to the individual Help Topic files can
be helpful in organizing your work.

My college registration example has five menu items: Contents, Search,
How Do I?, For More Information, and About. Note that this structure
has less reference-type information, and more process information. I chose
not to include context-sensitive Help, since this type of Help is oriented
toward feature and menu reference rather than process guidance.

The Contents section provides a listing of all courses offered, such as in the
example Help Topic file above, and organized by the department offering
the course. The Search menu is an alphabetical listing of all of the courses
by name. How Do I? provides step-by-step assistance in filling out the elec-

tronic registration form, along with information on how to complete the
registration process. Last, For More Information provides names and telephone numbers for academic advisors and administrators involved in the
course registration process.

Looking at one Help menu, Contents, gives an idea as to the overall organization of the entire Help system. The Contents file includes courses organized by department, in the manner of the preceding example file. Help
Topic files should be relatively small, usually between a half-screen page or
two in length. For smaller departments with only a few offerings, a single
Help Topic file will suffice. For larger departments with more offerings, the
Topic files can be broken down by course number—100 level, 200 level,
and so on.

The top-level Contents file lists all of the academic departments offering
courses. Selecting a department from this level will either display all offerings or the initial ones (100 level offerings in most cases). In these cases, a
button labeled Next will display the higher-level courses.

Note also that in the preceding example file, several key words and phrases
have single or double underlines. The single underlines will call pop-up
boxes that give a brief description of a concept. For example, the single
underline associated with Microsoft Access will display a box with a brief
description of Access. Double-underlined concepts will refer the user to
other courses. The double-underlined Pascal or C prerequisite, for example,
will jump the user to those course offerings and descriptions.

Bitmaps, Hotspots, and Help

The Help Compiler also lets you add graphics to a Help file. The graphics
can be used to illustrate concepts, make the Help more visually appealing,
or provide assistance by selecting graphical components in the file. Adding
graphics can be done in several ways. You can simply paste the graphic
directly into the Topic file. However, this requires using Microsoft's Word
for Windows as your word processor.

Alternatively and with more flexibility, you can reference the .BMP bitmap file within the Topic file, which will in effect include the graphic within that topic. This is referenced at the top of the Topic file, next to the context strings and keywords, and looks like this:

```
{bmc process.bmp}
```

The first instruction in this statement describes how to align the graphic in the file:

bmc aligns the graphic as a character.

bml aligns the graphic on the left margin.

bmr aligns the graphic on the right margin.

However, bitmap graphics can be used in the process of providing users help through the use of hotspots in the graphic. A *hotspot* is a graphic region in a window that is associated with some action. You use Hotspot Editor to create and edit hypergraphics. A *hypergraphic* is a bitmap that includes one or more hotspots. A hotspot can cover any portion of the bitmap. A bitmap can include multiple hotspots that link to Help topics or run Help macros when clicked.

Using Hotspot Editor, you can assign hotspots to a bitmap and assign attributes to each hotspot. Each hotspot includes the following attributes:

Context string

Link type (jump, pop-up, or macro)

Visible or invisible hotspot borders

Hotspot ID

Hotspot Editor saves hypergraphics in a special compressed file format. Hypergraphic files generally have a .SHG file name extension.

BUILDING THE HELP FILE

The key to the Help file is the Help Project file. This file tells the Help Compiler how to create the single Help file from the many topic and graphics files you may have. You create the Help Project file in ASCII format on any text editor or word processor, and save it with the file extension .HPJ. This file can contain up to nine sections that define which files are to be included in the compiled Help file. The sections are as follows:

Options. The Help Compiler can take up to 16 different options to control such things as which files are included in a build, the title of the Help window, and the font size used for the text. None of the options are required.

Files. This is a listing of all Topic files to be included in the compiled Help file.

Build Tags. Build tags are necessary if you plan on sharing files between different Help projects. They designate which files are included or excluded from different builds. This section is not required.

Config. The Config section is used to specify Dynamic Link Library and macro files to be included with the Help file. This section is not required if you don't plan on including such files.

Bitmaps. This is a listing of all graphical bitmap files to be included in the compiled Help file, and is required only if you are planning to use bitmap files.

Map. This section is used to associate context strings with context numbers, and is optional.

Alias. The alias section is used to assign context strings to topics, and is optional.

Windows. This section defines the appearance of any secondary windows used in a Help file, and is required only if you use secondary windows.

Baggage. The baggage section lists Topic files for assistance in using the Help file. A Help file for the Help file, if you will. This is also optional.

Since eight of the nine sections in the Help Project file are optional, or are required only if you want more than the basic Help file, the Help Project file can actually be quite easy to create. All it requires is a listing of the Topic files. You may also want to monitor the progress of the compiler as it works through your files. You can do this by setting the following options in the Options section of the Help Project file:

```
Warning = 3
ErrorLog = myproj.log
Report = on
```

These options will report all errors and warnings, write the error messages out to a file so that you can examine them later, and display all compiler messages generated during the compile process. With these options and a few Topic files, a typical Help Project file might look like this:

```
[OPTIONS]
        Warning = 3
        ErrorLog = myproj.log
        Report = on
[FILES]
        CS.RTF, BUS.RTF, ED.RTF, QUESTION.RTF, PROCESS.RTF
```

Once you have created this file, you simply apply it as an argument to the Help Compiler, which will do the rest of the work:

```
HC31
```

You must make sure that all of the files to be included in your Help file are in the same directory, or that you have specified their directory in the Help Project file. If you have no errors, the output of this process will be a compiled Help file with the .HLP file extension.

Hooking Help Files to Your Application

Once you have created the various Topic and other files and compiled them into the Help file, you must tell your application how to go about accessing the different topics in this file. There are two ways of doing this with Visual Basic. The first is to use the HelpFile property, which is a property of the global object App. The value of the HelpFile property is simply a string that specifies a Help file name to be called when the user selects Help from the menu or presses the F1 key, which has traditionally been the Help key for PC software. You specify the HelpFile property from the Project menu selection under the Options menu in Visual Basic by typing in the name and path of the file, or the name alone if the path is the same as the application. Figure 4.10 shows this menu.

To provide paths to specific Help Topic files, you have to use the HelpContextID property that is a part of all Visual Basic forms and controls. The value in this property can be mapped to the context strings that you can include as a part of your Help topic files, as described previously. The result is that by requesting Help on any Visual Basic form or control, you can call up the Help file that is specified by the HelpContextID property for that component.

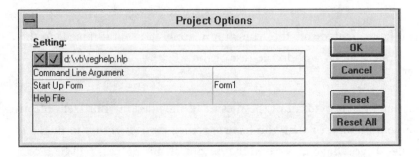

■■■■■■ **Figure 4.10** Using the Visual Basic HelpFile property to specify an application's Help file.

USING THE WINDOWS WINHELP FUNCTION

The Windows WinHelp function, which is a part of the Windows API, offers a more generic way to connect a Help file to your application. The WinHelp technique is designed to work with any Windows application. To use WinHelp, you first have to let your Visual Basic application know where to find it through a Declare statement (which is discussed in more detail in the next chapter):

```
Declare Function WinHelp Lib "USER" (ByVal hWnd As Integer, ByVal
lpzFileName As String, ByVal wCmd As Integer, dwData As Any) As Integer
```

You can then use the WinHelp function just as you would any Windows function, as described in the next chapter.

FROM THE USER INTERFACE

Most traditional programmers prefer to work with internal algorithms to tell an application how to perform its functions. These algorithms are frequently puzzles that are challenging but readily solvable and satisfying to work with. The graphical user interface, by contrast, is a difficult component of any application, and one that rarely has a single correct configuration. Rather, it is a product of trade-offs between efficiency and function, or between the novice and experienced user. This is why it's important in the user-centered design process to design the user interface first, and to get feedback and use the feedback to refine the design.

Once the design is largely completed, you can turn to the internal algorithms. In truth, you have probably started writing some code already, just as this chapter had to work with some code just to get the user interface working properly. The next chapter continues to lay down the underlying event-handling code that can bring your user interface to life.

5

ADDING FUNCTIONALITY

TO USER INTERFACE

OBJECTS

PROGRAMMING FOR VISUAL BASIC

Visual Basic uses an extension of the Basic programming language to instruct its components how to behave for different types of events. Anyone with experience in or an understanding of Basic should have little difficulty in working with the Visual Basic programming language. The language has been extended to add predefined functions, provide access to the Windows Application Programming Interface, and to support an event-driven programming model required by graphical user interfaces.

Basic code is associated with screen objects, forms, and stand-alone modules. Double-clicking on an object opens up a code window that will accept Basic instructions for that object (you may also choose Code from the View menu, or press the F7 key to do this). These instructions amount to activities that the application will perform in response to events, most of which are initiated by the user.

An event can be defined as a change in the state of the application. Most events are the result of the user directing the application through the use of the mouse. It may be a mouse click on a check box or command button, or a click on a window to make it the active window, or the selection of a menu item from a pull-down menu.

Each Visual Basic component, or object, is capable of responding to certain types of events. Different screen objects can respond to only a subset of the total number of events recognized by Visual Basic. The types of events different objects can respond to is very logical; it makes no sense, for example, to have a command button respond to a Resize event, since the user is not allowed to change the size of such a button.

Fortunately, you don't have to remember all of the events that each object can respond to. These are provided for you in the code editor windows for that object. At the top of these windows, there are two drop boxes. A sample editor window with its drop boxes is shown in Figure 5.1. The drop box on the left lists all of the objects available in that application. Selecting one of these objects will transfer you to the code windows for that object.

The drop box on the right lists all of the events for which the current object will respond. Selecting an event will change the focus of the code window to the code window corresponding to that event. Visual Basic also provides templates for the subroutine that handles that event. For example, the Load event of a form will display the following template:

```
Sub Form_Load ()

End Sub
```

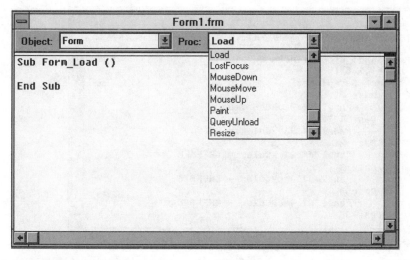

Figure 5.1 The code editing window along with the predefined events.

You've seen this subroutine format in earlier chapters, and now you can see how it's integrated into the individual Visual Basic components. This subroutine template isn't a great deal of help in writing your event-handling code, but it does prompt you with both the object and event that you're coding for. All of the objects open their code windows into default event subroutines that the object either has to respond to, or that it normally responds to. If you open the code window for a new form, the window will automatically default to the Load event and the Form_Load subroutine. Other objects default to the events most commonly associated with that object.

Once you write an event-handling subroutine for an object, Visual Basic also helps you locate the relevant events in the future. The events with code are displayed in boldface in the event drop box, as shown in Figure 5.2, letting you easily identify and access the events which have code associated with them. Visual Basic will also automatically open the first event handler that you have written code for when you double-click on that object.

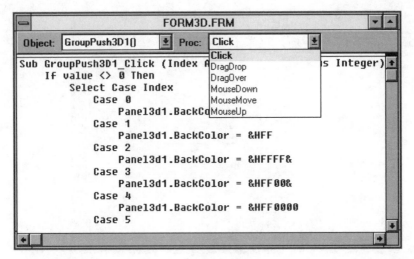

Figure 5.2 Event names with code are displayed in boldface.

IDENTIFYING AND USING OBJECT PROPERTIES

Further, each Visual Basic object has a set of properties that can be set for the application, or even changed while the application is running. The properties, like the events, vary, depending upon the object. Properties are attributes or characteristics that define the shape, color, location, or other features of the object. Sometimes, you set the values of these properties at design time to achieve a particular effect for the user interface. When doing this, you can change the properties directly, through the Properties window, which is commonly displayed in the development environment. The Properties window for a form is shown in Figure 5.3.

When changing values through the Properties window, Visual Basic often includes a set of possible values associated with each property. All you have to do to change the values is to double-click on the value of the property. For example, it is possible to quickly change between True and False on the Visible property, or between the colors available on the BackColor

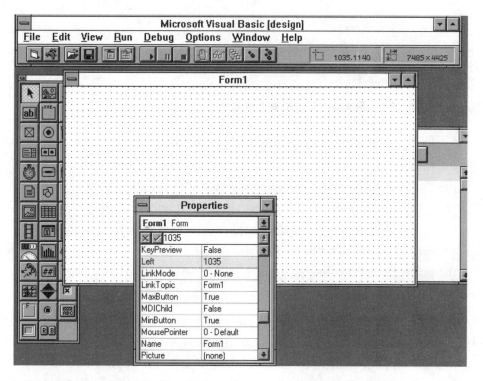

Figure 5.3 The Properties window associated with a form.

property. In some cases, these values only represent defaults; it is often possible to add unique values of your own.

In addition to setting up an application with a set of properties, the object properties are often manipulated or changed as a part of the execution of the application. When the application is running, these properties are changed by referencing the object and properties, and assigning a new value:

```
Objectname.property = NewValue
```

It is important to know the data type of the property if you plan to assign the property to other variables while the application is running. Some properties, such as Background Color, take hexadecimal values, while others, like the Enabled property, take Boolean values:

```
Form1.BackColor = &H8000005&
Form1.Enabled = True
```

PUTTING IT ALL TOGETHER

So the Visual Basic programming model is as follows: You create your user interface by placing user interface objects onto one or more forms. Once the user interface looks approximately as you intend, you decide what types of events to which each object should respond, and what types of behaviors each event should evoke. Then, you write event-handling code for each event in each object, as required. This code frequently manipulates the properties of the display objects, both to accomplish specific program activities and to send information to the user.

And then you're done. Or at least you begin the process again with successive refinements to the basic application. The concept of successive approximations is important to the development of software applications in general, and it is even more important to the making of an application in Visual Basic. In order to adapt to the needs of its users and to remain relevant as circumstances change, an application has to be able to adapt during its life cycle. This is related to the concept of rapid prototyping, to be discussed in the next chapter.

Once you are satisfied that the base application works properly, you can begin to enhance it. One type of enhancement is to permit existing objects to respond to more and different types of events. A second type is to add additional objects and even additional forms so that the application can do more. Then, of course, you have to write event-handling code for these new objects.

It is also possible to enhance this programming model by calling external code written in other languages, or by interfacing with other executable applications and exchanging data on the fly. When and how to do this will be discussed in later chapters of this book.

OBJECT NAMES IN VISUAL BASIC

Every Visual Basic object, from forms to buttons to boxes, all have names. The names make it easy to reference the object in the code. Visual Basic provides each object with a default name, which usually consists of the object's type and a number designating the instance of the object. For example, the name Form3 is simply the third form in the project you are working on. Any code referring to that form will reference it as Form3. You may also give Form3 a more descriptive name and refer to it by that name.

Objects within the form are designated with the object name and the instance of the object on that form, so the numbers for commonly used objects, such as buttons and text boxes, do not get too large. Since it is unlikely that code on one form will reference controls on other forms, this is a relatively safe practice. In the unlikely event that a control on one form has to reference a control on another, the control's name would be preceded by the form's name, like the following:

```
Form2.Option3.Value = True
```

This says that you are setting the third option button on the second form to True. You can easily refer to the default names of each control by its control name and the number of that type of control you have on a form.

The automatic naming convention of objects is useful in rapid prototyping, because it allows you to quickly lay out objects on the screen and give them some underlying functionality without worrying about filling in the name property on the objects. However, the default names quickly become unwieldy, because there is nothing in the naming convention to distinguish between the purpose or function of the control. When you have many controls on a form and have to refer to them in the Declarations section of your code or in a general subroutine, you will find yourself constantly checking back to make sure of the object name before you reference it in the code.

Therefore, you should make it a practice to give descriptive names to all of your Visual Basic objects, including the forms. While this seems like a distraction when rapidly prototyping an application, it will pay off when you get down to the work of making the controls behave in the required manner. This will also make it easier to modify the application in the future. Associating descriptive names with your objects will prompt your memory with code that you wrote in the more distant past.

Descriptive names might take the following format:

Forms	DialogForm, UserSelectForm, ConfirmForm
Option Buttons	GreenOption, ScoreOption, StatusOption
Text Boxes	NameField, AddressField, TelephoneField

The trade-off is that the more descriptive the name, the longer it is likely to be. While Visual Basic enables you to use names of up to 40 characters, these become tedious for you to type as you write code. Many application developers prefer to use short names because they may have to type these names dozens or even hundreds of times in the course of the application development process. Therefore, you should seek names that are not only descriptive but brief.

You should also look for a way to systemize your naming conventions. In other words, your names should follow a logical pattern. Visual Basic programmers often do this by making the object's name a combination of two words, such as FirstName or HomeAddress. This helps to organize the variable names so that they have a locational meaning as well as a descriptive one.

SUBROUTINE CALLS

Visual Basic has two types of subroutines: Subs and Functions. The Sub is the more generic of the two. It might be compared to a procedure in

Pascal. A Sub does not explicitly return values. However, by passing it parameters, you can modify the parameters within the Sub and return the modified parameters back to the calling routine. A Sub cannot be part of an assignment statement in a calling routine; rather, it is simply called as an instruction line:

```
Call SendTicket(0)
SendTicket 0
```

Both of these formats are functionally equivalent.

Visual Basic functions, like functions in other programming languages, are more specialized. They are designed to return a single value, and are often used to perform mathematical calculations. Functions can be called by assigning a variable to the function name and any parameters to be passed. In this way, the value returned by the function can be placed into the variable, just as you might with a normal assignment statement:

```
SqValue = Square(value)
```

Subs or functions that are not associated with any specific object and event are placed in the General object of an application. There are several ways of accessing the General object. To create the Subroutine, you can open the code window of any existing object, then choose the New Procedure menu item under the View menu. It will ask you if you want to create a Sub or a Function, then provide you with the template for the one you choose.

Once you have created your subroutines, you can return to them by selecting the General object in any object's code window. Then, like any other object, you can choose individual subroutines by scrolling through the right-hand drop box at the top of the window. Alternatively, you can scroll through the subroutines by choosing Next Procedure and Previous Procedure from the View menu.

General subroutines are stored in a file with a .BAS extension in the project window. They are referred to as modules in Visual Basic. You can open this file just as you would a form for the project, by double-clicking on the file name. This opens a code window for the General object, and normally displays the global declarations by default. You can then scroll through the other subroutines using one of the preceding techniques.

In practice, you use these types of general subroutines if they work with more than one object, or if they cannot easily be associated with any single object. You may also use the general section of the form for variable declarations that are global; that is, that apply across the applications. An example of this is shown in Figure 5.4. They are not invoked by a specific event; rather, they have to be explicitly called by some other part of the application. You also place any global declarations of variables in the General object. This makes their scope global; in other words, the variable name is accessible anywhere in the application.

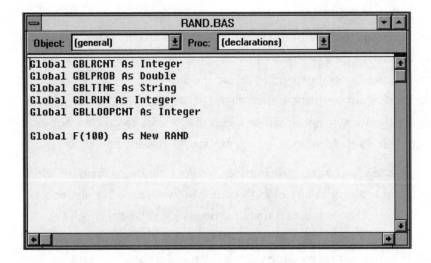

■■■■■■ **Figure 5.4** A Basic module used for global variable declarations.

STARTING AN APPLICATION

By default, Visual Basic will always start off running your application with its first form. You can also designate a startup form with the Project selection from the Options menu. Alternatively, instead of loading a form, Visual Basic can call a procedure to start an application. You may want to do this if your application has to perform some action, such as logging on to a server or connecting to the serial port, before turning control over to a user.

To specify a startup procedure, you write a general subroutine called Main and save it in a module. Then you choose the Project selection from the Options menu. Visual Basic displays the dialog box shown in Figure 5.5.

If you select Set Startup Form, Visual Basic will display a drop box of options, with all of the possible startup forms or a Sub Main option. If you choose the Sub Main option, your application will look for and execute a Main subroutine when it begins running. This lets you start off by connecting with another application or by performing some computations before displaying a form for user interaction.

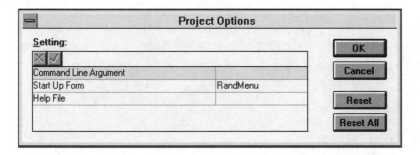

▰▰▰▰ **Figure 5.5** Setting a startup form or subroutine.

TYPING VARIABLES IN VISUAL BASIC

Most programming professionals have already learned to use variable names that describe the values they commonly hold. Variable names in Visual Basic are limited to 40 characters and must begin with an alphabetic character. This provides plenty of leeway to define variable names that are useful in identifying their purpose. The names can also be used to designate the data type, as described in the following.

Variables in Visual Basic may be explicitly or implicitly given type declarations, which define the characteristic of the value that variable can contain. Implicit typing is done simply by assigning to a variable a constant value of a particular type, or a variable of a particular type, or a function that returns a particular type:

```
NewValue = 3.0
NewValue = SingleFloat
NewValue = Square(Value)
```

In all of these examples, NewValue takes on the type of the value on the right-hand side of the equation, which is a single-precision floating-point value. This is known as a Variant type in Visual Basic. It is variant since the variable can potentially take on any type until the actual assignment is made.

Explicitly typed variables have to be declared through the use of the Dim or Global statements in the Declarations section of the application, or in individual modules. The Dim statement is often used to declare variables at module and procedure level.

The format is as follows:

```
Sub Form_Load ()
        Dim I, Start      ' Declare local variable.
        Load Form1        ' Load original Form1.
        For I = 1 To FORMCOUNT
```

```
        F(I).Caption = "Form" & I + 1
        F(I).Show
    Next I
End Sub
```

The Global statement works in much the same manner as the Dim statement, except that the Global statement makes a variable available to all subroutines in all forms and modules in the application. If necessary, it also defines the variable type, something that is not necessary in Visual Basic, thanks to Variant types. It is used in the Declarations section of an application to declare global variables and to allocate storage space for those variables. In fact, it cannot be used in forms or other objects, because form variables are available only to procedures within the form in which they are declared.

The Global statement has these parts:

varname	Name of a variable
subscripts	Dimensions of an array (you can declare multiple dimensions)
As type	Reserved word used to declare the data type of a variable
New	Creates a new instance of a specific object type

You can also use the Global statement to declare the data type of a variable so that the type declaration is explicit. For example, the following statement declares the variable TasksRemaining as an Integer:

```
Global TasksRemaining As Integer
```

This same technique can also be used with forms. For example, the following statement declares a variable for a new instance of a form:

```
Global Courses As New Form
```

Other examples of using the Global statement to declare new variables and their data types are as follows. All of these variables are used in an application described later on in the book.

```
Global GBLRCNT As Integer
Global GBLPROB As Double
Global GBLTIME As String
Global GBLRUN As Integer
Global GBLLOOPCNT As Integer
Global F(100)  As New RAND
```

Normally, if Visual Basic can discern the type of a variable by its use, not explicitly declaring a variable type is perfectly acceptable. I personally depend on this type of variable declaration when testing new concepts or creating rapid prototypes. The developer often has more important things to worry about than ensuring that all of the variables have been declared, and can depend on the development environment to perform this task properly.

However, there is a danger to letting Visual Basic perform declare variable types. If you mispell a variable name but use it properly, Visual Basic will in effect declare it to be a new and different variable, and will not detect a syntax error. This can cause application bugs that can be very difficult to track down. Therefore, under normal circumstances it is best to discipline yourself to declare all of the variables you use. You can also let Visual Basic assist in this task by flagging variables that have not been declared. You can do this manually by prefacing the Declarations section of the application with the following instruction:

```
Option Explicit
```

This requires that all of your variables be declared before you use them. You can also accomplish this automatically by selecting the Environment menu item under the Options menu and setting the following parameter:

```
Require Variable Declaration                    Yes
```

Variables may also be declared to be of a particular type by the structure of their names. Table 5.1 shows all of the available data types in Visual Basic, the range of values they can take on, and the suffix characters that can be added to variable names in order to declare them as that type.

▬▬▬▬ **Table 5.1** Visual Basic Variables

Data type	Suffix	Range
Integer	%	–32,768 to 32,767
Long (long integer)	&	–2,147,483,648 to 2,147,483,647
Single (floating-point)	!	-3.402823×10^{38} to $-1.401298 \times 10^{-45}$ for negative values; 1.401298×10^{-45} to 3.402823×10^{38} for positive values
Double (floating-point)	#	$-1.79769313486232 \times 10^{-308}$ to $-4.94065645841247 \times 10^{-324}$ for negative values; $4.94065645841247 \times 10^{324}$ to $1.79769313486232 \times 10^{308}$ for positive values
Currency (scaled integer)	@	–922,337,203,685,477.5808 to 922,337,203,685,477.5807
String	$	0 to approximately 65,500 bytes
Variant	None	Any numeric value up to the range of a Double or any character text
User-defined	None	The range of each element is the same as the range of its fundamental data type, listed above

Note that one the last types of variable is the user-defined data type. A user-defined data type is any data type that you define using the Type reserved word. User-defined data types can contain one or more of any of the predefined Visual Basic data types. This makes the user-defined data type analogous to the Pascal Type declarations or the C typedef, in that both provide the existing language constructs as templates that you can use to create new and unique data types.

THE WINDOWS APPLICATION PROGRAMMING INTERFACE

Developing Windows applications would be an incredibly long and detailed process without the existence of a set of building blocks known as the *Application Programming Interface*, or API. Rather than create a window one line at a time, for example, there is an API that lets you call a window fully constructed and ready for use. The same thing can be said of other Windows components, such as dialog boxes, menu items, and application controls.

The Visual Basic components and controls provide you with direct access to some of the more commonly used APIs. You need not make an API call directly in order to make use of these high-level Windows facilities. You simply place one of the Visual Basic predefined components within your application, and that component takes care of the appropriate API calls to implement that component.

However, Windows itself provides over 500 of these APIs, which is many more than the Visual Basic components use in implementing their operations. Many of these have to do with managing memory or other resources under Windows, or creating and positioning a window on the screen. Rarely if ever would you have to do some of these things from within your Visual Basic application, because Visual Basic itself has facilities for doing them. For the most part, Visual Basic deals with Windows automatically so that you have little need to do application housekeeping chores by interacting with Windows yourself.

Depending on what feature you're trying to implement, however, there may be times when you have to rely on a Windows API call directly from your code. You should invest some time in familiarizing yourself with the available API calls in order to know what's available for you to use in developing your applications even if you don't see a need for them immediately.

Using the Windows APIs can be an exercise in patience and discipline. Many function calls, such as in the following example, can require long lines of code and very long declaration statements. In addition to getting all of the function and parameter names spelled correctly, you must be sure you have the entire declaration or function call on one line. Microsoft recommends that you refer to the online reference to the Windows API provided with Visual Basic Professional to determine which APIs will meet your needs, then copy the examples provided and adapt them for your use. This saves you the time and effort of coding out the specific details of every call, and reduces the possibility of your making a typo or a more significant error.

You can make use of the Windows API simply by declaring the API functions as accessible to your Visual Basic application. For example, you can use this code to get the keyboard type from your Windows SYSTEM.INI file. It declares the Windows function **GetPrivateProfileInt** as located in the Kernel library, and declares the parameters and their types. To use it, the example simply assigns a variable to the function call.

```
Declare Function GetPrivateProfileInt Lib "Kernel" (ByVal
lpAppName As String, ByVal lpKeyName As String, ByVal nDefault As
Integer, ByVal lpFileName As String) As Integer

    Sub Form_Load ()

        Dim KeyboardType As Integer

        KeyboardType = GetPrivateProfileInt("Keyboard", "type", 2,
"C:\WINDOWS\SYSTEM.INI")

        MsgBox "Your keyboard type is "; KeyboardType
    End Sub
```

VISUAL BASIC PROGRAMMING
VERSUS TRADITIONAL PROGRAMMING

The event-driven model and outside-in development style of Visual Basic will be new to most programmers. These techniques make sense only if you can look at the application from the standpoint of the end user, who generates most of the events to which the Visual Basic controls are designed to respond.

Programmers experienced in the use of traditional programming languages should feel comfortable from the standpoint of developing and testing Visual Basic subroutines that respond to events. These subroutines work in very much the same way as do functions and procedures in traditional languages. The concept of the subroutine offers a good bridge between the two worlds, since programmers can start from the familiar and move to the new and different concepts that make up user-centered design.

Think of a Visual Basic application as a collection of subroutines that all perform a specific task that contributes to the overall functionality of the application. The traditional programmer normally writes these subroutines anyway, but also has to develop the code that connects them together and interfaces with the end user. These are the tasks that Visual Basic handles for you. If you can develop this type of mental image of programming, then making the step to user-centered application design with Visual Basic should not be difficult.

CHAPTER 6

RAPID PROTOTYPING

WITH VISUAL BASIC

SYSTEMS ANALYSIS AND DESIGN PROCESSES

One of the most important innovations in the software development process over the past several years has been the concept of *rapid prototyping*. Rapid prototyping means exactly what it says—quickly designing and assembling the essential components of an application. The resulting prototype actually runs much as the completed application would, and demonstrates some of what the application can do, but it does not include all of the features that the completed application will.

Rapid prototyping and rapid application development are increasingly popular ways to involve end users in the application development process, and to make applications available more quickly. This is critical because without the cooperation and active participation of the end users, the application may not serve their needs or may not be fully used. Fielding applications quickly means that it is more likely that the problem that they set out to address still exists and is still looking for a solution.

There is a growing literature base describing the rapid prototyping process, the systems planning and analysis needs of the techniques, and the organizational considerations. Instead of recounting the philosophies and considerations behind rapid prototyping in agonizing detail, this chapter will focus on the essentials of rapid prototyping from a design and development point of view, and how that process can be implemented using Visual Basic.

The steps in the rapid prototyping process can be described as follows:

1. Develop a substantial but incomplete set of requirements of what the software is supposed to do.

2. Prioritize the requirements in terms of importance to the end user.

3. Rapidly implement the most important requirements.

4. Show the prototype to the end user and solicit feedback on appearance and function. Use this as an opportunity to add to the collection of requirements.

5. Repeat steps 2 through 4 until both developer and user agree that the software can be usefully and reliably put to work.

6. Continue to develop, fix, and extend the software throughout its life cycle.

Preaching the concepts of rapid prototyping to programmers experienced in traditional languages, can end up with disastrous results. The most frequent complaint is that there is no defined completion point to the development process. I agree but argue that the completion point in most traditional efforts is artificial, anyway, because development and enhancement continue to occur after the software has been "completed." Today, most people readily admit that the first release of a software product is often a work in progress. Let us acknowledge this fact and recognize that a software application is never really completed. Rapid prototyping makes a lot more sense given this view of reality.

VISUAL BASIC AND RAPID PROTOTYPING

Visual Basic supports steps 3 and 4 of the preceding process. It's not like traditional languages, which have to start with a collection of very detailed, lower-level operations, which are then used as building blocks to create still higher-level functions, and so on. In many cases, it is not even possible to begin development with a traditional language until all of the requirements have been identified and placed into an overall application architecture.

Instead, Visual Basic lets you begin with a few major functions required by the application, and an idea of how those functions should work. The essentials of the application can be implemented in a way that both helps the users refine them and provides them with something that is useful almost immediately. Visual Basic and similar tools don't require that all of the needs be defined before beginning to implement them. In fact, as discussed in Chapter 4, it is possible to *run* a Visual Basic user interface with little or no supporting code behind it, letting the users get a feel for the interface alone.

Visual Basic also lets you experiment with radically different implementation approaches. It may be possible to prepare two or three applications that all address the problem in distinctly different ways. The end users may be able to decide for themselves which approach they prefer, once they see the alternatives. Further, there may be a high level of commonality between these applications underneath the surface. This lets you better address the needs of the users, while not greatly increasing the time and effort needed to do it.

RAPID PROTOTYPING AND THE JAD/RAD REVOLUTION

Joint application design, or JAD, has existed in one form or another since the early 1980s. While JAD has several variations, in general it refers to the participation by end users in defining requirements and designing the resulting application. The users gather for a series of meetings and often play very specific roles in the process. The roles include actual users of the software, those responsible for funding the project, a "champion" of the project, and a recorder of all the interactions.

The JAD team debates the need for the software solution, the various alternatives that might fill the need, and the design details of the software, all from the perspective of the preceding roles. Some may argue for a full-blown software development effort, while others may question the need for a change at all. The result is that the group is usually able to reach an agreement about a proposed software application after exploring all sides of an issue.

Rapid application development, or RAD, was popularized by software guru James Martin in a book by the same name published in 1991. The purpose of RAD is to quickly field applications that meet the needs of the intended end users. Martin presents RAD as a full-blown software development methodology, incorporating some of the JAD principles under the RAD umbrella.

In particular, Martin defines a team approach to applications development that results in a three- to four-month development cycle, as opposed to a normal one- to two-year cycle using traditional methodologies. Approximately one month of this time is spent in application design using the JAD concept, and the remaining time is used to develop the application and field it to the end users.

Once the JAD team has reached an agreement over the direction of a software solution, they frequently turn into the RAD team. In this role, the team members debate the requirements, the abilities of the users, the organization of the features in the software, and even the placement of individual controls and windows on the user interface. The overriding consideration, however, is the need to quickly put something worthwhile into the hands of users.

RAD is very relevant today, where business circumstances change rapidly, and the advantage goes to the organization that can make use of the best information in the shortest amount of time. Getting an application designed, built, and into the hands of those who need it represents a competitive advantage in more and more companies today. According to a 1994 survey in *Computerworld* magazine, 63 out of 100 companies surveyed used some form of JAD and RAD as their software design methodology.

RAD was not even possible until the early 1990s, when the software prototyping tools capable of quickly assembling the essential parts of an application became available. At first, these tools were simple screen builders, designed to represent only the appearance but not the operation of a user interface. Soon, however, they included resource bundlers and hooks into application code that made them a functioning part of a prototype. Today, some of these tools, such as Visual Basic, offer complete facilities for rapidly developing high-quality stand-alone applications.

JAD and RAD are frequently grouped together because they require one another in order to be successful. JAD would fail if the user teams had to wait months or even years before they could see the results of their efforts.

RAD depends on user input and feedback during the process in order to accurately reflect their needs and preferences. The result is a fast and powerful development methodology that promises to let you, the application developer, give the users what they want and when they want it.

APPLYING JAD AND RAD WITH VISUAL BASIC

Visual Basic assists in two phases of the JAD and RAD processes. First, it can be used as a rapid prototyping tool during the JAD sessions to quickly build screens and controls that can simulate the look and feel of many different types of applications. The rapid prototype described at the end of this chapter was first assembled within the space of two hours. With this kind of speed and flexibility, Visual Basic can be used during a JAD session to let users test out different configurations to determine the best application approach.

Second, Visual Basic can be used to design and develop the entire application, using a rapid prototyping methodology like the one described at the beginning of this chapter. Taking the screens and controls developed during the JAD sessions, you can quickly add functionality in phases, returning to the JAD committee to test the results and make further recommendations. The rapid prototype described at the end of this chapter was implemented in its essential parts within the space of an afternoon.

Often, Visual Basic alone may not satisfy the requirements of the application. In more and more computing environments, it is becoming increasingly important to add new applications that are able to work seamlessly, with existing ones, at least from the standpoint of the end users. That is the case of the rapid prototyping example described at the end of this chapter. This application is required to prepare data in a format readable by a mainframe application. In cases like this Visual Basic may be required to serve as a front end for another application, or it may be required to exchange data with other applications, especially those that run on different types of computers.

The following three chapters describe several ways that Visual Basic can work with existing applications or custom code. These include calling other applications from Visual Basic, establishing Dynamic Data Exchange links with applications and sharing data, and compiling and calling Dynamic Link Libraries written in other languages. All of these give you different options for working with existing code and making your applications more efficient and more useful.

Starting to Build the Prototype

The prototype must have a starting point. This starting point should be recognizable to the end users of the application, yet also show them what can be accomplished. If users are currently working with a manual paper process, the best starting point would be to prototype an application that emulates that paper process. Alternatively, they may be using a mainframe-based application without graphics, and may want the power and flexibility of a graphical user interface.

If you are engaged in JAD, users will have direct input and immediate feedback into the initial appearance of the prototype. However, they rarely know where to start and frequently depend on the prototype developer to propose a user interface design.

Before beginning to prototype, it is important to gain an understanding of the users' requirements and their expectations for a software solution. This means listening to the users describe their current tasks and their frustrations with those tasks, and devising solutions to those tasks through the use of a software application. The beginning of the solution is frequently as simple as assigning a series of controls to all of the needed tasks, and letting the users provide feedback from there.

Object-oriented design is frequently useful in translating the users' requirements into a working prototype. At its simplest level, object-oriented design involves taking objects in a real-life process or task, and describing the structure and behavior of a software application in the same terms.

For example, a time-scheduling application might consist of the user object, a calendar object, and a variety of objects that might represent different types of appointments and other activities that might be scheduled. Most of these activities objects cannot occupy the same times within the calendar object, so the time is a piece of data possessed by each of them. Each time an activity is scheduled, it communicates its time with the existing activities so that there can be no conflicts.

There is much more involved in object-oriented design than can be discussed in a few sentences, but this basic approach can be useful for rapidly conceptualizing a prototype's user interface. Each activity can be considered an object that possesses certain information and can do certain things. The application consists of the creation and interaction of these objects.

PROTOTYPING A DISPLAY

Prototyping a display begins with the form. By laying out controls on the form, it is possible to quickly produce a user interface that can be tested against both requirements and expectations. Consider the form to be your blackboard; if you don't like something, you can erase it and start all over again; or you can save it and copy its desirable features into a new project.

Groupings of controls are the next consideration for the prototype. Groups are controls that perform similar or complementary tasks, such as Yes/No buttons. Thinking about control groups at this time forces you to get down to some of the important details of the look and feel of the application. Consider using frames to define the groupings, and positioning different control groups in separate areas on the form.

Fortunately, many of the Visual Basic controls provide default behavior that is visible to the user, and can give an indication as to how the controls will behave when event-handling code is added to them. For example, option buttons will engage when the mouse is clicked on them. Option button groups will permit only a single option in the group to be selected at a time. Check boxes can be selected and deselected. Rapid prototypes in

Visual Basic can take advantage of these default behaviors to give the users a better idea of how the application will work.

Probably the most important thing to remember is that one of the principles of user-centered application design is that the users make the important decisions of the application's look and feel. You as the developer may propose a design that you think is perfect, but the users must have the final say over both the overall design and the individual details (if you are one of the users, this both helps you with an acceptable design, and makes it likely that other users will find it satisfactory).

This means that pride of authorship has little place in user-centered design. The contributions of the users may, in your opinion, make the application better or worse than your initial efforts, but the important thing is that those for whom it is destined believe that it can solve a problem or assist in a task.

Rapid Prototyping: An Example

This example of a rapid prototype is taken from an actual experience. Prior to beginning the prototype effort, the users were a diverse group, mostly with limited application software experience. In many cases, they had not even thought beyond the existing paper-based process, and were unaware that there might be a viable automated approach to the process. This prototype was also one that was developed from a look-and-feel user interface to a completed application, using the principles of user-centered design.

Many colleges and universities are attempting to modernize many of their processes in order to provide better services to their students while reducing their administrative overhead. One way of accomplishing these goals is through an electronic course registration process. Such a process can enable students to more easily and quickly register for courses, provide some measure of error checking in the registration process, and save administrative personnel from the time and effort of hand-keying registration data.

In the existing process, students filled out a registration form by hand. This form was manually entered into the college's mainframe computer by administrative staff and used for managing enrollment. This was expensive in both data entry and time, making it difficult to determine the enrollment in individual courses in time to cancel courses or add sections. In many cases, forms or associated paperwork were lost or incorrectly entered into the computer.

As a result, the college administration was seeking ways to automate this process. One way of doing so was to enable the students to enter their own registration information into the computer, subject to the approval of the academic advisors. The college decided to develop a Visual Basic application with a user interface similar to the existing registration form so that it was familiar to both faculty and students, and required little retraining and sustained few errors. This application saved individual student data in records that were directly readable by the student management software on the college's mainframe computer.

Colleges tend to be participatory work environments. Discussion and consensus-building are important parts of any decision-making process. Therefore, a rapid prototyping approach makes a good deal of sense as a development approach. Most participants in the process, from students to faculty to administrators, have ideas that may improve the look and feel of the application. They also determine the success of the application by their agreement to use it, or by disregarding it. However, while one of the primary attractions of an electronic registration process is the ability to enter such data automatically into the student management software, only a few of them are concerned about the underlying database connectivity.

The Rapid Prototyping Starting Point

The existing registration form is shown in Figure 6.1. This is an appropriate starting point for the Visual Basic application, although users will undoubtedly suggest improvements after examining the initial prototypes.

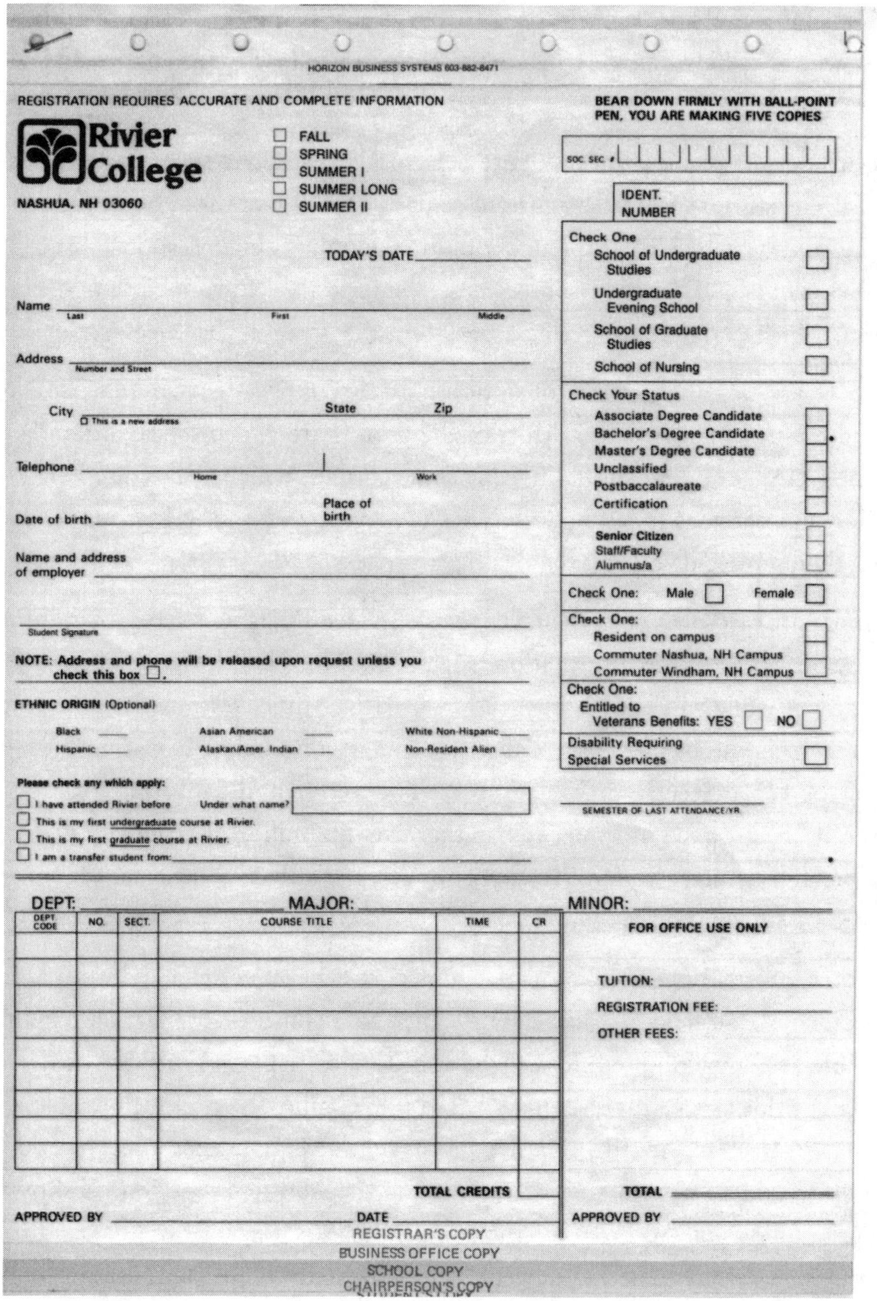

HORIZON BUSINESS SYSTEMS 603-882-8471

REGISTRATION REQUIRES ACCURATE AND COMPLETE INFORMATION

BEAR DOWN FIRMLY WITH BALL-POINT PEN, YOU ARE MAKING FIVE COPIES

Rivier College
NASHUA, NH 03060

☐ FALL
☐ SPRING
☐ SUMMER I
☐ SUMMER LONG
☐ SUMMER II

SOC. SEC. #

IDENT. NUMBER

TODAY'S DATE ____________

Name ____________ (Last / First / Middle)

Address ____________ (Number and Street)

City ______ State ______ Zip ______
☐ This is a new address

Telephone ______ (Home) | ______ (Work)

Date of birth ______ Place of birth ______

Name and address of employer ______

______ Student Signature

NOTE: Address and phone will be released upon request unless you check this box ☐.

ETHNIC ORIGIN (Optional)

Black ___ Asian American ___ White Non-Hispanic ___
Hispanic ___ Alaskan/Amer. Indian ___ Non-Resident Alien ___

Please check any which apply:
☐ I have attended Rivier before Under what name? ______ SEMESTER OF LAST ATTENDANCE/YR.
☐ This is my first undergraduate course at Rivier.
☐ This is my first graduate course at Rivier.
☐ I am a transfer student from: ______

Check One
School of Undergraduate Studies ☐
Undergraduate Evening School ☐
School of Graduate Studies ☐
School of Nursing ☐

Check Your Status
Associate Degree Candidate ☐
Bachelor's Degree Candidate ☐
Master's Degree Candidate ☐
Unclassified ☐
Postbaccalaureate ☐
Certification ☐

Senior Citizen ☐
Staff/Faculty ☐
Alumnus/a ☐

Check One: Male ☐ Female ☐

Check One:
Resident on campus ☐
Commuter Nashua, NH Campus ☐
Commuter Windham, NH Campus ☐

Check One:
Entitled to Veterans Benefits: YES ☐ NO ☐

Disability Requiring Special Services ☐

DEPT: ______ MAJOR: ______ MINOR: ______

DEPT CODE	NO.	SECT.	COURSE TITLE	TIME	CR

TOTAL CREDITS

FOR OFFICE USE ONLY
TUITION: ______
REGISTRATION FEE: ______
OTHER FEES:
TOTAL ______

APPROVED BY ______ DATE ______
APPROVED BY ______

REGISTRAR'S COPY
BUSINESS OFFICE COPY
SCHOOL COPY
CHAIRPERSON'S COPY

Figure 6.1 The existing paper-based registration form.

Since most users are concerned with the appearance of the form, the first prototype merely has to replicate the form, with little functionality underneath.

Consider the paper form in Figure 6.1 closely. There are several categories of information, such as the current semester for registration, degree level, and sex, for which the student should make only a single response. The obvious Visual Basic control for these responses is the grouped option button, which permits only a single option in the group to be selected.

There are two alternatives for option button groups—the two-dimensional and the three-dimensional. Most of the groups are set on the right-hand side of the form and should use the same format, whichever is decided. One alternative is to show both types of groups and option buttons, and let the user decide during the feedback process.

There are also places on the form where the user must enter personal information. Some of the information, such as name and address, can take on many possible values and must remain relatively unconstrained by the software. This can be accomplished with ordinary text fields. In two instances, for the Social Security number and the date of birth, the information should be grouped in some way so that event-handling code can apply to all of the elements equally. An appropriate Visual Basic construct for this type of information is the text array.

Other information, such as academic department, major field of study, and even course selections, can be constrained to a considerably greater extent. There are only a limited number of appropriate responses in these fields. These fields can be placed into Visual Basic combo boxes, which enable a user to select an input from a list and have it display in the box. The code used to add items into a combo box using the AddItem function, as shown in the following. AddItem for the combo boxes is a part of the boxes' form events, in this case the Load event, since the boxes themselves cannot load their own data.

Adding Items to a Combo Box

```
Sub Form_Load ()

        Combo1.AddItem "Business"

        Combo1.AddItem "Computer Science"

        Combo1.AddItem "Education"

        Combo1.AddItem "English"

        Combo1.AddItem "Modern Languages"

        Combo3.AddItem "CS 550 A Formal Languages M"

        Combo3.AddItem "CS 551 A Programming Languages R"

        Combo3.AddItem "CS 552 A Software Design R"

        Combo3.AddItem "CS 554 A Operating Systems T"

        Combo3.AddItem "CS 556 A Computer Architecture T"

        Combo3.AddItem "CS 558 A Compiler Concepts T"

    End Sub
```

Further, in many cases each of these selections can be further constrained by one of the others. If the student selects the business department, it may be appropriate to offer only business courses in the course selection combo box. Note that the combo box does not limit the user to the proffered selections; to enter a selection or value not on the list, the user simply types that alternative into the box just as if it were a normal text box.

The resulting Visual Basic prototype is shown in Figures 6.2a and b (one each for the two Visual Basic forms). I reconstructed the paper form on two separate Visual Basic forms, since the amount of information needed could not easily be displayed on a single form. An alternative would have been to provide a single scrolled form. Rather than making this design decision unilaterally, I'll leave it to the users to make their own suggestions.

The first iteration of the prototype contains little underlying code. Note that the option buttons and check boxes work pretty much as required already, at least from the standpoint of the user. In the final version, the option buttons may require default values, but these need not be applied to

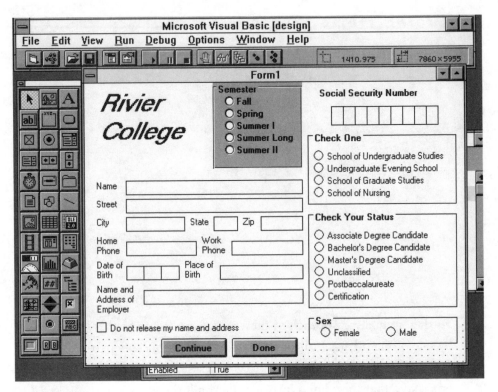

Figure 6.2a The initial Visual Basic application prototype.

obtain feedback from users. The text boxes must be left blank rather than relying on default values, so the Text property on all of the text boxes is changed to reflect a blank field. Also, to demonstrate how to use the combo boxes, I placed a set of default academic departments, majors, and course listings. I also defined their default Text properties as Enter Department, Enter Major, and Course Selection.

Other than default values and operations, only the command buttons contain code so that the users can move between the two forms and quit the application when completed. Calling another form is simply a matter of using the Show and Hide methods discussed in Chapter 4:

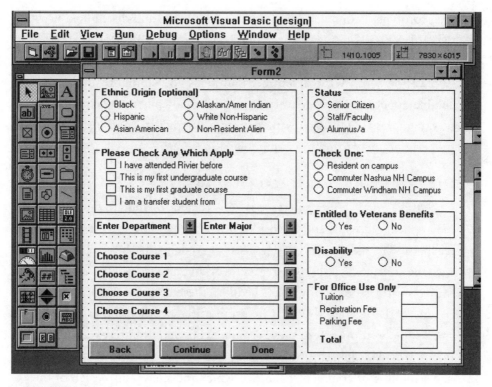

▬▬▬▬▬ **Figure 6.2b** The initial Visual Basic application prototype.

```
Sub Continue_Click ()
      Top.Hide
      Bottom.Show
End Sub
```

The application can be closed simply by using the End statement in the Close command button:

```
Sub Close_Click ()
      End
End Sub
```

This little code for the buttons was adequate for the users to get an idea of how the application worked. So that the varied user community could test the prototype, I compiled it into an executable file and distributed it with the DLL VBRUN400.DLL for Visual Basic 4.0, or VBRUN300.DLL for Visual Basic 3.0. For this purpose, Visual Basic Professional includes an Application Setup Wizard, a utility that helps you configure and set up executable applications for delivery. It will automatically include the proper files, compress the files, copy them onto a floppy disk, and install them properly on the destination computer.

DISTRIBUTING THE INITIAL PROTOTYPE

Once the electronic user interface is constructed to emulate the paper form, the application, while still a work in progress, can be shown to users for feedback. The users in this case consist of students, both traditional college-age students as well as part-time working adults, faculty, and administrative staff. Due to conflicting schedules, these users were not available to conduct JAD sessions. The first iteration of the prototype was given to a small sample from each of these groups, who were told to experiment with it and provide feedback. In the case of this application, these selected users had a number of comments, some of which reflected poor design of the form itself, while others reflected more general concerns about moving to an electronic format. Concerning the form itself, users made the following comments:

1. One of the most common causes of errors is that students do not fill in all of the necessary information on the paper form. These errors are generally caught before the form is approved, but may have to be resolved before registration is completed. Is there some way that Visual Basic can prevent students from omitting essential information?

It is a simple matter to include a subroutine as a part of the Done command button that checks to see if all necessary fields have had data entered into them. There is, of course, no way of ensuring that the entered data is correct, although it is possible to support a small level of consistency by permitting only certain combinations of inputs; for example, a graduate student may be discouraged from selecting an undergraduate course. Of course, the user should also have the ability to override these default limitations so that the system can respond to unique needs.

After the initial application is fielded and demonstrated in actual use, it should be possible to tie in access to the existing student management and course schedule databases so that mistakes in personal information and course selection can be caught more easily.

2. The course selection information is not in a format that can be read by the student management software. The course number, course section, course name, meeting time, and meeting day must be broken out into separate fields in order to put the data into a readable format.

This is an easily solvable technical problem, and it also represents an opportunity to improve the form's user interface. The technical solution is to provide combo boxes for each of the preceding data fields. This simply involves placing more boxes on the form. However, it is quickly apparent that there is no more room on the second form for more combo boxes. Rather than rearranging the existing controls on the form, or resizing the form itself, it makes more sense to add yet another form devoted to the selection of courses. It may also be possible to add Help buttons to aid in the selection, or buttons that access course descriptions if there is more form space available and users believe that such information is worthwhile.

I can also use this opportunity to constrain course selections so that users can select courses by the meeting date or time, or by the course number or name. If the user selects Monday, for example, the other combo boxes can display only those courses that meet on Mondays. This improves the user interface by letting the student decide how to select the desired courses. While not required by the registration process, it is also possible to add another combo box with the list of course instructors so that the student can select a recommended or favorite instructor and choose from courses taught by that instructor.

3. More generally, administrative users were concerned over the database interface between this application and the student management

software on the mainframe computer. Those who had used the software questioned the ability of a PC application and a mainframe application to pass data back and forth.

Interacting with a non-PC application limits the options available, but Visual Basic provides adequate facilities for even this situation. If all else fails, it is possible to write data from the electronic registration form into ASCII format, which can then be read directly by the student management software and translated into its database format. However, other formats, such as dBASE, FoxPro, Access, or ODBC-compatible databases, provide easy but sophisticated ways of exchanging data. This issue will be addressed in detail further along in the rapid prototyping process.

4. In general, users had few complaints about the format for the input. Since they were accustomed to working with the existing paper form, all of them were able to readily adapt to the same format on the computer screen. They indicated no preference between the use of two separate Visual Basic forms or a single scrolling form.

The following comments reflect general concerns on moving to an electronic format. Most organizations that are taking the step from a paper process to a reengineered electronic process should plan on receiving and airing concerns surrounding the doubts of the move so that all participants in the process can be informed and, as a result, better support the transition.

1. The paper form requires a signature from the academic advisor and the business office. It is not possible to incorporate a signature into the electronic form. How can the student obtain the appropriate approvals, and how can the college ensure that the registration process has been completed correctly?

This is possibly the only real disadvantage of converting to an electronic registration format. While there are several alternatives to a physical signature, none stand out as the obvious solution. Since other colleges have already offered alternatives to a paper-based registration process, however, this problem is not unsolvable.

One alternative is to require students to print out the registration form so that the necessary signatures can be obtained on the printout. The user then submits both the diskette or data file, and the paper form. The paper form is used only to provide proof of the approvals.

Another possibility is for students to e-mail their completed registration to the academic advisors, who indicate their approval by forwarding the data to the student management database. If there are any problems with the registration, the advisors e-mail the registration back to the students. This process, of course, requires that all faculty, staff, and students make use of e-mail, which up until now is voluntary.

2. Is the paper form an appropriate model to replicate in an electronic format? If the college is making such a radical move to begin with, should it consider a completely different user interface for student input?

There are probably better user interfaces than the existing paper form. In fact, once the prototyping process begins, users will probably find serious defects in the old, paper-based process. However, it is best to keep some recognizable aspects of the existing process so that users will be able to recognize elements of the new process and require less training to make use of it. In time, students may have to enter only their names or ID numbers, and their personal data and needed courses will be able to be automatically loaded from the student management database. Once all users are accustomed to using the electronic form, further changes can be made.

These are typical questions and comments that will arise from the initial rounds of the rapid prototyping process. Be prepared to deal with encouragement and skepticism, and enthusiasm and suspicion, as the prototype is examined by diverse users. While some will jump at the chance to try something new and different, others will wonder why things have to change at all. The advantage of the prototype is that it encourages user participation and can satisfy the concerns of even the most skeptical user before the application is even substantially begun.

One alternative to distributing the initial prototype so that users can try it out under their own circumstances, or the JAD process described earlier is to form a focus group to meet to jointly test and comment on the application. This may be appropriate if the completed application has to be fielded in a hurry, and you can gather together a representative group of users. However, a part of the rapid prototyping process is often to build user support for the application itself. This means that it must reach as many potential users as possible so that everyone can feel they participated in the design decisions.

FINE-TUNING THE USER INTERFACE

The next iteration of a rapid prototype is to incorporate user feedback into the user interface design, and to begin to add event-handling code into some of the objects. The user feedback in this case did not require many changes to the first prototype. Since it reflected the essential aspects of the older manual registration process, users largely accepted the same appearance in an electronic form.

To leave more room for a revised major department, program, course selections, and any other information that the college may want to collect in the future, I'll move these inputs to a third form. I'll also remove default selections for the option boxes simply by manually setting the Value property to False:

```
Option1.Value = False
```

Although it was not mentioned by the users evaluating the prototype, one attractive addition to this prototype is to enable the user to get a description of a selected course. In the future, this will probably involve interacting with an external database. However, it should be possible to add at least selected courses as text or as a database entry so that students will be able to get course descriptions of at least some of the courses. This is a part of this application's Help file, which was designed in Chapter 4.

This will work by selecting a course from those available, then pushing the Help command button. The key into the database will be the course number, which is a unique identifier for all of the courses offered. The Help button will be active only when the user selects a course number that corresponds to an available description.

The resulting application is shown in Figure 6.3, which shows only the added third form that is substantially different than the first round of prototyping. The first form remained substantially the same as in the first iteration. The second form changed to remove the course information and reposition the other fields slightly. The third form is completely new and lets students select courses by course name, number, meeting days, or academic department.

In addition to providing the look and feel of the manual process, the end result of this application is that it lets students select courses from combo boxes, flip back and forth between forms, obtain course descriptions of elective courses, get Help and contact information for the registration process, and ensure that all necessary information is filled in before closing. All personal and course information will be saved in the next section so that it can be written into the student management database.

BUILDING IN THE BACK END

The remaining concerns and suggestions from user feedback largely reflect function rather than appearance. This is a natural development in the rapid

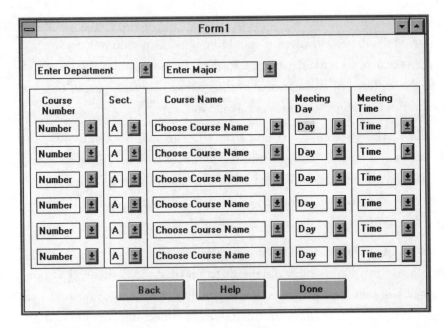

Figure 6.3 The result of the second round of rapid prototyping.

prototyping process. Once users begin to see what they expect, they also want it to work the way they expect. Therefore, the next step is to begin adding functionality behind the user interface controls. These are still user interface issues, however, because user expectation as to how the controls behave constitutes an important part of the user-centered design effort.

As a result, the second iteration of the prototype has to start incorporating functionality underneath the user interface. Where should you begin with the process of adding code? To be consistent with user-centered design principles, these functions should be those that are apparent to most end users as a result of user actions.

In the case of this prototype, that means constraining the inputs between academic department, major field, and course names and numbers. To a lesser degree, it also means starting to build in some error-checking in some of the other information fields. Error-checking without access to external databases won't be very robust, but it is possible to make sure that users make valid entries for such inputs as the Social Security number, which must be all numbers, and the name, which must be all alphabetical characters. This can be done by taking the Text or Value field in each object and making sure it contains a value appropriate to that particular box.

For example, when testing the Social Security number, you can simply check for the range of whole numbers after the user moves away from that box, using the LostFocus event handler:

```
Sub SSAN_LostFocus (Index As Integer)
   If SSAN(1).Text <"0" Or SSAN(1).Text > "9" Then SSAN(1).Text = " "
End Sub
```

While this is fast and simple, there are better ways of doing this, because you are not informing the user why you are deleting their input. Ultimately, the best thing to do is to display a pop-up dialog box, explaining the reason for the error. This was demonstrated using the MsgBox function in Chapter 4.

The Help file and course descriptions designed in Chapter 4 and just described can also be added in. Last, the user should not be able to complete the registration form without filling in essential information. You have to be careful here, because the users may partially complete the form and want to complete the rest at a later time, so you can't tell when they consider it to be complete. You may have to let them close an incomplete application, trusting that they will complete the input at a later time.

WRAPPING UP THE PROTOTYPE

The rapid prototyping process can continue until there is an acceptable application from the standpoint of the users. The danger in this process is that users may not agree on the feature set, or they may continue to ask for more features as they gain an understanding of the power of the application to their problem. There may also be a portion of the user community that objects to any automated solution, and could stonewall the prototyping process. These are largely management rather than technical issues, but are very real problems that have to be recognized as natural consequences of rapid prototyping.

The last step in this rapid prototyping effort is to complete the database connection to the college's administrative computer. This is the last step because only those responsible for data entry and database management are concerned with this step. Before it occurs, we have to ensure that the application will be accepted and used, and that this was done by concentrating the bulk of the efforts on the user interface portion of the application.

Utilizing database objects to save the resulting registration information in machine-readable form will be discussed in Chapter 12. However, the data can also be simply written out to an ASCII file, where it can then be read into other applications. This was the requirement for the back-end database to this prototype.

BEYOND THE PROTOTYPE

The preceding description accurately portrays the steps involved in a typical rapid prototyping design effort using Visual Basic. However, rapid prototypes can be used for much more than designing electronic forms. Virtually any application with a significant user interface component can be developed using rapid prototyping or JAD/RAD.

User participation in the application design and development process is making applications easier to use and more relevant to users. It also lets you deliver applications more quickly than with traditional development methods. With Visual Basic, rapid prototyping together with user-centered development techniques can be used in the development of Windows user interfaces, along with the internal application engines.

RAPID PROTOTYPING AND REENGINEERING

Prototyping plays a role in what is currently known as *business process reengineering*, or simply reengineering. This concept, popularized by Michael Hammer and James Champy, involves the radical change of an existing process to achieve quantum leaps in performance and efficiency. It usually involves eliminating the existing process altogether in favor of an entirely new approach to performing the task. In practice, this "new approach" almost always involves the application of modern software technology in new and imaginative ways.

For example, the prototype just described effectively reengineered the process of student registration. It took a manual, paper-intensive process with a large number of steps, and helped to condense it into a simple, auto-mated process. A key feature of a reengineered process is that it transfers tasks to those more capable of performing the task, which was also a result of this effort. Data entry of the individual student registration information into the student management database required a tedious and time-con-suming effort by administrative personnel that was highly error-prone. This step of the process also proved to be a bottleneck, since two or three clerks were entering data for over 2,500 students within the period of a few days.

Now, however, that task has been transferred to the student, who effec-tively enters his or her own registration information into the database sim-ply by filling out the form. Not only has the student taken over a task previously done by administrative personnel, but it benefits the student by removing a source of error from the process, and gives the student greater control over the contents of the registration.

This software effort has shortened and simplified the registration process, reduced the likelihood of errors, removed the data entry bottleneck, and given greater control to the customers. Further, it would not have been possible without the ability to quickly develop highly usable and effective software, solicit feedback from users, and field a solution that has already been agreed upon by all interested parties. These are the strengths of using Visual Basic as a rapid prototyping tool.

SUCCESSFUL PROTOTYPING FOR REENGINEERING

A similar example of using prototyping to reengineer a process is the development and distribution of package tracking software by overnight package delivery services, such as Federal Express and United Parcel Service. Prior to the use of such software, customers interested in tracking a package had to call a customer service representative, who checked the package number in the company's database and relayed the information back to the user.

In effect, the service representative was simply a conductor of information. Many customers could eliminate this step entirely simply by giving them direct access to the package-tracking database. By putting customized application software capable of searching this database for a particular package number into the hands of users (and distributed free; the software and diskette are inexpensive, while the true value is in the data the customers are seeking), these package-delivery services were able to effectively get customers to perform the work of service representatives, eliminating the need for a number of these people, while putting better service and more control into the hands of the customers.

As a result of more user participation in the application design and development process, the need to reengineer to improve results and performance, and the need to field applications more quickly, rapid prototyping is an increasingly important software development methodology. Visual Basic, with predefined user interface components and a comprehensive event-handling programming model, is an ideal application development tool to use to achieve these goals.

7

WORKING WITH

OTHER APPLICATIONS

EXCHANGING DATA ACROSS APPLICATIONS

Much of the interest in visual languages today is geared toward modifying and exchanging data with existing applications. These applications may be commercial Windows applications, or they may be custom applications written to perform specific tasks. Often, a single application does not contain all of the features or all of the data necessary to satisfy the needs of end users, so it is important to get separate applications to work together with as little effort as possible.

There is also an increasing interest in equipping applications with the ability to share data with one another. Data formatted in a spreadsheet may be needed in a report written in a word processor, for example. While it is possible to cut and paste such data, at least within Windows, this can render the data stale; that is, the data may be modified in the original spreadsheet but will not be updated in the report itself. The user can manually perform the update, but this is inconvenient and subject to forgetfulness, especially if there are large numbers of such documents.

To address this problem, Windows offers a type of Dynamic Data Exchange, or DDE, where applications can pass data back and forth to one another while both applications are running. *Live* data from one application can also be embedded in another application, using a technique called *Object Linking and Embedding*, or OLE.

Visual Basic can be used as a front end for existing applications, or it can exchange data with other Windows applications. Visual Basic can also be used to exchange data between two Visual Basic applications, using similar techniques. This chapter discusses both ways of working with existing programs.

Applications working with one another can increase usability by putting information into the hands of the user without regard to where that information originally resided. This abstracts two important details from the user: the origin and location of data. If these are not important considerations for the user's purpose (and they usually are not), then it is extraneous information that we need not require the user to know. DDE and OLE both contribute to abstracting these details from the user.

DYNAMIC DATA EXCHANGE

Dynamic Data Exchange, or DDE, is the real-time transfer of data between two running applications. The distinction between DDE and OLE is subtle but real. DDE assumes a live transfer of data, where both applications are running and passing data back and forth (or simply in only a single direction) in real time. OLE consists of a data object taken from a file of one application and embedded in the file of another. The object is connected to the original application by a link so that when the original data is changed, the embedded data is automatically updated through the link.

Visual Basic can perform both DDE and OLE. DDE uses a set of properties and expressions that are used to establish the link and pass data across the link. OLE embeds a data structure referred to as an *object* from one file into another, using a variation of the Windows Cut and Paste operations. When you update the data in the OLE source file, you also update the data structures in the OLE destination file.

Both DDE and OLE work only with commercial applications that have been written to accept DDE conversations. Fortunately, an increasing number of Windows applications now support both forms of data exchange, including virtually all of the popular productivity applications. You need not interact with an existing commercial application; you can also write you own Visual Basic applications to perform DDE and OLE with one another.

USING VISUAL BASIC FOR DDE

Visual Basic provides properties and functions for establishing DDE links between running applications, and for passing data across these links. The key Visual Basic object properties involved in the process are LinkMode, LinkTopic, and LinkItem.

The Visual Basic model for DDE works something like this: Two applications that communicate with one another using DDE are said to be having a conversation. The application that initiates the conversation is called the *destination*, while the one that responds to the destination is called the *source*. The destination opens the link and requests information from the source, and then receives it via the DDE link. Applications can have more than one DDE link active at the same time, and can be serving as either the source or destination on each of the links. For the most part, the source is also the application that makes the request for data, while the destination is the application that supplies the data.

To begin a DDE conversation, a destination application has to specify two things: the name of the source application, and the subject of the conversation. The subject, or topic, is simply a unit of data that has meaning to both applications. For most applications, the topic is simply the file name containing the desired data.

The last necessary piece for a DDE conversation is the *item*, which is the piece of data that is being passed between the applications during a DDE conversation. This may be a text stream, a cell or defined range in a spreadsheet, or a field in a database table. If the Visual Basic application is the source or data, the item can be the names of text boxes, labels, or pictures on a form.

Now the ideas behind the LinkMode, LinkTopic, and LinkItem properties should start to fall into place. LinkMode describes the type of link as well as the source and destination applications; LinkTopic the document or file within that application; and LinkItem the piece or pieces of data being exchanged.

How to Use LinkMode

The LinkMode property applies to forms, labels, picture boxes, and text boxes; determines the type of link used for a DDE conversation; and activates the connection. With a Visual Basic control, LinkMode allows a destination control on a form to initiate a conversation, as specified through the control's LinkTopic and LinkItem properties. With a Visual Basic form, LinkMode allows a destination application to initiate a conversation with a Visual Basic source form, as specified through the destination application's LinkTopic or LinkItem expression.

The syntax used to reference the LinkMode property is as follows:

```
ComponentName.LinkMode = Value
```

For controls used as data destinations in DDE conversations, the possible values for the LinkMode property are:

0. **None.** There is no DDE interaction specified. This is the default value.

1. **Automatic.** Visual Basic will update the destination control each time the linked data changes.

2. **Manual.** Visual Basic updates the destination control only when the application invokes the LinkRequest method.

3. **Notify.** A LinkNotify event occurs whenever the linked data changes, but the destination control is updated only when the LinkRequest method is invoked.

As mentioned previously, LinkMode is also used for the other side, or the data source, of the DDE conversation. If you also use a form in a Visual Basic application as the source in DDE conversations, the LinkMode property settings are:

0. **None.** There is no DDE interaction with the form. No destination application can initiate a conversation with the source form as the topic, and no application can send data to the form. If LinkMode is 0 at design time, it is not possible to change it to 1 while your application is running. This is the default value for the property.

1. **Source.** Allows any label, picture box, or text box on a form to supply data to any destination application that establishes a DDE conversation with the form. If such a link exists, Visual Basic automatically notifies the destination whenever the contents of a control are changed. In addition, a destination application can insert data into any label, picture box, or text box on the form. If LinkMode is 1 at design time, you can change it to 0 and back while your application is running.

LinkMode has some special conditions that you also have to be aware of. The following conditions may affect how you use the LinkMode property:

1. Setting LinkMode to a value larger than 0 for a data destination control causes Visual Basic to attempt to initiate the conversation that you specified in the LinkTopic and LinkItem properties. The source updates the destination control according to the type of link you specified (in other words, automatic, manual, or notify).

2. If a label, picture box, or text box has established an automatic link with a source application, a Change event occurs for that control each time new data is entered, regardless of whether the value of the data differs from the control's current contents. Note that this is the only way a Change event can occur for a label control, since it is otherwise impossible to change a label control.

Using the LinkTopic Property

The next step in the establishment of the DDE link is the LinkTopic property. For the destination control, the LinkTopic property determines the source application and the topic. For a source form, the LinkTopic property specifies the topic that the source form responds to in a DDE conversation:

```
Component.LinkTopic = Value
```

The LinkTopic property consists of a string that supplies part of the information necessary to set up either a data destination link or data source link. The string you use depends on whether you're working with a destination control or a source form. Each string corresponds to one or more elements of the standard DDE syntax, which will be demonstrated below.

To set LinkTopic for a destination control, use a string with the syntax *application | topic*, as defined in the following:

1. Application refers to the application from which data is requested, usually the executable file name (without the .EXE extension).

2. The *pipe* character (|) separates the application from the topic.

3. Topic is the fundamental data grouping used in that application; for example, a worksheet in a spreadsheet application.

In addition, you have to set the related LinkItem property in the destination control to specify the item for the link. A spreadsheet cell reference such as R1C1, for example, would correspond to an item in a worksheet for a spreadsheet application.

To set LinkTopic for a source, change the default string to the identifier for the form. The application used as the DDE destination uses this string as the topic argument when it establishes the DDE link with the form. Although this string is all you need to set LinkTopic within Visual Basic for a source form, the destination application itself also needs to specify the application element that the destination application uses, which is the Visual Basic application name without the .EXE executable file extension. You also need the item that the destination application uses to receive the data. This is usually the Name property for the label, picture box, or text box on the source form.

To activate the data link set with LinkTopic, you have to set the LinkMode property to the appropriate value to specify the type of link you want. After changing LinkTopic for a destination control, you must set LinkMode to one of its three appropriate values, described previously, for establishing a DDE link:

1. Automatic

2. Manual

3. Notify

Alternatively, you can also establish a permanent data link at design time with the Paste Link command from the Edit menu. This also sets the LinkMode, LinkTopic, and LinkItem properties to their necessary values. This operation establishes a link that is saved when you save the form from within Visual Basic. Each time the form is loaded, Visual Basic will attempt to reestablish the DDE conversation with the application specified in the Paste Link command.

LinkItem Property

The LinkItem property specifies the data passed to a destination control in a DDE conversation with another application. Its general use is as follows:

```
Component.LinkItem = Value
```

To set this property, specify a recognizable unit of data in an application as a reference; for example, a cell reference in a spreadsheet worksheet. You use LinkItem along with the LinkTopic property to specify the complete DDE data link for a destination control to a source application. To activate this link, you simply set the LinkMode property as described in the previous section.

You set the LinkItem property only for the control you're using as the DDE destination. When you use a Visual Basic form as the source in a link, the name of any label, picture box, or text box on the form can be the item argument in the string used by the destination.

A DDE control can potentially act as destination and source simultaneously, which has the potential of creating an infinite data exchange loop if a destination-source pair is also a source-destination pair with itself; in other words, if the two applications are passing data to and from one another. For instance, a text box may be both a source and destination of the same cell in a spreadsheet. When data in a Visual Basic text box changes, sending data to the spreadsheet, the cell in the spreadsheet changes, sending the change to the text box, and so on, causing the loop. To avoid such loops, don't use identical controls for destination-source and source-destination links in both directions between applications.

Using the DoEvents Function in DDE

A key to using Visual Basic for Dynamic Data Exchange is the Visual Basic DoEvents function. DoEvents causes Visual Basic to yield execution so that

Microsoft Windows can process events. DoEvents exists as either an instruction or a function, the difference being that the DoEvents function returns the number of visible forms.

DoEvents passes control to the Windows environment. This control is not returned until the Windows environment has finished processing all of the events in its queue, and all keys in the SendKeys queue have been sent. This means that either part of the DDE link that cannot respond to its messages may not be able to work properly. Your DDE link may break down if both the source and the destination lack the processing time they need.

DoEvents is an important part of many Visual Basic applications, regardless of whether they use Dynamic Data Exchange. A Windows application relies on Windows to perform a number of activities, and the application has to yield control of the CPU in order for that to happen. For example, in order to receive asynchronous input, such as from a serial port, the application must, in many cases, yield to Windows, which will then inform the application of incoming data.

As a result, it often makes sense to add a DoEvents statement into a portion of code that interacts with the outside environment in some way. Many Visual Basic developers report difficult-to-discover bugs in their applications, because the application was not able to hand off control to Windows periodically so that Windows could take care of normal operating system tasks.

Therefore, you should use the DoEvents instruction to interrupt processing so that the Windows environment can respond normally to other events, such as keyboard input and mouse clicks. If parts of your code take up too much processor time, you may have to use DoEvents to relinquish control to the Windows environment.

Using DoEvents is simple—it's a stand-alone function that requires no arguments, and can be used in any section of code:

```
DoEvents
DoEvents
```

Knowing where to insert it can be somewhat more difficult. In general, you should use DoEvents after a loop that occupies a good deal of processing time, or during a pause in a DDE conversation. If you find that your application is not responding as you expect, and you cannot find the problem, try inserting several DoEvents statements into sections of your code.

CREATING MULTIPLE INSTANCES OF AN APPLICATION

DDE gives the application developer enormous control over how two applications can work together. You can even let the user define some of the parameters of an application, and let this definition drive some of the operation of DDE.

For example, the following application simply generates random numbers based on a specification provided by the user. You literally create several instances of a random number generator window, which are provided with random numbers dynamically by a single random number generator running as another application. It uses multiple instances of a single form, using the technique introduced in Chapter 4, each of which is given a dynamic link name. The second part of the example is a form that links to all instances and collects information.

One caution: If you run this application, do not specify too many instances of the random number generator. You can specify 100 or more, but the performance on your PC will probably be so slow that it will take a great deal of time to execute. The following illustrates the make file used to load this application: It takes a long time to generate random numbers and to establish and perform a DDE conversation across 100 forms.

Following is the .MAK file used in this application:

```
RANDMENU.FRM

C:\WINDOWS\SYSTEM\THREED.VBX
```

```
RAND.BAS
RAND.FRM
ProjWinSize=152,402,248,215
ProjWinShow=2
IconForm="RandMenu"
Title="RANDOM"
ExeName="RANDOM.EXE"
```

The opening screen of the application is shown in Figure 7.1. It requires that the user input the number of new form instances to create, and the average probability desired for the resulting random numbers.

Following are the global declarations for this example, defined in the Declarations section of the application. They consist of the prefix GBL-, and then a description of their purpose. For example, the GBLRCNT variable is the user input on the number of random number form instances to create.

```
Global GBLRCNT As Integer
Global GBLPROB As Double
Global GBLTIME As String
Global GBLRUN As Integer
Global GBLLOOPCNT As Integer
```

This limits the number of new instances of forms to a maximum of 100.

```
Global F(100) As New RAND
```

Figure 7.1 The opening screen of the sample DDE application.

The following code is the heart of the application. When the user clicks on the Go button, the random number generator application is launched and the new forms are created. The DDE link is established with LinkMode and LinkTopic properties, and the random numbers are written into the appropriate fields in the forms, which are identified with the LinkItem property. The running application is shown in Figure 7.2.

```
GoButton_Click()
Sub GoButton_Click ()
If GoButton.Caption = "Pause" Then
   Timer1.Enabled = False
   GoButton.Caption = "Resume"
   Exit Sub
Else
   If GoButton.Caption < > "Go" Then
     Timer1.Enabled = True
     GoButton.Caption = "Pause"
     Exit Sub
   End If
End If
```

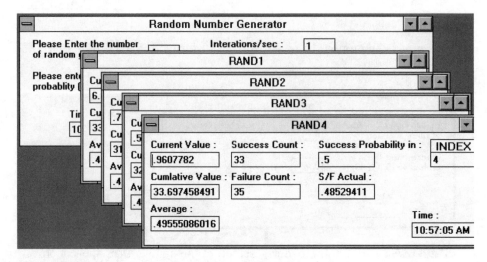

■■■■■ Figure 7.2 The running DDE application.

```
GBLRCNT = Text1.Text

GBLPROB = text2.Text

GBLLOOPCNT = Text4.Text

For i = 1 To GBLRCNT

   F(i).Caption = Trim$("RAND" + Trim$(Str$(i)))

   F(i).LinkTopic = F(i).Caption

   F(i).Text9.Text = i

   F(i).Text6.Text = GBLPROB

   F(i).Show             ' Load and display new instance

   ' Move and color new instance

   F(i).Move Left + (i * 400) + (Width \ 10), Top + (i * 400) + (Height
\ 10)

   ' F.BackColor = RGB(Rnd * 256, Rnd * 256, Rnd * 256)

   DoEvents

   DoEvents

Next i

Timer1.Enabled = False

Timer1.Interval = 100

Timer1.Enabled = True

GoButton.Caption = "Pause"

End Sub
```

The following code is associated with the DDE destination forms when
new instances of the form are created and loaded. It sets the LinkMode
and LinkTopic properties, prepares to create random numbers, and initializes the values in its text boxes.

```
Sub Form_Load ()

      Rand.LinkMode = 0

      Rand.LinkTopic = Rand.Caption

      Rand.LinkMode = 1

      Randomize

      EVENTCNT = 0

      DBLA = 0

      Text1.Text = 0
```

```
        Text2.Text = 0

        Text3.Text = 0

        Text4.Text = 0

        Text5.Text = 0

        Text6.Text = 0

        Text7.Text = 0

    End Sub
```

This is associated with the text field labeled Time, and advances the time on all of the new form instances at the time that the forms are updated with new random numbers.

```
    Sub TimeText_Change ()

    For m = 1 To GBLLOOPCNT

       EVENTCNT = EVENTCNT + 1

       Text1.Text = Rnd

       DoEvents

       DBLA = CDbl(Str(Text1.Text))

       If Trim$(Text2.Text) < > "" Then DBLA = DBLA + CDbl(Str(Text2.Text))

       Text2.Text = DBLA

       If EVENTCNT > 0 Then Text3.Text = DBLA / EVENTCNT

       DBLA = Text1.Text

       DBLB = Text6.Text


       DoEvents

       If DBLA < DBLB Then

          Text4.Text = Text4.Text + 1

       Else

          Text5.Text = Text5.Text + 1

       End If


       DBLA = Text5.Text

       DBLB = Text4.Text
```

```
    If DBLA > 0 Then Text7.Text = DBLB / (DBLA + DBLB)
    DoEvents
Next m
End Sub
```

CREATING THE DDE SOURCE

The source application is the one that creates the random numbers on request from the RANDMENU form. This application has two global variables defined in the Declaration section of the form.

```
Global RTEMAPPSSRC As String
Global RANDCNT As Integer
```

The remaining code is all contained within a Basic module (.BAS) file. The CheckLink function establishes the DDE conversation and tests it to see if it is working properly. If it is not, it will send the user a message using the MsgBox function.

```
Function CheckLink () As Integer
On Error Resume Next
  RandRes.Text1.LinkMode = 0
                      ' Set the application name and topic name.
  RandRes.Text1.LinkTopic = "Random|randmenu"
  RandRes.Text1.Text = ""              ' clear all
  RandRes.Text1.LinkItem = "text1"      ' Set the LinkItem.
  RandRes.Text1.LinkMode = 2         ' Activate the link to Manual
' Automatic.
  If Err Then
     MsgBox ("App not rseponding")
     CheckLink = -1
     Exit Function
  End If
    CheckLink = 0
    RandRes.Text1.LinkMode = 0 ' disconnect
End Function
```

Function GetAll identifies all of the destination text fields and sets the appropriate LinkItem properties.

```
Function GetAll () As Integer
    RandRes.AText.LinkMode = 0
    RandRes.BText.LinkMode = 0
    RandRes.CText.LinkMode = 0
        ' Set the application name and topic name.
    RandRes.AText.LinkTopic = "random|randmenu"
    RandRes.BText.LinkTopic = "random|randmenu"
    RandRes.CText.LinkTopic = "random|randmenu"


    RandRes.AText.Text = "" ' clear all
    RandRes.BText.Text = "" ' clear all
    RandRes.CText.Text = "" ' clear all
    RandRes.AText.LinkItem = "Text1"        ' Set the LinkItem.
    RandRes.BText.LinkItem = "Text2"        ' Set the LinkItem.
    RandRes.CText.LinkItem = "Text4"        ' Set the LinkItem.
    RandRes.AText.LinkMode = 2              ' Activate the link to
Manual                                     ' Automatic.
    RandRes.BText.LinkMode = 2              ' Activate the link to
Manual                                     ' Automatic.
    RandRes.CText.LinkMode = 2              ' Activate the link to
Manual                                     ' Automatic.
    RandRes.AText.LinkRequest
    RandRes.BText.LinkRequest
    RandRes.CText.LinkRequest
    RANDCNT = RandRes.AText.Text
    RandRes.AText.LinkMode = 0 ' disconnect
    RandRes.BText.LinkMode = 0 ' disconnect
    RandRes.CText.LinkMode = 0 ' disconnect


End Function
```

Function LinkToAll actually passes the data from source to destination.

```
Function LinkToAll () As Integer

Dim i As Integer

On Error Resume Next

For i = 1 To RANDCNT


    RandRes.Label1(i - 1).LinkMode = 0

        ' Set the application name and topic name.

    RandRes.Label1(i - 1).LinkTopic = Trim$("Random|RAND" +
Trim$(Str$(i)))

    RandRes.Label1(i - 1).Caption = ""' clear all

    RandRes.Label1(i - 1).LinkItem = "text7"' Set the LinkItem.

    RandRes.Label1(i - 1).LinkMode = 2' Activate the link to Manual
' Automatic.

    If Err Then

        MsgBox ("App not rseponding")

        LinkToAll = -1

        Exit Function

    End If

    RandRes.Label1(i - 1).LinkRequest

    LinkToAll = 0

Next i

End Function


Function ReadAll () As Integer

Dim i As Integer

On Error Resume Next

For i = 1 To RANDCNT


    RandRes.Label1(i - 1).LinkRequest

    ReadAll = 0

Next i

End Function
```

UnLink breaks the DDE link after the DDE conversation has been completed.

```
Function UnLink () As Integer
Dim i As Integer
On Error Resume Next
For i = 1 To RANDCNT


    RandRes.Label1(i - 1).LinkMode = 0
    UnLink = 0
Next i


End Function
```

Any attempt to run the source application without the destination application will send a message that the link cannot be established because the destination is not running.

```
Sub Form_Load ()
Dim xcount As Integer
    xcount = GetAll()
    If xcount = -1 Then
        MsgBox ("Random not running")
        End
    End If
    For i = 1 To AText.Text
        label1(i - 1).Caption = "0"
        label1(i - 1).BackColor = &HFFFF00
    Next i
    xcount = LinkToAll()
    If xcount = -1 Then
        MsgBox ("Random not running")
        End
    End If
    Timer1.Interval = 300
    Timer1.Enabled = True
End Sub
```

This subroutine catches any errors in establishing the DDE link, and informs the user with a pop-up dialog box using the MsgBox function described in Chapter 5.

```
Sub Form_LinkError (LinkErr As Integer)
Dim Msg
    Select Case LinkErr
        Case 1
            Msg = "Data in wrong format."
        Case 11
            Msg = "Out of memory for DDE."
        Case Else
            Msg = "DDE Error occured"
            cmdstat.Text = "SUCCESS"
    End Select
    MsgBox Msg, 48, "MyTextBox"
```

Last, Timer function associated with the Timer control performs some calculations that fill in some of the other fields in the destination application.

```
Sub Timer1_Timer ()
Dim i As Integer
Dim xcount As Integer
Dim prob As Double

    xcount = ReadAll()
    If xcount = -1 Then
        MsgBox ("Random not running")
        End
    End If
    DText.Text = "0"
    For i = 1 To RANDCNT
        prob = CDbl(Str$(DText.Text))
        prob = prob + CDbl(Str$(label1(i - 1).Caption))
```

```
              DText.Text = prob
        Next i
        prob = prob / RANDCNT
        DText.Text = prob
    End Sub
```

OBJECT LINKING AND EMBEDDING (OLE)

Object Linking and Embedding (OLE) is a technology that allows you to create an application that can display data that originated in other Windows applications. In some cases, the user can even edit the data from within the Visual Basic application. The Visual Basic OLE custom control provides the development interface to this technology.

There are two major versions of OLE available. Most existing applications, and Visual Basic 3.0, support OLE 1.0. Newer applications, especially those from Microsoft, and including Visual Basic 4.0, support OLE 2.0. OLE 2.0 provides for advanced OLE capabilities, including editing a pasted object in place, rather than opening the originating application.

You use the Visual Basic OLE custom control to display an OLE object on a form. You either create the object when you're building your application using standard OLE dialogs, such as Insert Object and Paste Special from the Edit menu, or while the application is running by assigning the appropriate properties in the OLE object itself.

USING THE OLE CONTROL

Each time you draw an OLE control on a form, Visual Basic will display the Insert Object dialog box, shown in Figure 7.3. You use this dialog to create a linked or embedded object, or to create a new document for the object, by calling up any application that supports OLE. While you're working on your application, you can click the OLE control box with the

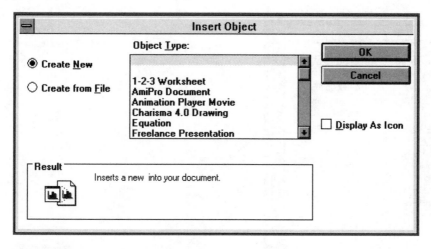

▬▬▬▬▬ **Figure 7.3** The OLE Insert Object dialog box.

right mouse button to display a pop-up menu. The commands displayed on this pop-up menu depend on the state of the OLE control as displayed in the following list. Following are the possible commands on this pop-up menu, and when you have access to them:

Insert Object. This is always available.

Paste Special. This is available when the Clipboard contains an OLE object.

Delete Embedded Object. This is available when the OLE control contains an embedded object.

Delete Linked Object. This is available when the OLE control contains a linked object.

Create Link. This is available when the object's SourceDoc property is set.

Create Embedded Object. This is available when the object's Class or SourceDoc property is set.

The properties available in the OLE object are shown in Figure 7.4.

Properties	
OLE1 OLE	
✗ ✓ 2 - DoubleClick	
AutoActivate	2 - DoubleClick
AutoVerbMenu	True
BackColor	&H80000005&
BorderStyle	1 - Fixed Single
Class	AmiProDocument
DisplayType	0 - Content
DragIcon	(none)
DragMode	0 - Manual
Enabled	True
Height	495
HelpContextID	0
HostName	
Index	
Left	1800
MiscFlags	0
MousePointer	0 - Default
Name	OLE1
OLETypeAllowed	2 - Either
SizeMode	0 - Clip
SourceDoc	
SourceItem	
TabIndex	0
TabStop	True
Tag	
Top	1200
UpdateOptions	0 - Automatic

Figure 7.4 The OLE object properties.

THE OLE OBJECT

An OLE object is actually the piece of data supplied by an OLE application. An application can show many different types and ranges of data in OLE. For example, a spreadsheet application can show a worksheet, macro sheet, chart, cell, or range of cells, all as different types of objects. You use the OLE control to both embed the object and to create the link so that the object is automatically updated.

When a linked or embedded object is created, it contains the name of the application that supplied the object, its data (or, in the case of a linked object, a reference to the data), and an image of the data. A single OLE control can contain only one embedded object at a time. There are several ways to create a linked or embedded object:

1. You can use the Insert Object or Paste Special dialogs when you create the object.

2. You can set the Class property for the object in the Properties window, then click on the OLE control with the right mouse button to get the command menu.

3. While the application is running, the user can perform an action that results in setting the Action property of the OLE control.

The class of the object determines the application that provides the object's data and the type of data the object contains. You can get a list of the class names available to your application in a dialog box when you create the object, or by selecting the Class property in the Properties window and clicking on the three dots in the Settings box.

LINKED AND EMBEDDED OBJECTS

You use an instance of the OLE custom control to incorporate data from another application into a Visual Basic application by linking or embedding data from another application. There is a difference between a linked object and an embedded object, and the difference is reflected in how the data is stored. Data associated with a linked object is stored by the application that supplied the object, rather than in your Visual Basic application. Your application stores only link references that enable display of the source data. The data associated with an embedded object is contained in an OLE control, and can be saved by your Visual Basic application.

The link is more limited in that it requires the application and the data to be at a known place on the computer. However, it is also more flexible in that changes in the data are reflected in the Visual Basic application. This kind of OLE is good when the user works in one application and needs up-to-date data from that application in the Visual Basic application.

When an object is linked, the object's data can be accessed from any application containing a link to that data and can be changed from within any of them. For example, if a text file is linked to a Visual Basic application, it can be modified by any other application linked to it. The modified version will appear in all the documents linked to this text file.

When you use an OLE control to create an embedded object, all the data associated with the object is contained in the instance of the OLE control in your application. For example, if a spreadsheet were an embedded object, all the data associated with the cells would be contained in your Visual Basic application, including any formulas. The name of the application that created the object is saved along with the data. If the user clicks on the embedded object while working with the Visual Basic application, the spreadsheet application can be started automatically for editing those cells. When an object is embedded into an application, no other application has access to the data in the embedded object. Embedding is useful when you want your application to maintain only data that is produced and edited in another application, rather than keep the most up-to-date data.

DATA EXCHANGE AND USER-CENTERED DESIGN

The OLE and DDE techniques make data seamlessly available to the end user when it is needed, no matter what application it happens to reside in. As commercial applications provide better support for both concepts, there will be an increasing need for custom applications that can accept and work with this data. You will be able to count on most Visual Basic applications requiring support for DDE and OLE in the future. Visual Basic provides a quick and easy way of adding this technology to your application.

8

DEVELOPING UNDERLYING CODE IN OTHER LANGUAGES

INCORPORATING DYNAMIC LINK LIBRARIES INTO VISUAL BASIC APPLICATION

At times, it becomes necessary to write some of the code for Visual Basic applications in traditional programming languages. There are several reasons for this. First, your expertise may be in a traditional language, and you may feel more comfortable developing an underlying computational engine in that language. Second, the problem you're trying to solve may not be very easy to accomplish in Visual Basic. As mentioned in Chapter 1, Visual Basic is not the best language choice for all types of computing problems. Last, you may have efficiency considerations—the code may have to run in limited memory, for example, or it may have to run at the fastest possible speed. Visual Basic is great for prototyping, but is not the most efficient language available.

For whatever reason, it is possible and often even desirable to write parts of a Visual Basic application in another language. How do you do this? Through a mechanism known as Dynamic Link Libraries, or DLLs. For those of you experienced in Windows programming, the concept of DLLs may already be a familiar one. For others, the concept may be new and different. However, to develop applications in Windows in general, and in Visual Basic in particular, DLLs make up an important tool. DLLs also contribute to the concept of reusable code, discussed in more detail in the next chapter.

The DLL can contribute to the concept of user-centered application design in several ways. By using a more appropriate language, you can improve the response time of a particular set of operations that may not run very quickly in Visual Basic. Other languages may help you add user-centered features that may be difficult or impossible to do in Visual Basic, such as in developing custom controls, and even to share them across multiple Visual Basic applications.

Clearly, under most circumstances, Visual Basic should be used for user interface development. The range of predefined controls and events, and the ability to lay out and rapidly test a user interface, make Visual Basic almost unbeatable for user interfaces. However, for many people who have existing code for computations, or when the application spends relatively little time responding to user events, subroutines written in other languages often make sense.

What Is a DLL?

The DLL is a function library that can be shared among different applications. While it is not itself executable, its contents are compiled just like an executable application. When an application needs to make use of a particular function that is not in its own executable file, it goes off and looks for that function in a DLL. The application links with the DLL only when it needs access to that function. After the link occurs, that function and all of the other functions in that library are accessible to the application, just as if they were a part of the executable file.

In practice, the DLL is simply a list of subroutines that accomplish specific, stand-alone tasks. They could easily be included in the stand-alone application file itself, but for reasons discussed later, are broken out into separate files. These files are loaded into memory only when needed by the executable application.

DLLs can be shared among applications. This makes it possible for generic libraries to be developed for multiple applications. This is how DLLs can support reusability. DLLs also make it popular to update or enhance applications by writing new DLLs and replacing the old ones. Ideally, changing existing applications is much less difficult with this approach. As a result, some commercial applications may have tiny executable files, but extensive DLLs that provide many of the features of that application. The vendor can then enhance the application by providing new or modified DLLs, which will work together with the same executable files to deliver those new features to the user.

Subroutines in DLLs may also call subroutines in still other DLLs, and the DLLs need not be written in the same programming language, as long as the DLL and subroutine interfaces are coordinated. I have written DLLs using the C language, which contained procedures that were called from the main program. These functions, in turn, called functions and procedures in another DLL written in Borland Pascal.

DLLs can be developed in many traditional languages that support Windows programming. The use of DLLs is not confined to Windows applications, although that is the most popular use today. The C and C++ languages, especially Microsoft's Visual C++ and Borland International's Borland C++, are popular languages for writing DLLs. So is Borland Pascal, the language I will use for my examples. I prefer Pascal as my traditional development language because it is a simple and easy to understand language with enough power to accomplish all but the most complex programming tasks. The examples discussed here can easily be translated into C and run in one of the aforementioned compilers. I will also briefly discuss how to produce a DLL using Borland C++.

DLLs Using Borland Pascal

Writing a DLL in Borland Pascal is not much different than writing a stand-alone application. In fact, it is somewhat easier, since the DLL does not have to perform very many of the housekeeping chores required of the executable application. For example, it usually does not have to implement a graphical user interface, or handle user-generated events, or worry about how to display its results. These are all tasks usually handled by the executable application.

In fact, the DLL is usually just a collection of functions and procedures that perform specific tasks. These functions and procedures are called from Visual Basic when the user or the application generates an event that requires the use of that routine. While Visual Basic may call only one subroutine at a time, Windows will load the entire DLL whenever the first routine is called. The entire DLL is rarely if ever run at a single time. Rather, your Visual Basic application will pick and choose routines from the DLL whenever it needs them.

Telling Borland Pascal that you are compiling a DLL rather than an executable application is simply a matter of using the appropriate statements in the program file to tell the compiler what kind of file to produce. Rather than the program statement at the beginning of the file, a DLL requires a library statement, used as follows:

```
library waiting_line;
```

You must make use of the appropriate Pascal units, just as in a Windows application. A unit is similar to a header file in C; it provides some declarations and definitions that are required by all programs. In a Windows

DLL, the following units must be used at a minimum, which are required for all Windows applications in Pascal:

```
uses WinTypes, WinProcs;
```

You may also require other units to be loaded into your DLL, depending on the contents of your code.

The actual program file consists of a series of Pascal functions and procedures that the executable file expects to find when it runs. You must declare any constants or variables and define any data types that you expect to use in the library code, but you don't have to worry about any of the variables or structures that are used in the executable file itself. Of course, it is important that the function or procedure calls in the executable file use the same number and type of parameters expected by the actual subroutine in the DLL. For example, if the procedure defined in the DLL uses the following three parameters of type double:

```
procedure server(var param, inV,outV: double);
export;
```

then the calling routine in the main part of the program must also contain the same number and type of parameters:

```
server(param, inV,outV);
```

where **param, inV,outV** are also all of type double. The var declaration means that the parameters are being passed by reference so that they can be modified in the DLL, and the modified values will be returned to your application.

The subroutine in the DLL must also be defined as being exportable, which is done by simply using the instruction **export** as a part of its definition. Exportable refers to the fact that the function can be called by and taken from its existing file and used in another executable file. This is the only way your DLL function will actually be recognizable to your application. If you don't declare your DLL function as exportable, you will not generate an error compiling the DLL, but your Visual Basic application will not be able to find the function, generating an error at run time. The C language has an analogous requirement for exporting, but it is taken care of automatically by the compiler, or in a separate definition file.

```
function sim_timeEvent(var h: HWND; msg,wParam:integer; lParam: longint):
PChar;

export;
```

A Borland Pascal DLL also requires that each library function be assigned an index number in order to export that subroutine to the main part of the application. One of the ways that the subroutine in the DLL is identified by the calling program is by this number:

```
exports

        exponential             index 1,

        poisson                 index 2;

    end
```

where **poisson** and **exponential** are functions in the DLL.

This declaration is performed at the end of the DLL file, after the declaration of the functions and procedures in that file. All functions and procedures that you intend to call from your Visual Basic application must be declared as exportable and given an index number. If you forget to give it an index number, the DLL will compile, but the Visual Basic application will not be able to access those subroutines. A Visual Basic application will respond with an error message when you attempt to call such subroutines. On the other hand, including an index number for a nonexistent subroutine will cause a compile error in the DLL.

The last two lines of a Pascal DLL file simply finish up the essentials of any Pascal program, the main part of the program. Since no calls are to be made from the DLL itself, this last declaration is simply the main begin and end of the file:

```
begin

    end.
```

With these small modifications to the normal application structure, it is possible to create a DLL in Borland Pascal that contains subroutines that can be called from Visual Basic.

DLLs in Borland C

Developing a DLL in Borland C++ is only slightly more complicated than in Borland Pascal. More compiler settings have to be changed in order to accomplish the result, but the files are constructed in similar ways. Like Pascal, the C DLL bears a strong resemblance to the source code for an executable application. Within the source code file itself, the primary difference between an .EXE and a .DLL file in C is that the .DLL file does not contain a main function.

One distinct difference between C and Pascal is that C requires the explicit use of a WEP function (WEP stands for Windows Exit Procedure). This is known as a callback function, which ensures that Windows returns control back to your application after the DLL function finishes execution. If you leave out the WEP function, Borland C++ provides a default function that accomplishes the same purpose.

A typical C project contains at least one other file of significance. This is a *definition file*, which uses the file extension .DEF. The definition file lets you tell Windows how to manage the executable code within the file. To designate your file as a DLL, you must use the line **LIBRARY <filename>** in the definition file. Following is a common definition file for a Windows DLL written in Borland C++:

```
LIBRARY menus
DESCRIPTION 'Sim  DLL'
EXETYPE WINDOWS
CODE PRELOAD MOVABLE DISCARDABLE
DATA PRELOAD MOVABLE SINGLE
HEAPSIZE 4096
```

Last, the compiler has to be informed that you are creating a DLL rather than an executable application. In Borland C++, this is done in three places in the Options menu. The most general place to set the compile option is under Applications, where you have the choice between Windows EXE and Windows DLL. Second, under Linker Settings, you have to set the output to Windows DLL rather than Windows EXE.

Under Entry/Exit Code Generation, you have to set the Prolog/Epilog Code Generation option to Windows DLL. Here, you have the choice of setting all functions exportable, or explicit functions exportable. DLLs with simple functions that do not call other functions within the DLL should all be exportable, since the intent of all of these functions is to be used directly in the executable file. When your exportable functions call other functions within the DLL, you should limit exportable functions to those you specifi- cally declare as exportable. This is not only a more careful and accurate structuring of your code, but it can also slightly reduce your memory requirements.

OTHER ASPECTS OF DLLs

One other Borland C option of interest is in selecting a memory model for the DLL. The memory model you choose determines the default method of memory addressing. The concept of memory models is a throwback to compatibility with earlier Intel processors and with MS DOS (so that oper- ating systems not based on DOS usually don't require a choice of memory models, because they address all memory equally). The trade-offs are between performance and the size of code and/or data. You have the choice of Small, Medium, Compact, and Large memory models.

Use the Small memory model for small-size DLLs, and where performance is critical. The code and data segments are different and don't overlap, so you have 64K of code and 64K of data and stack. Near pointers are always used; in other words, pointers that are confined to just a single Windows 64K memory segment. This tends to make the functions run faster, because the system doesn't have to map pointers into other 64K memory segments.

Use the Medium model for larger DLLs that don't keep much data in memory. Far pointers are used for code but not for data. As a result, the DLL's data and stack together are limited to 64K, but the code itself can occupy up to 1Mb.

Use the Compact model if your code is small but you need to address a lot of data. Far pointers are used for data but not for code; code is then limited to 64K, while data has a 1Mb range. Both the Medium and Compact models offer a compromise between performance and flexibility, accommodating large amounts of either code or data, but not both.

Use the Large model for very large DLLs only. Far pointers are used for both code and data, giving both a 1Mb range. All functions and data pointers are far by default. The use of far pointers by both will decrease your performance somewhat, but gives you the greatest flexibility in terms of expanding your code or managing larger amounts of data while DLL functions are running.

Functions and procedures in DLLs can call subroutines in other DLLs. You might want to do this in order to have a DLL with a number of generic functions that can be applied to several different DLLs that directly support different applications.

This is easier in C, where subroutine definitions need not occur in any particular order. In Pascal, it makes more sense to compile such second-level calls as Pascal units, and make them accessible to the DLL by inserting the uses instruction in the Pascal file.

Enter Visual Basic

As mentioned previously, the DLL usually does not have to implement highly complex application features, such as a graphical user interface, or handle user-generated events, or worry about how to display its results. These are all tasks handled by the executable application. Programming event handlers, menus, and dialog boxes in a traditional programming language can be very labor-intensive, as up to 50 percent of the effort in developing a graphical application involves work on the user interface.

Fortunately, these types of complicated housekeeping chores are what Visual Basic does best. This means that for some types of applications, the combination of a set of DLLs written in a traditional language with a Visual Basic executable application can be the best of both worlds. Visual Basic performs many of the user interface-oriented chores that a programmer in a traditional language would have to be concerned with. In return, developing a computational engine in a traditional language is often easier and more efficient than it would be in Visual Basic (although I know of developers who have written low-level network access routines in Visual Basic to take advantage of the rapid prototyping facilities and integrated development environment).

You must ensure that your Visual Basic application is properly informed about the DLLs you use, and can call them properly and make use of their results. Visual Basic has several requirements and options in this regard.

First, you have to identify the functions and procedures contained in any DLL you use as Global Declarations within your Visual Basic application. Technically, you can identify the DLL functions you intend to use in the event-handling code in any form or control in the Visual Basic application, but identifying them as Global Declarations means that they can be called from anywhere in the application, rather than just a particular form or control.

Global declarations are nonexecutable code statements that name external procedures, constants, or variables and define their attributes (such as their data type). You can write declarations for forms or code modules. To enter module-level declarations, go to the Declarations section of the form or module. To enter global declarations, go to the Declarations section of a module and use the Declare statement to make the subroutine visible to Visual Basic. For example:

```
Declare Sub server Lib transact
```

This Declare statement declares the subroutine server (in this case, a Pascal procedure) as being within the DLL named **transact**.This makes the procedure server accessible to the form (if used in a form) or an entire application (if used in a module). In general, the Declare statement takes one of the following forms:

```
Declare Sub globalname Lib "libname"


Declare Function globalname Lib libname As typename
```

The first declares a DLL subroutine as a Visual Basic sub, which is analogous to a Pascal procedure or C void function. The second is analogous to a Pascal function or ordinary C function. As in either traditional language, Visual Basic requires that you declare the return type of the value being returned from the function.

Parameters can be passed by reference or by value, just as in a subroutine call in a traditional language. Passing by reference lets you modify the values within the subroutine and have the modified values returned to your Visual Basic application. Pass by Reference is the default behavior and requires no special instructions. Pass by Value simply passes the actual value, and requires use of the ByVal instruction along with the Declare statement.

You can also enter procedure-level declarations that can be used within any Visual Basic procedure.For whatever code level and technique you use to declare a variable or constant, specific scoping rules may apply to your declarations, so be careful that your declarations match how you intend to use the subroutines in the DLL.

To open the Declarations section for a form, you double-click the form (or any control on the form) to open the Code window, then in the Object box, select the General identifier. When you do this, the Procedure box automatically displays Declarations. The Declarations code window will appear, letting you enter the declarations you want, following the guidelines for entering and editing code.

To open the Declarations section for a module:

1. In the Project window, select the module you want to open and click the View Code button.

2. In the Procedure box, select (Declarations).

3. Enter the declarations you want.

Once you have declared the function to be globally available in your Visual Basic application, you can make use of it, just as you would any Visual Basic sub or function. This opens an entire new world of capabilities and uses for Visual Basic applications.

CALLING THE DLL FROM A VISUAL BASIC APPLICATION

Once you have declared any DLL subroutines as accessible from Visual Basic, you can use them in your Visual Basic code. The mechanism you use to actually call a function in a DLL is the Call statement. The syntax of the Call statement is as follows:

```
Call function_name (parameter_list)
```

The Call keyword indicates to Visual Basic that you are referencing an external subroutine. Beyond that, all you have to do is specify the subroutine name and any parameters it requires to be passed. The Call statement, in conjunction with the subroutine declaration, will take care of the work of finding the external subroutine and passing the appropriate data.

Since you use the same Call statement to call a Visual Basic subprocedure as you do a DLL subroutine, it is not always apparent which you are calling. This is especially true because the optional syntax for the Call statement leaves out the Call keyword altogether. That's not a problem, however, because calls to a DLL subroutine are handled in exactly the same way as calls to other Visual Basic subroutines. The optional syntax is:

```
function_name parameter_list
```

When you leave out the Call keyword, however, you also leave out the parentheses around the parameter list. This is usually the appropriate syntax for calling a function that you expect to return a value, since you would usually want to assign that returning value to a Visual Basic variable:

```
VB_variable = function_name parameter_list
```

As described previously, you have to tell your Visual Basic application about any DLL subroutine you call so that it knows where to look for it. This is done with the Declare statement, which is normally used in the Declarations section of an application:

```
declare server(var param, inV,outV: double);
```

Visual Basic doesn't care which programming language is used for the DLL, as long as a few simple rules are followed:

1. The language must allow you to compile into a DLL.

2. The language must have a mechanism for creating functions or procedures.

CALLING FUNCTIONS FROM WINDOWS DLLS

Since the calling conventions for external functions are the same for all DLLs, it doesn't matter if you wrote the DLL, or if the DLL was provided by an outside party. In the case of Windows itself, many of its capabilities are contained within DLLs provided with Windows, so you can call Windows functions directly from your Visual Basic application in the same manner as previously described. Chapter 5 introduces the concept of calling functions using the Windows API. The following broadens the concept by introducing the Windows API functions as a part of a set of Dynamic Link Libraries that you can use just as you would your own DLL functions.

The Declare statement can also be used to call functions in the Windows API. This gives you access to many of the routines used by traditional languages to access Windows-related functions. These include access to special data-handling functions, drawing and graphical functions, and memory management routines. The Visual Basic Professional package provides a complete reference for the Windows API. Here are some examples of Windows API functions you can declare, and how to declare them:

```
    Declare Function GetWindowsDirectory Lib "Kernel" (ByVal P$, ByVal S%)
As Integer

    Declare Function GetSystemDirectory Lib "kernel" (ByVal P$, ByVal S%)
As Integer

    Declare Function GetWinFlags Lib "kernel" () As Long
```

The actual calls can then be made as described in Chapter 5, with special attention to passing the proper parameters and including them all on the same line.

WHEN TO USE A DLL

Much of an application can and should be developed in Visual Basic. Over the course of several years and four major releases, Visual Basic has become fast and flexible enough to be used in real-world applications. However, there are often good reasons for using a DLL, and you should not hesitate to use one if the situation justifies it.

Consider an application for which code already exists. I have worked on a Visual Basic application that involved adding a graphical front end to some engineering data analysis programs. These programs, originally developed in Fortran and C, required the user to enter dozens of precisely formatted data items in an ASCII text file that could be read by the programs. Any incorrectly formatted data would often not produce a program error, but rather deliver incorrect results that were in many cases not easily distinguishable from the correct results.

The code was computationally intensive, often requiring hours or even days to run, and the program developers considered computational efficiency more important than usability. My task was to deliver the best of both worlds—the same level of performance accorded by the original program, with the usability inherent in a Windows-based graphical user interface. The solution to this challenge was to compile the existing code as a Windows DLL, and access the procedures through Visual Basic components. The Visual Basic front end provided descriptions of variables, on-screen prompts and Help, and boxes to enter variable values, then took these values and put them in the ASCII file in the required order so that the analysis program could use them in its run.

PERFORMANCE CONSIDERATIONS

Does it matter whether you use a Visual Basic routine or a DLL function to perform a particular operation? In particular, do you pay a performance penalty in making a call to a DLL? If so, do you gain in performance in your DLL function, written in a more optimized language, so that you may offset any performance penalty in using a DLL, and hopefully even gain a performance advantage?

These questions are not idle ones, and are of concern to those interested in user-centered application design. One important consideration in user-centered design is response time. When I was first introduced to computers in the late 1970s, it was not unusual to wait seconds for a text-only response on an interactive terminal. Today, with personal computers that are orders of magnitude faster, users are considerably less inclined to wait for the computer to respond, even though the software is correspondingly far more complex.

Some of the preceding questions can be answered directly, but others depend on the type of application and the purpose of the DLL. For instance, there is never a performance penalty in calling a function in a DLL over a function compiled as a part of the executable application. This is because of the nature of the DLL and its link to the executable application. The DLL is compiled code, just like the application, but cannot be executed on its own. Once the link has been established, the DLL becomes resident in memory, again just like the application itself. Therefore, the application makes no distinction between a function call within the application, and a function call to a DLL. The result is no performance distinction between the two.

How long are users willing to wait in modern interactive applications before usability suffers? Generally, most research on software human factors indicates that an acceptable response time is about half a second. Trying to plan for acceptable response times can cause problems when an application is performing an action that may require more time, such as searching a large database, opening a file, or formatting a document.

To ease the waiting time, or to cue the user that the application is working, many applications change the screen pointer into the hourglass icon. Visual Basic gives you a number of different mouse pointer shapes to use, including the hourglass. Whenever you have to make the user wait a perceptible period of time for an application activity, you should change the mouse pointer into the hourglass.

Since most forms and controls, including the MDI form, have the MousePointer property, the best approach would be to change the MousePointer property on the form or MDI form to the hourglass just prior to calling a long-running DLL subroutine, then change it back immediately after the subroutine call returns control to your application, like this:

```
MDIForm1.MousePointer = 11  ;;The number designating the hourglass shape
Call server (param inV outV)
MDIForm1.MousePointer = 0   ;; The default shape for the mouse pointer
```

A DLL ENGINE FOR A
VISUAL BASIC APPLICATION

One of my Visual Basic projects was a visually oriented application for performing *discrete event simulation*. Discrete event simulation, also known as the simulation of waiting line systems, involves any use of a scarce resource. It is used to model supermarket and ticket-counter lines, computer resource utilization, telecommunications networks, and a large number of other resource-intensive systems.

I've used Visual Basic to create the user interface of my simulation application, which consists of a number of graphical blocks designating high-level simulation activities, statistics, and displays. You can indicate an interaction between these blocks by connecting them with a line. The code that makes these blocks perform as they should is written and called from a DLL.

My DLL, written in Borland Pascal, consists of a collection of about 24 procedures and functions that create transactions, queue up the transactions into a waiting line, service the transactions, collect statistics on the behavior of transactions in the system, and provide utilities such as random number generators. One of the advantages in working with a language other than Visual Basic is that it enables you to dynamically allocate memory using pointers, something that is not possible in Visual Basic. The following code makes extensive use of pointers, which enables it to create as many simulation components and transactions as needed.

The entire DLL consists of about 3,000 lines of Pascal code. Rather than show you all of that code, the following listings will show just a few of the procedures that can be called by Visual Basic from the DLL.

The first part of the code consists of the declarations, including the library heading necessary to define the file as a DLL, and the type declarations. The transaction is represented by the **transact record**, and is accessed by the **transactptr** pointer variable. Note that the transaction record contains a great deal of information about individual transactions, including a unique ID number, priorities, and waiting and service times.

```pascal
library waiting_line;

    uses WinTypes, WinProcs;


type


        SimArg = array[0..18] of double;
        user = array[1..10] of double;
        transactptr = ^transact;
        transact = record
                transact_number : double;
                priority : double;
                wait_time : double;
                serve_time : double;
                preempt_time : double;
                qid : double;
                t_mgr : double;
                use : user;
                link : queueptr
        end;
```

This procedure, CREATE, creates the transaction and initializes values in its fields:

```
procedure create(var param, inV,outV:SimArg);
export;
var i: integer;

begin
if param[0] <> 0 then
        q_number := trunc(param[0])
        else
        begin
                q_number := 1;
                param[0] := q_number
        end;
c[q_number] := false;

if (inV[0] > 0) and q_remaining[q_number] <= 0 then
begin
        new(next[q_number]);
        created[q_number] := true;
        q_remaining[q_number] := InV[0];
        cust_created[q_number] := cust_created[q_number] + 1;
        customer_id[q_number] := customer_id[q_number] + 1;
        next[q_number]^.customer_number := customer_id[q_number];
        next[q_number]^.qid := q_number;
        next[q_number]^.priority := inV[1];
        next[q_number]^.wait_time := 0;
        next[q_number]^.serve_time := 0;
        next[q_number]^.preempt_time := 0;
        next[q_number]^.link := nil;
        next[q_number]^.use[1] := InV[2];
        if inV[3] <> 0 then
```

```
            if first[q_number,1] = 0 then
                    next[q_number]^.use[1] := InV[2]
                    else
                    for i := 1 to max_data do
                            next[q_number]^.use[i] :=
first[q_number,i];
end;
if created[q_number] = false then
        outV[0] := 0
        else
                outV[0] := q_number;
end;
```

This procedure, FIFO_QUEUE, takes newly created transactions and places them in a line in first-in, first-out order:

```
procedure fifo_queue(var param, inV,outV:SimArg);
export;
var trailer : qlist;
begin
if param[0] <> 0 then
        q_number := trunc(param[0])
        else
        begin
                q_number := 1;
                param[0] := q_number
        end;
if param[1] <> 0 then
        t_number := trunc(param[1])
        else
        begin
                t_number := 1;
                param[1] := t_number
        end;
```

```
if param[2] <> 0 then

     q_capacity := trunc(param[2])

     else

     begin

          q_capacity := 0;

          param[2] := q_capacity

     end;

q_init[q_number] := false;

if (inV[0] <> 0) and (inV[0] = q_number) then

begin

     created[q_number] := false;

     if next[q_number] <> nil then

          next[q_number]^.t_mgr := t_number;

     if (q_capacity <> 0) and (q_capacity <= q_length(q_number)) then

     begin

          dispose(next[q_number]);

          next[q_number] := nil;

          lost_index[q_number] := lost_index[q_number] + 1

     end

     else

     if (front[q_number] = nil) and (back[q_number] = nil) then

          begin

               front[q_number] := next[q_number];

               back[q_number] := next[q_number];

               next[q_number] := nil

          end

          else if front[q_number] <> nil then

               begin

                    back[q_number]^.link := next[q_number];

                    back[q_number] := next[q_number];

                    next[q_number] := nil
```

```
                              end;
         end;
         if front[q_number] <> nil then
                 outV[0] := q_number
                 else
                         outV[0] := q_number
         end;
```

The SERVER procedure is passed transactions from the head of the queue, and retains them for a set period of time. It also advances the time and checks for events happening in other parts of the simulation:

```
procedure server(var param, inV,outV:SimArg);
export;
begin

if param[0] <> 0 then
        s_number := trunc(param[0])
        else
        begin
                s_number := 1;
                param[0] := s_number
        end;
t_number := trunc(inV[0]);


s_init[s_number] := false;


s[s_number] := trunc(inV[0]);


if halt_ops[s_number] = false then
begin
if init_s[s_number] = true then
begin
```

```
        s_remaining[s_number] := inV[1];

        serve_sum[s_number] := s_remaining[s_number];

        init_s[s_number] := false
end;
if (preempt_server[s_number] = true) and
(serve_customer[s_number]^.preempt_time = 0) then
begin

        s_remaining[s_number] := inV[1];

        preempt_server[s_number] := false
end
else if (preempt_server[s_number] = true) and
(serve_customer[s_number]^.preempt_time > 0) then
        begin

                s_remaining[s_number] := inV[1];

                preempt_server[s_number] := false

        end;


if (s_busy[s_number] = false) and (s_remaining[s_number] <= 0) then
        begin

        s_remaining[s_number] := inV[1];

        serve_sum[s_number] := serve_sum[s_number] + s_remaining[s_number];

        outV[0] := s_number <0 }

        end

        else

                if (s_busy[s_number] = false) and (s_remaining[s_number] <> 0)
then

                        outV[0] := s_number;


if s_busy[s_number] = true then

        if s_remaining[s_number] <= 0 then

        begin

                outV[0] := s_number; {serve_customer[s_number]^.customer_number;}

                server_wait[s_number] := server_wait[s_number] +
```

```
                        serve_customer[s_number]^.wait_time;
            done_service[s_number] := true;
            depart_customer[s_number] := serve_customer[s_number];
            snapshot_s(s_number);
            serve_customer[s_number] := nil;
            cust_served[s_number] := cust_served[s_number] + 1;
            s_busy[s_number] := false;
            s_remaining[s_number] := inV[1];
            serve_sum[s_number] := serve_sum[s_number] + s_remaining[s_number]
        end
        else
            if (s_busy[s_number] = true) and (s_remaining[s_number] > 0) then
            begin
                outV[0] := s_number
                {serve_customer[s_number]^.customer_number;}
                cust_served[s_number] := cust_served[s_number] + 1
            end;
    end
    else
        outV[0] := s_number
    end;
```

The statistic QUEUE_LENGTH calculates the number of transactions in a queue.
It works simply by starting at the front of the queue and traversing the list:

```
procedure queue_length(var param, inV,outV:SimArg);
export;
var count : integer;

begin
q_number := trunc(Inv[0]);
current[q_number] := front[q_number];
if front[q_number] = nil then
    outV[0] := 0
```

```
else
        begin
        count := 0;
        while current[q_number] <> nil do
        begin
                count := count + 1;
                current[q_number] := current[q_number]^.link
        end;
        outV[0] := count
        end
    end;
```

The last example procedure, UTILIZATION, calculates the utilization rate of each server. The utilization rate is simply the proportion of time the server is in use servicing transactions. It works by making use of data collected in the SERVER procedure, by dividing the time the server is in use by the total simulation time:

```
procedure utilization(var param, inV,outV:SimArg);
export;
var temp_time : double;

begin
s_number := trunc(inv[0]);
outV[0] := 0;
if total_time = 0 then
    outV[0] := 0
    else
    begin
        temp_time := serve_sum[s_number] / total_time;
        if temp_time > 1. 0 then
            outV[0] := 1.0
            else
                outV[0] := temp_time;
```

```
          end
     end;
```

The last few lines assign index numbers to the procedures being exported into the Visual Basic application, and complete the Pascal file with the begin/end statements:

```
   exports


         create            index 1,
         server            index 2,
         utilization       index 3,
         queue_length      index 4;


   begin
   end.
```

With the appropriate variable declarations, Borland Pascal will compile the preceding code into a DLL.

CALLING PROCEDURES FROM VISUAL BASIC

Within Visual Basic, the simulation application utilizes picture boxes to represent each of these simulation components. The picture box contains an icon symbolizing the type of component, along with an unique ID identifier. Startup data, such as time between new transactions and service time, is generated with random numbers in a .BAS file. The components represented by the icons are labeled at the bottom of the form for information purposes. There is also a Graph control that can be configured to display queuing statistics generated from the simulation, such as average waiting time in the queue or average service time. A typical simulation using these components is shown in Figure 8.1.

Each of these components is designed to respond primarily to user-generated events, but they also respond to Timer events. The Timer control is located in the upper left-hand portion of the display, and advances the clock for the application. At each step of the clock, each of the other components calls its subroutine in the DLL and recomputes its state.

For example, at **Time = 0**, each of the two Create Transaction components generates a new transaction and passes it to its respective Queue. The first Queue determines that the Server is idle and passes its transaction directly to the Server. The second Queue holds its transaction until the Server is again free.

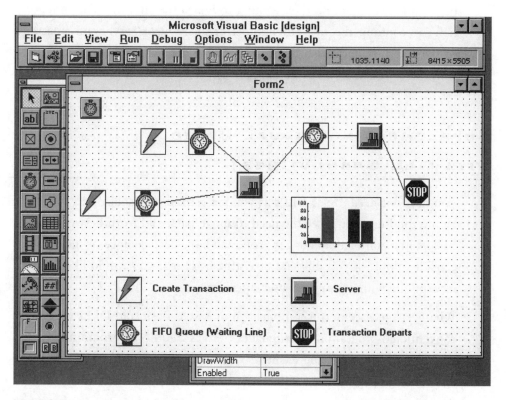

▬▬▬▬**Figure 8.1** A simple graphical simulation using controls that call DLL subroutines.

At each subsequent time signal, each component checks its progress. The Create Transaction components check to see if it is time to create new transactions. The Queues check to see if the Server is free. The Server checks to see if the service time is up. Based on the answers to these queries, the simulation advances by creating, queuing, and serving more transactions.

Transactions that finish service on the first Server are passed to a subsequent queue to await service from the next Server. This is analogous to a person having to wait in two consecutive lines, as when buying an airline ticket at the counter and then waiting to board the aircraft. The simulation can continue through any number of such Queue/Server combinations. At the end of the process, the transaction is removed from the application with the Transaction Departs component.

SUPPLEMENTING VISUAL BASIC WITH DLL SUBROUTINES

You may not need to use DLLs as you get started in Visual Basic, but before too long, you'll see the need to move back and forth between Visual Basic and traditional languages. You may have performance or memory considerations, or you may have existing code that you would like to incorporate with a graphical user interface.

Whatever the reason, the combination of Visual Basic and DLLs written in conventional programming languages bridges traditional programming with the user-centered and event-driven model of the future. You can leverage existing programming skills to make yourself more effective in Visual Basic.

9

DEVELOPING

VISUAL BASIC

COMPONENTS FOR REUSE

SOFTWARE REUSE AND
USER-CENTERED DESIGN

One of the supposed advantages of object-oriented software development was that it was intended to promote the reuse of code and objects. That is, you could conceivably develop a set of objects for use in one application that could be used with little or no modification in other applications. The objects themselves could act like *black boxes,* where data flows in, is operated upon in predetermined ways, and then flows out. Neither the application developer nor the end user has to worry about what goes on inside the black box, since it has already worked as needed in other applications.

This solution potentially addressed one of the major problems in software development; that is, that software was becoming too complex and too expensive to continue writing one line at a time. A library of standardized objects could be used across multiple applications, lowering the cost of all software projects. These reusable objects would have the side benefits of delivering a common look and feel to the users, and making the underlying code easier to maintain and enhance.

Unfortunately, few solutions for object reuse developed in practice. There were few guidelines on how to develop software objects for reuse, and most object-oriented systems had no way of sharing objects across computers. Those few organizations that have developed effective reusable object libraries are reluctant to share them, since they represent an investment of effort that may give them a competitive advantage.

Reusability contributes to user-centered application design in several ways. Most important, it provides you with a tool to achieve consistency in appearance and behavior across your applications. By using the same components and code across multiple applications, your users can easily transfer their skills and experiences, and take less time learning to use the applications.

Second, it assists you in keeping and reusing your best design ideas. When you don't have to work from scratch, you can make sure that your usual work is your best work. Your inspirations are saved for routine use, rather than for special circumstances and then lost.

Third, it supports rapid prototyping, discussed in Chapter 6. If you have a library of tried and proven components, then you can rapidly assemble not only the look and feel of an application, but also much of its underlying operations. This can deliver a better and more reliable application into users' hands faster than if you started from scratch.

However, your reuse libraries have to be constructed and organized to take advantage of the work you have done in the past. This includes proper naming of reusable components and variables; knowing what type of components can be reused and when; designing generic rather than specialized components; and cataloging your components so that you know where to look when you need something.

VISUAL BASIC AND COMPONENT REUSE

Visual Basic represents a step in the right direction toward object, or component, reusability. The predefined components themselves, such as forms, buttons, and dialog boxes, go a long way toward establishing a standard set of structures or templates that are easily transportable between applications, at least on PCs. To develop these components from scratch in each application would be a complicated and time-consuming process that would greatly lengthen the time and effort needed to produce modern applications.

However, predefined Visual Basic components are not the only structures that can be reused. It is possible to include the underlying event-handling code with the component, and write this code so that it can be used, whole or in part, in more than one application.

Unfortunately, the Visual Basic development environment is not optimized for easily creating and reusing both components and the code in these components. There are few good ways to save individual components other than forms. However, by planning carefully and by understanding what Visual Basic can and can't help you with, you can create components, event-handling code, and subroutines that you can use across many applications.

Also, as the Windows software development world moves into the world of OLE, detailed in Chapter 7, the potential to develop components that can be shared across applications becomes greater. Any Visual Basic developer who is thinking about and implementing plans to write reusable components will enjoy advantages over the coming years.

THE MANY WAYS OF LEVERAGING SOFTWARE

This book discusses many ways to leverage the investment in software to and across Visual Basic applications. These include:

1. Dynamic Link Libraries (DLLs), which let you call functions and procedures written in other languages, just as if they existed in the Visual Basic application.

2. Dynamic Data Exchange (DDE), which lets you work with some commercial applications and specialized custom applications by dynamically passing data between these applications and your applications.

3. Object Linking and Embedding (OLE), which lets you work with some commercial applications and specialized custom applications by embedding data from them into your Visual Basic application.

4. The Windows API, which gives you access to many standard and well-documented Windows functions through external subroutine calls.

5. Visual Basic Custom Controls (VBXs) and OLE Custom Controls (OCXs), which allow you to use traditional programming languages to extend the features of the Visual Basic development environment.

6. The Visual Basic controls themselves, which give you the same user interface components with the same structures, properties, and events across every application.

All of these techniques promote reusable software, and many of them are used in day-to-day Visual Basic development activities. However, there is still more leveraging of software to be done in the Visual Basic environment, through reusing parts of your own designs and your own event-handling code from application to application.

LIMITATIONS TO USABILITY IN VISUAL BASIC

Creating a library of reusable components is not a simple matter of copying and pasting controls. When you copy a Visual Basic control from one form and paste it to another, you copy only the appearance of the control and its properties. You do not automatically copy the underlying event-handling code, at least not across forms within a project or across projects.

Further, when you save a form, you normally save it in a binary format; that is, a format that is specially designed for working with Visual Basic and not with any other applications. Such a form, and the controls on that form, cannot be used or even edited outside of Visual Basic. While it is possible to save forms in text format, when you try to load them, Visual Basic will attempt to load them into a code window.

Controls, which are the natural units for creating reusable components, cannot be saved as separate entities. There is no mechanism in Visual Basic to save the appearance and behavior of individual controls, and apply them from application to application. Rather, they are saved collectively, as parts of individual forms. The means of the basic unit of application management in Visual Basic is the form. In order to save, copy, and load your reusable components, all of these components have to be associated with forms.

There are yet additional problems when you attempt to load a text file into a form. The code from the text file automatically loads into a Basic module, rather than into the form. This means that your event-handling routines for both the form and the controls residing on the form will be in the wrong place in the application.

Nevertheless, there are ways to get around all of these limitations, and it is worthwhile to expend the effort to do so. The primary reason is that even though Visual Basic speeds the development process through the use of graphical controls, hundreds or thousands of lines of supporting code are still required for many applications. The question is one of determining what types of operations are common across many different applications, and how to encapsulate these operations so that the same techniques can be used over and over again. These are problems that are faced by all software developers, and while Visual Basic solves some of them with reusable controls, how to achieve better reusability still takes planning and forethought.

Using Forms as Reusability Tools

Despite its limitations, your first primary weapon in developing reusable software is the form. This is because controls, as such, cannot be saved and reused. Forms, however, can be saved in a binary format, along with all of the controls they contain. This is the way to save both forms and controls, along with all of the code associated with both.

There are two ways of using this feature. The first and easiest is to design forms, complete with controls, that you can use between similar applications. While this is easy to do, it is the least flexible method of reusability, because it means that you have to work with forms that are general enough to be useful across multiple applications. While it sounds like a challenge to do this, it is not as difficult as it seems. The next section will discuss how to start and then build on a library of reusable forms.

The second way of using forms in your reuse library is as a platform for saving controls that you would like to reuse, along with their code. You're not so much interested in the forms themselves, but rather the controls on the forms. In other words, the controls are simply the medium on which the controls are stored. The form is the reuse library, so to speak.

Creating and Building on Reusable Forms

What kinds of forms can you reuse from application to application? The answer to this depends a great deal upon the type of application you commonly develop. You may be able to save and reuse large parts of forms and associated controls, or only smaller parts. If it is not clear to you when you start your reuse library, then you should start with more general forms and make them more specific as your knowledge and confidence increase.

Consider starting with a form like the one in Figure 9.1. This is a form that simply contains two command buttons at the bottom, labeled Continue and Done. The code associated with them will just call another form, or end the application, respectively.

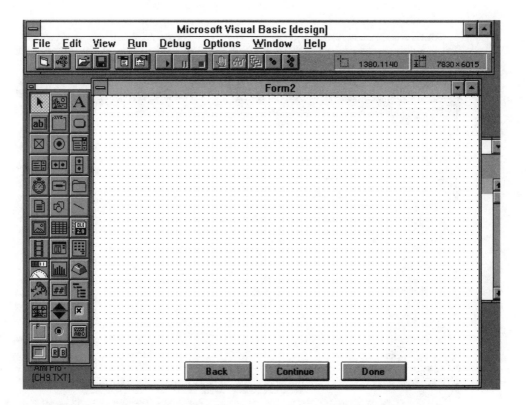

Figure 9.1 A simple form with the potential to be reused.

This particular form does not save a great deal of time and effort. However, it can be an appropriate starting point; once you gain a better understanding of your reuse needs, you can add controls to it. Alternatively, from the standpoint of creating a formal reuse library, you can leave the original form in the library and add enhancements as more specialized instances of that form.

For example, we can add name and address text boxes to this particular base form if we use those types of information on a regular basis. Figure 9.2

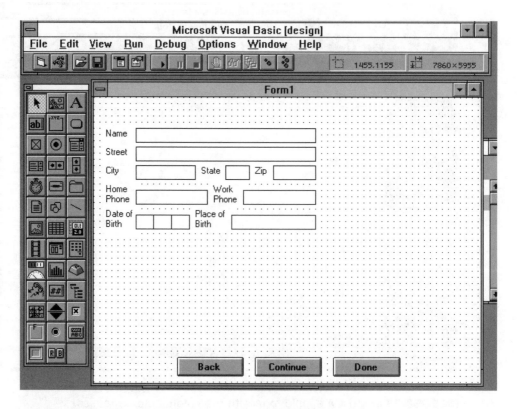

Figure 9.2 A more specialized example of a reusable form.

shows just such a form that may suffice to provide you with more reusability. Underneath, the code associated with the LostFocus event in the text boxes can check to ensure that data has been entered properly before moving on.

The most common type of form that can be reused is the pop-up modal dialog box. It would be very easy to create a library of such dialog boxes that provide you with ready access to a number of routine messages. Some examples are shown in Figures 9.3 through 9.5, and include such common messages as "Are You Sure You Want to Exit the Application?", "Do You Want to Save Your Work?", and "You Cannot Perform That Operation at This Time."

These dialog boxes can be implemented using the MsgBox function, and associated with a form or other control. The following event procedure associates it with the Click event of a command button.

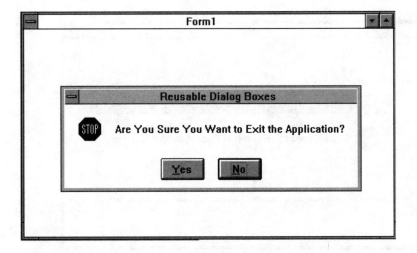

Figure 9.3 Examples of reusable dialog boxes.

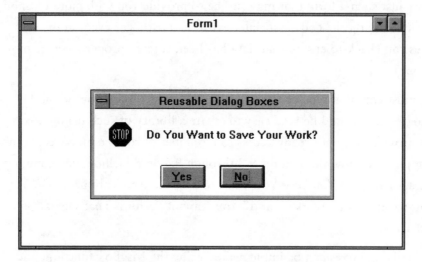

Figure 9.4 Examples of reusable dialog boxes.

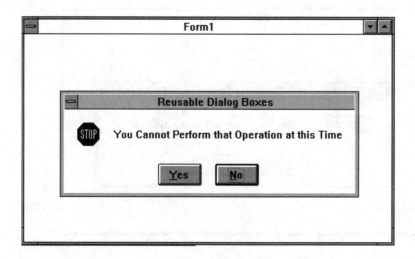

Figure 9.5 Examples of reusable dialog boxes.

```
Sub Command_Click ()
    ' The following are already defined as a part of the MsgBox function.
    Const MB_OK = 0, MB_OKCANCEL = 1
    Const MB_YESNOCANCEL = 3, MB_YESNO = 4
    Const MB_ICONSTOP = 16, MB_ICONQUESTION = 32
    Const MB_ICONEXCLAMATION = 48, MB_ICONINFORMATION = 64
    Const MB_DEFBUTTON2 = 256, IDYES = 6, IDNO = 7
    Dim DgDef, Msg, Response, Title

    Title = "Reusable Dialog Boxes"
    Msg = "You Cannot Perform that Operation at this Time"
    DgDef = MB_YESNO + MB_ICONSTOP + MB_DEFBUTTON2
    Response = MsgBox(Msg, DgDef, Title)
End Sub
```

One other item you may want to save and reuse in conjunction with a
form is a company logo, picture, or other unique visual component that
you may use as a common part of all or most of your applications. While
it is possible to save most of these types of images as bitmaps or icons, and
import them into a picture box or other control for every new application,
you will find it easier and more convenient to have them already prepared
and on a form that is ready to load and use again.

MODULES AND REUSABILITY

Your second primary weapon in reusability in Visual Basic is the Basic
module. A module is a set of declarations and subroutines stored in a single file, independent of any form or control. Modules therefore make an
ideal way for storing reusable code that is not associated with any specific
control. This gives you two possibilities for module reusability—*global declarations* and *global subroutines*.

Global declarations are more difficult to reuse, because they apply to the entire application rather than to individual components. Variable names and types can vary from application to application, because their names (and sizes, in the case of array or other size-dependent variables) should be adapted to describing their use or behavior, something that is not normally possible to do across applications.

Therefore, you should concentrate your reuse efforts on global subroutines. The only global declarations you can reasonably reuse are those associated with these subroutines.

SETTING UP A MODULE LIBRARY

As you work in Visual Basic, you will write modules to perform a variety of different activities. However, you will find that you will write many of the same types of subroutines over and over again. The global module concept in Visual Basic is partly intended to facilitate the ability to reuse operations at several different points within an application. It can also be used to facilitate reusability across applications.

Visual Basic modules can be treated as black boxes, in that once you have demonstrated that they work, you have to know only the necessary inputs and the resulting outputs. This means that an important part of your module reusability structure is to document the required inputs and outputs. You can do this as part of a comprehensive reusability database, or simply in a text editor.

Developing these modules involves recognizing what types of features make a module reusable and why. There are no hard and fast rules in doing so, but some pointers or hints can be applied to the problem. First, you should develop subroutines for things that are clearly generic; in other words, things that are done in all applications. These may include such operations as common mathematical computations (mean or standard deviation, or calculations common in your business), basic file manipulation operations, and the more often used Windows API calls. These will likely be called from higher-level (and more application-specific) subroutines, so it is easy to make them independent of any particular application.

Second, your subroutines should be written so that they can be easily modified or extended. You do this by not relying on data being in a specific location on a form, or in a specific format. If you have to do this, then it should be through a subroutine call that can be specifically tailored to individual applications.

Third, you should clearly document the behavior of your modules, so you will be able to quickly determine at some point of time in the future if you can reuse them. This will involve detailing the required inputs and resulting outputs in both a database or a reuse notebook, and within the module itself. Normally, you can do this for your modules after the application has been completed, rather than when writing the module itself; but the only way you have a chance of reusing a module is if you know what it contains.

CONTROL ARRAYS AND REUSABILITY

The concept of the Visual Basic control array lets you practice a limited form of control reusability with relative ease. A control array is made up of a group of controls of the same type (for example, all text boxes) that share a common control name and a set of event procedures. Each control in the array has a unique index number within the array so that each can be individually identified. All items in a control array must have the same setting of the Name property.

When a control in the array recognizes an event generated by user actions, such as entering text or pushing a button, Visual Basic calls an event procedure for the entire group of controls and passes the index as an additional argument, allowing you to determine which control recognizes the event.

Figure 9.6 shows a couple of typical control arrays. The following subroutine takes data from sequences of text boxes designed as control arrays, and writes their data to a text file when the form is closed. These particular

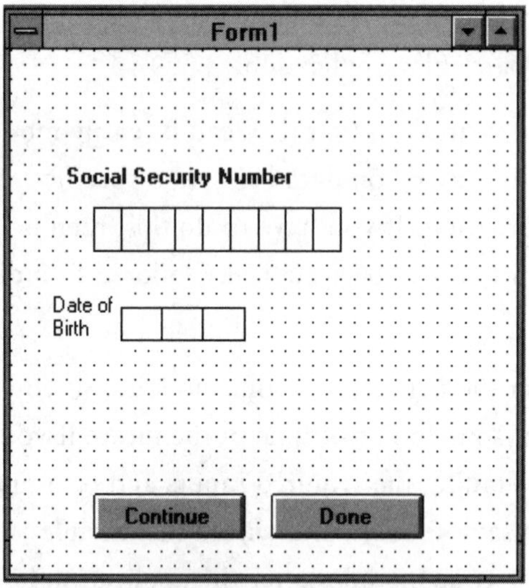

■■■■ **Figure 9.6** Control arrays for collecting discrete but related information.

control arrays ask the users to enter their Social Security numbers and dates of birth. Each control array uses a FOR loop to perform the same actions on all elements of the control array. Note that the first element of a control array is designated 0 rather than 1, a convention more familiar to C programmers than Basic programmers.

```
Sub Command2_Click ()
Dim i
Open "TESTFILE" For Output As 1
  For i = 0 To 8
    Write #1, Head.SSANText(i).Text
    Next i
  For i = 0 To 2
    Write #1, Head.DOBText9(i).Text
    Next i
  Close #1      ' Close file.
End

End Sub
```

NAMING YOUR COMPONENTS

One important consideration in designing reusable controls is naming conventions. While the information displayed to the user (the Text or Value properties of controls) is likely to be changed from application to application, the internal names used to reference the controls can and should remain constant. That reference name should not be the default name provided with the control, since it then becomes possible for your application to end up with multiple controls with the same names. Even though this is acceptable on different forms, it can make for confusion when you are writing Visual Basic code that performs operations across those forms.

The names should be both generic and descriptive of what the component was designed to do. The generic nature of the name is necessary so that it can be used with little or no modification in what may be very different applications. However, the name should also be able to communicate to yourself or to others the general purpose of the form or control.

Further, you have to manage the variable naming process so that you are instantly aware of the purpose of each variable, and the type of data it holds. Ideally, this means maintaining a database of variable names so that you can immediately search and identify relevant variables, and easily add new variables when necessary. You at least have to keep a manual listing of these variables, organized by control or module, data type, whether they are global or local, and their purpose in the application.

ORGANIZING YOUR REUSE LIBRARY

Most software developers prefer not to deal with the administration necessary to set up and manage a formal reuse library. Most of us who use traditional libraries cringe at the discipline and arcane knowledge necessary to catalog and store books or other types of information. Many of us would do without reusability if it involved this kind of effort to set up and maintain.

Fortunately, the object-oriented model provides a good structure for the easy creation of a reuse library. This model provides a hierarchy of related structures, with the more general classes at the top of the hierarchy, and a tree of more detailed and specific structures below. In an ideal object-oriented world, the forms and controls would inherit elements from general to specific components down the class hierarchy. However, Visual Basic does not support such an automatic inheritance mechanism.

That means that while you can't count on a class hierarchy and inheritance to do most of your work for you, you can still structure a reuse library in a similar manner. In other words, your library can be structured like a class hierarchy or a tree, with general reusable components at the top of the tree, and more specific components below.

An example might use Figure 9.1 as the top of a data input form tree. The most basic and general *class* simply lets you close the application or continue on to another form. At one level below this might be several different types of forms typified by Figure 9.2, where the structure asks for more specific information. You might have a form that requests name and address, another that requires entering product ordering information, and a third that requires credit card or financial arrangements information. As your needs become more specific, you can add still more detailed reusable forms beneath these.

Each form in this tree includes all of the structure and code of the one above it, and adds another layer of detail. By organizing your library in this way, you know exactly where to go to get the level of detail you need in adding already developed components to a new application.

As for storing these forms, your best option is to use the default PC directory structure and a good file manager, such as the one that comes with Windows, or a third-party file manager, such as the one available from the Norton division of Symantec Corporation.

USING YOUR REUSE LIBRARIES

An important part of the reusability equation is the discipline and application development practices that you need to make use of your reuse libraries. Many professional programmers feel uncomfortable in using components that they did not develop specifically for the application at hand, and will actually put in the extra time and effort to do so, even though a perfectly acceptable module may exist in the reuse library.

Because prototyping application user interfaces and simple application behaviors in Visual Basic is so easy, you may be inclined to bypass your reuse libraries altogether, in favor of making every form and module unique. Getting beyond this is a matter of establishing trust that your forms and modules behave in the way you expect, and making it a part of your normal practice to turn to your reuse library.

If you developed all of your reuse library, the issue of trust shouldn't be a problem. If, on the other hand, you're using components that were at least partially developed by others, you will have to do some testing and evaluation before you've reached the level of confidence necessary to use them. While you can't test all of the components under all circumstances, you should build a number of sample applications using them, in order to understand how they work and to feel comfortable that they work as advertised.

Making it a part of your normal development practice depends more on your own personal discipline. If you are committed to component reuse, then you should make it a practice to look at your library every time you begin a development project to refamiliarize yourself with its contents. You should then begin by selecting reusable components that are close to what your project needs, and begin with them. You will probably have to modify the appearance or the behavior of these forms or controls somewhat, but even so, you have given yourself a head start on your new application.

After you have completed the new application, look for forms and controls that you can add to your reuse library. They may be more specialized versions of the components you began with, or they may be entirely new components. You can then add these into your reuse library, and document them appropriately.

MOVING TO VISUAL BASIC 4.0

One question on the minds of many Visual Basic application developers is how to move their applications from Visual Basic 3.0 to Visual Basic 4.0. Are existing applications and code reusable in this and subsequent versions of Visual Basic?

The short answer is Yes, they are. Every Visual Basic 3.0 application should load and work without modification in the new 4.0 release. I have tested a large number of my own 3.0 applications with the new release, and have found no problems with loading, modifying, and running a wide variety of applications utilizing all control types.

However, once you make the transition to Visual Basic 4.0, you must make it for good. Don't expect to be able to go back and forth between 3.0 and 4.0. An application developed in 4.0, or ported to and modified in 4.0, is not backward-compatible with 3.0. There are different file formats, and slightly different control structures, that prevent moving from 4.0 back to 3.0.

For compiled applications, you also have to make use of a new version of the run-time DLL, VBRUN400.DLL. This works with the new file format, and includes support for the new and redesigned controls. In terms of size, you will find it slightly larger than the VBRUN300.DLL for Visual Basic 3.0.

However, with proper planning and forethought, you can expect a smooth transition to the greater power and flexibility found in Visual Basic 4.0. You should anticipate making the transition within a year after the availability of the product. All of your existing applications should be able to be reused.

10

DEVELOPING
CUSTOM CONTROLS
FOR VISUAL BASIC

Anyone who has used the Professional version of Visual Basic has an idea
of what a custom control is. Several of the controls that Visual Basic
Professional loads by default into the toolbox, such as the 3D buttons,
Crystal Reports, and the spin control, are all Visual Basic custom controls,
or VBXs.

These controls extend the functionality of Visual Basic in ways not done
by Microsoft in the base package for a variety of reasons. They can add
new user interface components into the development environment, or
extend the package to perform certain types of activities, or make application development easier or more convenient. These custom controls are
written by programmers in traditional programming languages, and connected to Visual Basic through a set of interfaces provided internally by
Visual Basic in the development environment. They are for the use of
Visual Basic application developers.

Custom controls support the principles of user-centered design in several ways. First, custom controls on the commercial market can give the application developer a wider selection of user interface components to use, and also enable the user interface to perform more activities. These custom controls can make it easier to produce applications with innovative user interfaces.

Second, your own custom controls can be tailored for your specific needs. A good example might be a collection of touch-screen controls that are designed to control machinery. Such controls might be larger than the ones provided with Visual Basic itself, and may respond to different kinds of events. This lets you use Visual Basic for applications for which it may not have been originally designed.

It's important to make clear that the custom control is a tool for the application developer, rather than for the end user. The end user ultimately benefits in that the developer has more and possibly better user interface controls available for building an application. However, the custom control aids in building an application more than in using it. It also need not be a user interface control; many programmers develop custom controls to aid in internal aspects of an application, such as data communication and networking.

Custom controls are written in a traditional programming language, such as C or Pascal, and compiled into a .VBX file, and can be loaded into Visual Basic as a part of a project's .MAK file. They will then be automatically added to the toolbox, and can be used in application development just like the other components.

Visual Basic 4.0 has introduced a new type of custom control, the OLE custom control, or OCX. The OLE custom control is intended to be more generic and portable than the VBX, and Microsoft hopes that the OCX will become a standard for the creation of reusable objects. However, Visual Basic 4.0 still supports the VBX component, and Microsoft will undoubtedly continue to do so for a long time to come. Also, while the details of the development process are different, the principles underlying the design of a custom control remain the same.

DEVELOPING A CUSTOM CONTROL

A custom control is, in effect, a DLL, which I described in Chapter 8. The difference is that this control, with the file extension .VBX, includes a structure that conforms to that used in the Visual Basic controls provided with the base package. It has routines that enable it to be recognized by Visual Basic and loaded on the toolbar, properties defined that can be modified by the Visual Basic developer, and events defined that it can intercept and respond to. This means that the custom control designer has to devise in the program itself how the control works internally, including what to do when presented with the different types of events.

Visual Basic Professional will let you develop custom controls with any programming language that supports the compilation of DLLs. This includes many implementations of C, Pascal, and Fortran for the PC. However, Microsoft also makes it easiest to do the development in C, its own high-level language of choice. The Visual Basic custom control development kit, or CDK, includes C libraries for programming interfaces, and also includes files that can be placed directly in or called from the code for your custom control.

However, there are several possible strategies for developing custom controls in other languages. My practice has been to develop the actual control functions in Pascal, my language of choice, then tie them into Visual Basic using a C module that contains the code that enables Visual Basic to register the control and load it into the toolbox. In other words, the C module is the actual .VBX file, and it calls a Pascal DLL that contains the operations for the custom control. This lets me work in the language in which I am most comfortable, yet I can also take advantage of Microsoft's bias toward C. If C is not your first traditional language, you might also want to consider this approach.

THE CUSTOM CONTROL MODEL

Microsoft refers to the addition of a custom control to Visual Basic as the creation and addition of a control class to the development environment. While the Visual Basic control structure is not in a true sense the same as a class hierarchy in object-oriented systems, the concept is understandable in the same way. There is no hierarchy to use to help create new classes, and Visual Basic does not support the concept of inheritance, which would enable classes to automatically inherit the characteristics of classes farther up on the inheritance tree.

However, you can view each control that you use in an application as an instance of the control class that is represented on the toolbar. All of the characteristics of that class are available with each instance you create. While not truly object-oriented, it is enough alike to not cause confusion on the terminology. The control class model is more consistent if you're enhancing an existing MS Windows control from the Windows control libraries, rather than creating a new one from scratch. This way, you can inherit some of the characteristics of the Windows control, especially many of the functions that perform the memory and display housekeeping chores. This approach follows the object-oriented model more closely, but only if your own custom control is an extension of an existing Windows control.

Each Visual Basic control class has two parts—a *control model* and a *control procedure*. The control model provides Visual Basic with information about the control, such as its name, its properties, and the events to which it responds. The control procedure intercepts event messages from the application (usually, but not always, from the user), and dispatches them to the appropriate event handler.

When you add the name of a custom control to your .MAK file, Visual Basic registers it within the development environment and mounts it on the toolbar. To register the custom control properly, Visual Basic calls a function called VBINITCC, which you define in your VBX file. This calls VBRegisterModel, which provides Visual Basic with the memory location of the control's control model. The control model, in turn, provides the memory location of the control procedure. All of this is necessary in order for Visual Basic to recognize and work with the new control.

It is possible to set up a .VBX file so that it creates more than one custom control. For example, a SHAPES.VBX can actually load controls for drawing rectangles, triangles, and any other shapes you may care to include. However, under most circumstances, you will want to use a separate .VBX file for each control, unless the controls make use of many of the same operations. Otherwise, the file will become too large and unwieldy for you to debug and enhance.

VISUAL BASIC CUSTOM CONTROLS: AN EXAMPLE

The goal of a custom control is to provide the application developer with application-building tools that are not available with Visual Basic itself. These tools may enhance the existing application building blocks, or they may adapt Visual Basic for a specialized type of application development. My sample application, which builds on previous examples in this book, does the latter by making it possible to design and simulate computer networks.

The ultimate goal of the discrete event simulation application described in Chapter 8 was to devise a visual way of designing a prospective computer network as a graphical application, and simulating the behavior and performance of that network. A network is, after all, little more than the creation, queuing, and servicing of packets carrying data. These components can be used to reproduce the behaviors of computer network components, and that is the goal of the following custom control.

The continuation of the earlier project, then, involved the development of bundled components to represent different network components, such as a client workstation, a host computer, a hub, and a gateway. Each software component represents a discrete set of functions and operations based on a combination of the discrete event-simulation operations from Chapter 8, which emulate the behavior of the real-life computer network component.

Custom controls such as these can be offered with very little modification to Visual Basic developers interested in working with network simulations built from components from a set of custom controls. I'll describe the development of a custom control for a network host system, using Pascal routines for discrete event simulation as described in Chapter 8, and using C routines for connecting it into the Visual Basic development environment. This example demonstrates and describes code that will take you through the .VBX file compilation process.

The component I'll concentrate on for this example is a *network host* system. A network host receives data packets from multiple local workstations and routes them to the appropriate destinations, whether they are local or distant. It also receives packets from distant locations and parcels them out to local workstations, or reroutes them to other distant sites. Since the host is a finite resource, it can be considered a server in a discrete event-queuing system. The discrete event transactions described in Chapter 8 are analogous to network packets.

SETTING UP A CUSTOM CONTROL

A custom control requires a potentially large number of definitions, which are best made in a separate header file. These include function prototypes and other library references, if required, property and event definitions and structures, and the custom control model. In this example, HOST.H contains all of these definitions.

Here, for example, is where you define the properties that are associated with your control class, and the events to which they respond. You define properties in two ways—by giving them index numbers, and by placing them in the PPROPINFO data structure. The following defines the index numbers on the properties of my own Network Host control:

```
#define          IPROP_HOST_BACKCOLOR          0

#define          IPROP_HOST_CAPTION                      1

#define          IPROP_HOST_DRAGICON                     2

#define          IPROP_HOST_DRAGMODE           3

#define          IPROP_HOST_ENABLED                     4

#define          IPROP_HOST_FORECOLOR          5

#define          IPROP_HOST_HEIGHT                       6

#define          IPROP_HOST_HELPCONTEXTID               7

#define          IPROP_HOST_INDEX              8

#define          IPROP_HOST_LEFT                         9

#define          IPROP_HOST_MOUSEPOINTER                10

#define          IPROP_HOST_NAME              11

#define          IPROP_HOST_TOP                         12

#define          IPROP_HOST_VALUE                       13

#define          IPROP_HOST_VISIBLE                     14

#define          IPROP_HOST_WIDTH                       15

#define          IPROP_HOST_HWND              16
```

The following declaration takes these properties and places them in a property information table. The defined properties get placed in alphabetical order in the Property window in Visual Basic, but for identification purposes, Visual Basic refers to them, in order, by their index number.

```
PROPERTIES Host_Properties[ ]

{

        PROPINFO_STD_BACKCOLOR,
```

```
        PROPINFO_STD_CAPTION,

        PROPINFO_STD_HOST_DRAGICON,

        PROPINFO_STD_HOST_DRAGMODE,

        PROPINFO_STD_HOST_ENABLED,

        PROPINFO_STD_HOST_FORECOLOR,

        PROPINFO_STD_HOST_HEIGHT,

        PROPINFO_STD_HOST_HELPCONTEXTID,

        PROPINFO_STD_HOST_INDEX,

        PROPINFO_STD_HOST_LEFT,

        PROPINFO_STD_HOST_MOUSEPOINTER,

        PROPINFO_STD_HOST_NAME,

        PROPINFO_STD_HOST_TOP,

        PROPINFO_STD_HOST_VALUE,

        PROPINFO_STD_HOST_VISIBLE,

        PROPINFO_STD_HOST_WIDTH,

        PROPINFO_STD_HOST_HWND,

        NULL

    };
```

In addition to defining the available properties, you have to determine how Visual Basic gets the value of the property, sets the property, and loads and saves the current value of the property. Many of these properties are already defined in Visual Basic as default properties, so Visual Basic itself takes care of setting them. Of this group, the only one you have to write code for is the BACKCOLOR property. Visual Basic can accept messages for the Backcolor property, but needs direction on just what in the control composes the background.

DEFINING AND HANDLING EVENTS

The second concern is defining the events to which the control will respond. While the event-handling code is written in the source code file itself, you have to assign index numbers to each event, just as you did with the properties, and define each event in the event information table.

My host computer custom control responds to a total of six events. This is enough to give it some basic functionality as a computer network host, although it can be further enhanced in order to make it behave in a more realistic fashion. These events are defined in the following event information table, and are described in detail further on in the chapter.

```
PEVENTINFO Host_Events[ ]
{
      PEVENTINFO_STD_CHANGE,
      PEVENTINFO_STD_CLICK,
      PEVENTINFO_STD_DBLCLICK,
      PEVENTINFO_STD_GOTFOCUS,
      PEVENTINFO_STD_LOSTFOCUS,
      PEVENTINFO_STD_MOUSEDOWN
};
```

Also like the properties, you have to assign index values to the events (or rely on default values based on their ordering):

```
#define        IEVENT_HOST_CHANGE            0
#define        IEVENT_HOST_CLICK             1
#define        IEVENT_HOST_DBLCLICK     2
#define        IEVENT_HOST_GOTFOCUS     3
#define        IEVENT_HOST_LOSTFOCUS    4
#define        IEVENT_HOST_MOUSEDOWN         5
```

The last required step in the header file is to assemble the VBX control model. This is the data structure that defines all of the information needed by Visual Basic to register and process the control. It has a number of components. My own control model for the network host VBX looks like this:

```
MODEL modelNetNode =
{
        VB_VERSION,
        0,
        (PCTLPROC)NetNodeCtlProc,
        CS_DBLCLKS,
        WS_BORDER,
        sizeof(NetNode),
        IDBMP_NETNOD
        "Network_Host",
        NetHost",
        NULL,
        NetHost_Properties,
        NetHost_Events,
        IPROP_NETHOST_BACKCOLOR,
        IEVENT_NETHOST_CLICK,
        -1
    };
```

You also will want to choose an icon that represents the custom control when it's mounted on the toolbar: To do this, choose the icon name and provide Visual Basic with a bitmap resource ID number:

```
#define IDBMP_NETNODE                    0000
```

You will probably also want to include any function prototypes in the header file. The function prototype is required in ANSI-compliant implementations of C to define the type and parameters of all functions, and is commonly inserted into the header file. At the very least, you will be required to have a function prototype for your control procedure:

```
LONG FAR PASCAL _export NetNodeCtlProc(HCTL, HWND, USHORT, USHORT, LONG);
```

All of your event-handling functions in the custom control file will also require function prototypes. If, of course, you develop your custom control functions in another language, as I do, then you don't need the function prototypes.

There are a couple of optional things you can also include in the header file. The first is to fill in some fields that define what your VBX is and who owns any copyrights and trademarks on it. A sample of these fields and possible inputs is as follows:

```
#define VBX_COMPANYNAME          "Peter D. Varhol\0"
#define VBX_FILEDESCRIPTION      "Network Simulation\0"
#define VBX_INTERNALNAME         "NetNode\0"
#define VBX_LEGALCOPYRIGHT       "Copyright \251 Peter D. Varhol\0"
#define VBX_LEGALTRADEMARKS      "Trademark Peter D. Varhol\0"
#define VBX_ORIGINALFILENAME     "NetNode.VBX\0"
#define VBX_PRODUCTNAME          "Network Host Simulator\0"
```

The following definitions designate the version number of your VBX:

```
#define VBX_VERSION              4,00,0,00
#define VBX_VERSION_STR          "4.00.000\0"
```

Of course, the header file can include any other definitions and references that you need in implementing your custom control. These may include references to other header files, code files, or libraries; references to other DLLs; or references to Windows or Visual Basic functions that can be called from your custom control. Beyond that, you are ready to define your actual custom control.

THE CUSTOM CONTROL REQUIRED FUNCTIONS

The first step in setting up a custom control is to declare the VBINITCC function. This function serves as the entry point into the VBX, and is called

when the VBX is first loaded into memory, but before it is registered by
Visual Basic.

```
Bool Far Pascal _export VBINITCC
{
        ushort        usVersion,
        bool          fRuntime
}
{
        fRuntime = fRuntime;
        usVersion = usVersion;


return VBRegisterModel(hmodDLL, &modelNet);
}
```

The parameters **usVersion** and **fRuntime** are required by this function, and
their assignment to themselves is simply to prevent a linker warning that
the variables are declared but not used. The real key to this function is the
call to VBRegisterModel, the Visual Basic function that registers the new
custom control as a new control class.

Another important function is the LibMain function. LibMain, like the
normal main function, is the entry point for any calls into the .VBX file.
The memory handle hModule is passed via hmodDLL to VBRegisterModel,
so that Visual Basic knows where to find the DLL functions. Like
VBINITCC above, the other parameters are required by Visual Basic but
are not assigned in a relatively simple LibMain file, so as to prevent linker
warnings from occurring.

```
Int Far Pascal LibMain
{
        HANDLE        hModule,
        WORD wDataSeg,
        WORD cbHeapSize,
```

```
        LPSTR lpszCmdLine

}

{

        wDataSeg = wDataSeg;
        cbHeapSize = cbHeapSize;
        lpszCmdLine = lpszCmdLine;
        hmodDLL = hModule;


        return 1;

}
```

The custom control's control procedure is needed to receive messages and respond to them. The C structure is shown in the preceding function proto-type form. You can also write it in a Pascal language that supports Windows programming, such as Borland Pascal. The following is an abbre-viated example of a control procedure written in Pascal. It looks at the messages from Visual Basic and passes them to the appropriate message-handling procedures. The message handlers perform the actual operations necessary to emulate the behavior of a computer network host.

```
Function NetNodeCtlProc(var c: HCTL, var h: HWND; msg, wParam: integer;
lParam: longint):

PChar;

export;

begin


if msg = WM_VBM_GET_FOCUS then
        Process_Transactions;
        else
        if msg = WM_VBM_CLICK then
                DisplayData
          else

                . . .
```

```
                    .  .  .

        end

        NetNodeCtlProc = '  '

    end;
```

The last thing you have to be concerned about is the Windows Exit
Procedure, or WEP, function. The WEP is a callback function; it returns
control back to the Windows application after all of the executable applications are finished using the VBX operations. The WEP is a very simple
function, and some compilers will automatically assign a default WEP if
you leave it out. If you are required to include a WEP, the most basic one
looks something like this:

```
int Far Pascal WEP

{

        int fSystemExit

}

{

        fSystemExit = fSystemExit;

        return 1;

}
```

Once again, the assignment of the required parameter to itself is to prevent
a compiler warning.

USING THE TIMER CONTROL
WITH THE CUSTOM CONTROL

Now you are ready to define the functions that perform the actual operations of your custom control. I'm doing this in the Pascal language to take
advantage of the code developed for the DLL in Chapter 8, and will call
these routines from Visual Basic through the C .VBX file.

I will not repeat the code already illustrated in Chapter 8. However, I will describe and code the high-level event handler for one of the events defined previously. One of the most difficult design decisions in a custom control is how the control will respond to events.

The event described here is the GotFocus event. Since much of the operation of a network host simulation control occurs without user intervention, other controls have to pass the focus to this custom control. In this case, as in other custom controls in this series, the Timer control in Visual Basic serves this function.

When the Timer advances the clock, it calls the SetFocus method for each of the custom controls in turn. The network simulation custom controls perform most of their activities as the result of getting the focus. When the simulation custom control, such as the NetNode control, is performing its activities, it disables the Timer. When NetNode is done, it reenables the Timer control, which passes SetFocus on to the next control.

The time period that passes between Timer events is controlled by its Interval property, but the time interval does not matter, since all the Timer event does is enable the advancement of the simulation. The Timer Interval property can be changed to look at the effect of different computer host speed conditions on overall network performance.

```
Sub Timer1_Timer ()
        NetNode1.SetFocus
        NetNode2.SetFocus
        NetNode3.SetFocus

        .  .  .

        .  .  .

End Sub
```

MAKING THE CUSTOM CONTROL WORK

All that is needed now is the message-handling procedures that are called from the NetNode custom control's control procedure, illustrated previously. For the NetNode custom control, this code consists largely of the procedures shown in Chapter 8, since the operation of a network host is largely a matter of creating, receiving, and transferring packets of information, both out over the local network, and across other network branches.

Together, the network host CPU, memory, and disk resources are limited resources that take time to perform these functions. If packets pass through very quickly, then they will have to be queued in first-come, first-served order until they can be processed.

The code to perform these operations has already been illustrated earlier in the book. It merely has to be organized so that it performs the necessary queuing operations in the proper order. It also requires supporting code to tie it together so that the messages passed into the procedure are interpreted and handled properly.

FINISHING UP

While the C language routines that connect to the Visual Basic development environment can be modeled after the examples in the Visual Basic Professional reference material, the concepts and implementations of the custom control, its properties, events, and behaviors are entirely up to you. The preceding description provides a template that can get you started in your own control.

The custom control previously described implements the behavior of a single network host computer for use in a computer network simulation. I've also implemented custom controls for a single client computer, and for an internetworking hub. The icons used for all of these custom controls were included as samples in the Visual Basic Professional package. Alternatively,

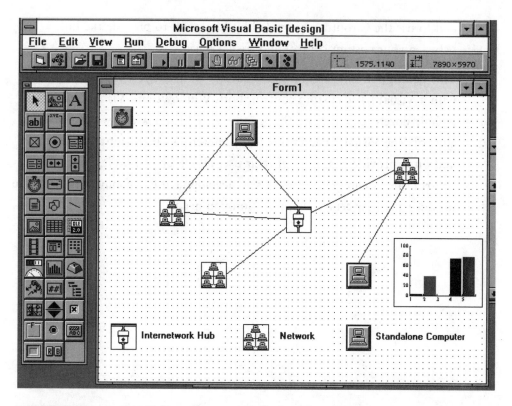

Figure 10.1 Using custom controls in an application.

you can develop your own icons, using any Windows bitmap editor. A sample implementation of a simulation application making use of these custom controls is shown in Figure 10.1.

OTHER CUSTOM CONTROLS

Using the same techniques described here to create and load the network host custom control, you can also create separate controls for other computer network components. You may find it less complicated to develop your entire custom control in C; however, if you already have programs written in other languages, or if you have a greater amount of experience in another language, it is easy and convenient to work with that language and to use the C routines provided by Microsoft to provide the link between your custom control and Visual Basic.

This description only scratches the surface on what you can accomplish with a Visual Basic custom control. Both Windows and Visual Basic itself include dozens of functions that can be called from within your custom control. The Visual Basic Professional references document these functions and often provide examples of their use. However you do it, the custom control can extend your Visual Basic development environment to help you produce any user-centered application you need.

11

UTILIZING VISUAL BASIC 4.0 AND ITS 32-BIT FACILITIES

With the coming of Visual Basic 4.0, there are a number of additional capabilities that will interest even the most experienced application developer. Among the most compelling are OLE 2.0 and OLE custom controls, better database access facilities, and better ways of navigating the Visual Basic development environment. Another advantage to Visual Basic 4.0 is the ability to develop 32-bit applications in addition to the 16-bit applications that earlier versions of Visual Basic have been able to deliver.

There are several reasons why it is important to be able to develop both 16-bit and 32-bit applications under Visual Basic: First, with the launch of Windows 95, and growing support for Windows NT, it is clear that the average user will be moving toward a 32-bit computing environment. While all of the 16-bit Visual Basic applications will run in the 32-bit world, they have a performance disadvantage.

Another reason for developing 32-bit applications is that these applications can access much more memory than their 16-bit counterparts. 16-bit applications are limited to approximately 2^{16} bytes of memory, or about 32Mb. 32-bit applications, on the other hand, can access 2^{32} bytes, or approximately 4Gb of memory (in practice, system needs usually limit these values to half of the theoretical limit).

Third, new applications using new 32-bit features will be able to take advantage of the new capabilities of these operating systems. These include, most importantly from the standpoint of this book, new user interface facilities, but they also include networking, multimedia, and better database access.

However, the 16-bit Windows is not going to go away overnight. Over 50 million copies are currently running, many on slower systems that will be hard-pressed to make the transition to the 32-bit world. Windows 3.1 will likely be the dominant desktop operating system moving into the next century, and 16-bit applications will continue to be needed for the next several years.

As a result, developing applications that take full advantage of both Windows 95 and Windows 3.1 will be an important part of Visual Basic development for the next several years. This will involve a great deal of common components and Basic source code, but it will also mean some differences—mostly small ones scattered about your application, but occasionally bigger ones.

Your task is to manage the two separate code bases, while keeping the portions of the application that don't change the constant between the two. While this may seem like a simple task, it is very complex and fraught with potential for error. It is not uncommon to make changes to common components that should apply to only one version, and to make changes to only one version that should apply to the common base.

And then there are the demands of user-centered application design. You may make an interface design decision that requires the use of a 32-bit Windows API not available in the 16-bit version, or you may call your own 16-bit custom control that you have to consider porting to the 32-bit world to get its benefits for your 32-bit application.

VISUAL BASIC 4.0 AND 32-BIT OPERATIONS

Visual Basic 4.0 comes in both 16-bit and 32-bit versions. The 16-bit version will run on any Windows-based operating system, but the 32-bit version will run only on Windows NT and Windows 95. However, as previously mentioned, there are compelling reasons to produce 32-bit applications. Therefore, it may make sense to do both—if only it can be done without a great deal of additional effort. The following sections describe the considerations involved in developing for both 16-bit and 32-bit Windows concurrently.

Functionally, both the 16-bit and the 32-bit versions are the same. You can produce identical applications with identical behaviors. However, the 32-bit version gives you some added advantages. These include:

- The ability to store and manage large amounts of data

- Greater flexibility in the amount of data that can be associated with objects

- The ability to more easily internationalize your applications

- The ability to take advantage of new user interface facilities in newer Microsoft operating systems

There are many issues surrounding Visual Basic 4.0's 16-bit and 32-bit versions, and the moving from Visual Basic 3.0 to both versions of 4.0, from the standpoint of user-centered development. Visual Basic 4.0 does not have new controls, but there are new visual features in Windows 95 that may change the overall look of your applications. You can also use the enhanced controls to provide your users with greater flexibility in using your applications.

CHARACTERIZATION AND LIMITATIONS OF VISUAL BASIC 4.0

The Visual Basic 4.0 development environment is very similar to its immediate predecessor. Microsoft has added some menu items that make accessing code edit windows and forms easier. Perhaps the largest change to the environment is that you now have the ability to load custom controls dynamically; that is, while you are in the environment. In the past, the custom control had to be in the .MAK file for your project. If you wanted to add a custom control to a particular project, you had to exit the environment and edit the .MAK file.

In general, any application written for Visual Basic 3.0 will run in Visual Basic 4.0 The limitations have, for the most part, been relaxed rather than constrained. This is what you would expect, since 32-bit addressing and memory offers more space and more flexibility than its 16-bit counterparts. However, there are still certain aspects of a Visual Basic project and an application that the 32-bit world still limits. For the most part, these limitations deal with the amount of data a project or a control can deal with.

A project can contain up to 32,000 identifiers. An *identifier* is every type of control, label, variable, and anything else that is named in the project. Since an average Visual Basic project will generally have no more than about 1,000 of these identifiers, this is not a big problem except for very large projects.

The number of forms is limited by the amount of resources on the system. Resources include memory and process handles, and room in the Windows system data structures. Therefore, the maximum number of forms allowable will vary from system to system, and will also vary depending on what you have running on individual systems. In general, a system running no other applications may be able to manage up to 100 forms in a project.

However, there are several considerations that should limit your applications to well under 100 forms. First is a capacity issue—you can't be sure of the amount of resources on the systems your application may ultimately run on, or how many other applications your users may be running at the same time. While it is perfectly reasonable to have minimum memory and resource requirements for your application, you can't usually expect to have access to all or most of what an average system has to offer.

Second, and more important from the standpoint of this book, multiple forms in a user interface makes the interface crowded and difficult to use. Under most circumstances, displaying any more than two or three forms at one time to the user will make your user interface harder to understand. Your use of forms should be governed by how much information makes sense to present to the user at one time, as well as by the resource capacity of the computer.

A Basic procedure is limited to 64K in size. Further, the amount of source code that you can associate with any control, module, or form can be no longer than 64K (65,534) lines The number of procedures and variables you can use in a module is unlimited.

There are also limitations associated with controls and individual properties in controls. Most of the properties affected are those that incorporate text data in some way. These include the list and combo boxes, text properties, caption properties, and tag properties. In 16-bit Visual Basic applications, the data that can go in these properties is, for the most part, limited to the same 64K segments used in managing 16-bit memory. There are also some other restrictions on the size of individual items in these properties (see Table 11.1 for details).

Table 11.1 Differences in Limitations between 16-Bit and 32-Bit Visual Basic 4.0

Feature	16-bit	32-bit
Procedures	64K of code	64K of code
	65,534 lines	65,534 lines
Strings	64K characters	2^{**31} characters
Arrays	Range of –32,768 to 32,768	range of -2^{**31} to 2^{**31}
Stack space	20K fixed	20K removable
List property	64K / 5,440 items	32,768 items
(list box or combo box)	1K per item	No size limitation per item
ListCount property	64K / 5,440 items	32,768 items
(list box or combo box)	1K per item	No size limitation per item
Text property	32K	2^{**32} characters
(text box)		
Caption property	1K	1K
(label control)		
Tag property	32K	2^{**32} characters

With the 32-bit version of Visual Basic, the limitations on property data are generally either higher or nonexistent altogether. Once again, Table 11.1 has details.

One last limitation is with the stack. The stack is a memory area that is used to temporarily hold data that will be needed later on in the execution of your application. It is limited to 20K, although on the 32-bit version you can remove this limit. The purpose of the limit is to prevent an out-of-control application from taking all available memory, so you should remove it in the 32-bit version with care. Consider doing this only if your application is working with large amounts of data or many different windows.

DATA TYPE CONSIDERATIONS

There should be no need to change any of the data types for your variables between 16-bit and 32-bit source code. Integers, characters, floating-point numbers, and other standard data types are used in both versions. Most of the underlying details are hidden from you, so variable conversion between the two versions is almost automatic.

However, there can be differences in how much memory they take up, and the legal range of values they can hold. Both string and array data types have differences based on whether they are used in the 16-bit environment or 32-bit environment. In addition, variables declared as user-defined data types—that is, those that you create, rather than those defined by the system—also have limitations. These limitations are summarized in Table 11.1. The important thing to remember is that in order to enable your application to have common code between both 16-bit and 32-bit operating systems, you have to observe the size and data limitations of the 16-bit Visual Basic world.

MAINTAINING A COMMON CODE BASE

One of the challenges in this transitional era between 16-bit and 32-bit Windows is writing applications that can take advantage of the facilities offered by Windows NT and Windows 95, while also running on the large installed base of Windows 3.1. Your existing 16-bit applications will run on both, but you may be losing some of the capabilities that can make your application more appealing or more useful to users. Taking advantage of both 16-bit and 32-bit capabilities means that you may have to change certain aspects of your source code in order to run on the different versions of Windows. If that's the case, then your goal should be to keep all of the source that doesn't matter the same between the two versions, while carefully separating the source code that is system-specific.

All Visual Basic language and components are completely portable between 16-bit Windows (Windows 3.1) and 32-bit Windows (Windows 95 and Windows NT). The object model between the two versions is the same, and the controls are the same between the two. If you use variables of the normal data types in one, they will translate seamlessly to the other; this goes for Integers, Long, Single, Double, Currency, and String (although the constraints between 16-bit and 32-bit implementations may be different; see the previous section). This makes the prospect of maintaining separate 16-bit and 32-bit versions of your application easier, but the process is still not automatic.

WORKING WITH CHARACTERS

Many of your considerations for developing a common code base will revolve around the use of characters and character data types. This represents the most significant change between the 16-bit and 32-bit world in Visual Basic. Some of these considerations are due to different ways Microsoft operating systems use characters, but there are also differences within the two versions of Visual Basic.

THE UNICODE CHARACTER SET

The Unicode character set is a new way of encoding characters that first appeared in Windows NT, and then in Windows 95. It replaces the ubiquitous ASCII character set used almost universally in computing over the last 30 years. The rationale behind Unicode is that ASCII, which used a single byte to encode characters, was insufficient to meet the demands of software that was translated to other written languages. With $2^8 - 1$, or 255 characters, available in a single byte, there are not enough different representations available for languages that are made up of hundreds or thousands of symbols, such as the Japanese Kanji or Chinese Mandarin.

The Unicode character set, in contrast, uses two bytes to store each character. While this ends up using more memory and storage than the one-byte representations, it makes it possible to represent up to $2^{16} - 1$, or 65,535 characters—more than enough for any language on the planet.

There is a way of representing different and longer languages through a variation of ASCII, called the Double Byte Character Set, or DBCS. Up until this time, Microsoft and other application vendors that developed for non-English languages used the DBCS variation for software development for international markets. DBCS uses the first 128 ASCII characters in the first 7 bits, but then uses the eighth bit as a lead bit into a second byte of character representations. While it works well enough, it is awkward to use, since without testing the lead bit there is no way of telling whether the character uses one byte or two.

As software becomes more international in nature, representing your application in the native language for users is an important software feature. While most computer users worldwide up until now were capable of reading at least some English, as computers are used by more and more people, an increasing number are unlikely to speak and read American English. As a result, there is a greater opportunity to tailor applications to international users.

In Visual Basic 4.0, the 16-bit version uses the ASCII character set, while the 32-bit version uses Unicode. Since this is an underlying feature rather than a visible feature, under many circumstances you need not worry about this distinction for your applications. The primary problem is when you use 16-bit external objects with the 32-bit version of Visual Basic, or 32-bit objects with the 16-bit version of Visual Basic, discussed in the following section. It can also be an issue when using Microsoft's only Unicode-based operating system, Windows NT.

UNICODE AND FILE INPUT/OUTPUT

Since the 32-bit version of Visual Basic uses the Unicode character set, it automatically converts ASCII values in files to Unicode values in the application, and then back to ASCII when the values are written back to the file. This means that your files must contain ASCII values rather than Unicode.

While this may seem like a convoluted process, it serves to help make your applications more portable between the two versions. Since they require the same type of file inputs, and produce the same kind of file outputs, you don't have to prepare two different sets of files for your application to use, depending on whether it is 16-bit or 32-bit.

You can also use a Unicode file with a 16-bit Visual Basic application in order to facilitate it running on a 32-bit Unicode operating system, such as Windows NT. You simply have to apply a string conversion function, called StrConv, to the incoming data.

OLE AND 32-BIT VISUAL BASIC

Within Visual Basic 4.0, OLE has become the preferred way of accessing external data and structures. The Visual Basic custom control (VBX) is being supplanted by the OLE custom control (OCX). Both VBX and OCX controls are available for 32-bit Visual Basic, but only VBX controls can be used with the 16-bit version.

All of the VBX controls included with Visual Basic 3.0 Professional are available as OCX controls with Visual Basic 4.0. However, this may not be the case with third-party developers of VBX controls, especially until Visual Basic 4.0 has had a chance to establish itself in the market. If you use third-party VBX controls, you may have difficulty in finding OCX equivalents, which will make it more difficult to upgrade your applications.

These issues have substantial implications for those trying to develop for both 16-bit and 32-bit operating systems and maintaining a common code base. If you use custom controls of any type, and plan on developing 16-bit and 32-bit versions of your applications, then you have to work with OCX controls, or ensure that your VBX and OCX controls are all functionally equivalent. If you need custom controls, and can't ensure that the controls are the same, then maintaining a common code base will be difficult.

To upgrade any VBX custom controls to their OLE equivalents, choose the Tools menu and Environment Options selection. You'll see a dialog box like that shown in Figure 11.1. This dialog box includes a check box that asks if you want to upgrade your custom controls. If you select it, it will display any VBX custom controls in any subsequently loaded project that can be upgraded to their OLE equivalents. You can select all displayed controls or only those you want to upgrade, and your project will be upgraded with the new controls. Of course, if you have no custom controls, or there are no OLE control equivalents, then nothing will happen.

OLE also lets you make use of objects from other applications that follow the OLE standard. This includes MS Access and Excel, both of which have their own object libraries. In time, it will probably include other vendors' applications. You may be able to take advantage of them either as custom controls, if they are designed in that manner, or as objects called from your Basic source code. This gives you the added flexibility to customize your user interface (as well as other aspects of your application) to make it appear and behave like other familiar applications on the market.

To obtain access to application objects that are not custom controls, you open the Tools menu and choose the References item. You will be shown a list of application objects that you can make available to your application (see Figure 11.2). Click on any that you plan on using. If there are objects

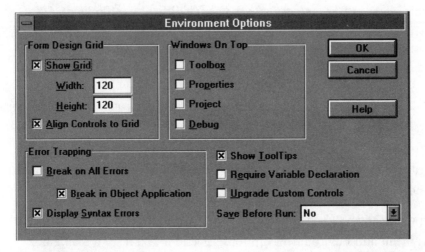

■■■■■■■■■■**Figure 11.1** The dialog box that lets you convert VBX custom controls in your project to OLE custom controls.

checked that you don't plan on using, deselect them; otherwise, Visual Basic will look for them to attempt to resolve external references, which can greatly lengthen the time it takes to compile an application.

SYSTEM APIs AND 32-BIT APPLICATIONS

When dealing with Windows API calls, you have to be careful with ASCII versus Unicode issues when passing data back and forth. You can use the 32-bit calls when they are available in either 16-bit or 32-bit applications, but you may have to perform a character conversion operation before making use of the data. Windows NT provides both ACSII and Unicode versions of its 32-bit APIs for use by calling applications. To develop common 16-bit and 32-bit applications, you should always use the ASCII library. Use Unicode only if you want 32-bit-only applications for an international market. To use ANSI versions of these APIs, you have to specify an alias to the appropriate ASCII library. That library is the same as the

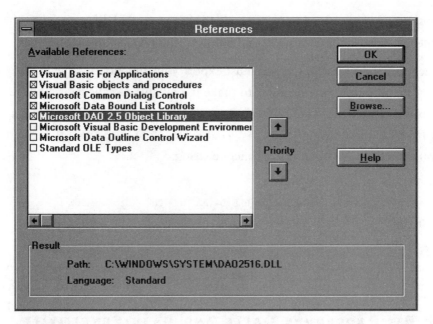

Figure 11.2 The dialog box that lets you use OLE objects from other applications.

API name with an *A* added onto its end. For example, to call the GetClassName API function, you call it just as you normally would, but with the alias keyword at the end followed by "GetClassNameA" immediately afterward:

```
Declare Function GetClassName Lib "User" (ByVal hWnd As Integer, ByVal
lpClassName As String, ByVal nMaxCount As Integer) As Integer Alias
"GetClassNameA"
```

32-Bit DLLs

Calling a function in a DLL is very similar to calling a function from the Windows API. You declare the function as an external in the global declarations section, and then you can use it just as you would any other function. However, your DLLs, even if they are 32-bit DLLs, will always use ASCII character strings. Since the 32-bit Visual Basic 4.0 will make the appropriate conversions to its Unicode format, a single DLL can return the appropriate string types for either 16-bit or 32-bit Visual Basic.

When writing 32-bit DLLs, you must export your function via the DEF file. The purpose of exporting is to make it available to calls from outside of its executable file. The following example demonstrates how to write a 32-bit DLL and return a string to Visual Basic. Note once again that the string is an ASCII string, not a Unicode string.

```
; The DEF File LIBRARY TestDLL
CODE   PRELOAD MOVEABLE DISCARDABLE DATA      PRELOAD MOVEABLE
EXPORTS
ReturnString
BSTR WINAPI ReturnString()
{    this API function returns SysAllocString("Testing string transfers"); }
```

32-BIT PROCEDURE CALLS AND CASE-SENSITIVITY

On Windows NT and Windows 95, the function names are case-sensitive; for example, createBlock is different from CREATEBLOCK. This means that there is the potential for typing errors in calling external functions. It is very possible for developers who are used to working with DOS and Windows 3.1 to be inconsistent in the use of case, since it didn't matter in these environments.

Fortunately, Visual Basic 4.0 can help somewhat with this potential problem. Visual Basic will convert a function or procedure name to the same case as the last occurrence of that name associated with a definition statement, such as Declare, Dim, Sub, or Function. For example, if you declare the following:

```
Declare Function GetClassName Lib "User" (ByVal hWnd As Integer, ByVal
lpClassName As String, ByVal nMaxCount As Integer) As Integer
```

and then redeclare it further along as:

```
Declare Function getclassname Lib "User" (ByVal hWnd As Integer, ByVal
lpClassName As String, ByVal nMaxCount As Integer) As Integer
```

then the function will be redeclared as getclassname, with all small letters. Since this may not be what you had in mind for either call, this may make more difficulties for you than if Visual Basic did nothing at all.

From the standpoint of creating a common code base, this means that you should always be careful about the case of your function declarations, even in 16-bit versions. This is because you may eventually want to use your 16-bit calls on a 32-bit operating system. Mixing the cases between function calls, or using a convention of all small or all capital letters, may result in unresolved references or inadvertent function calls. As a result, you should use the names as they are displayed in the API library.

COMMON CODE APPLICATIONS

Everything that you develop within the Visual Basic environment is portable between 16-bit and 32-bit versions. Even accounting for the differences previously mentioned, Visual Basic itself performs the necessary conversions between the two versions. However, to create a single source code base that will build both 16-bit and 32-bit versions of your applications, you have to consider the user's operating system, the custom controls you use, the legal values your controls can accept, and the APIs and DLLs you call.

First, to create 32-bit versions of your applications, you must be running Visual Basic on Windows 95 or Windows NT. Using Windows 3.1 will give you access to only the 16-bit versions of your applications. Even with the 32-bit extensions to Windows 3.1, 32-bit Visual Basic will not load.

Second, you must have both versions of Visual Basic 4.0. This may be a given, but it is important to realize that the 32-bit version cannot be used to produce 16-bit applications. You may want to run both versions on the same Windows 95 or Windows NT system, or you may want to run them on separate machines, depending upon your available system resources. Running on the same machine is preferable, since this will allow you to more easily use the same source files for both 16-bit and 32-bit versions.

Beyond these basic points, to maintain an application that can run natively in both 16-bit and 32-bit Visual Basic, you have to remember the following points:

- Make sure your application and its controls abide by the data limitations of 16-bit Visual Basic.

- Whenever possible, limit the users' access to data, especially in external files, to 32K.

- Work in the ASCII character set whenever possible in external function calls. Even with 32-bit applications, Visual Basic will make the appropriate function calls.

If you manage to keep these rules, your application will compile unmodified on 16-bit and 32-bit Visual Basic 4.0. To the extent that you have to break one or more of these rules, your code will be less portable between the two versions. You will have to identify these differences and maintain two separate versions of those parts of the application.

THE RETURN FOR YOUR INVESTMENT

It is exciting to begin to use Visual Basic 4.0 to develop full 32-bit applications for Microsoft's newer operating systems. You have more APIs with which to work, better user interface facilities, and faster running applications as a result. This new version of Visual Basic gives you more tools to add a wider variety of custom controls, and to communicate via object linking and embedding to data residing on other applications.

However, it also makes sense to continue to be able to run applications under 16-bit Windows. This is the operating system with the largest

installed base, and it also has fewer hardware needs than the 32-bit implementations. You have to plan your application carefully to take advantage
of both types of operating systems, but you will find that your application
will be able to take advantage of user-centered design principles to enable
more end users to accomplish more activities.

12

WHERE TO GO

FROM HERE

Up until now, the book has discussed ways to design effective Visual Basic applications using conventional software techniques—better command buttons, better explanations, more readable fonts, and so on. While there is much that can be done with these tools, such techniques largely fail to take advantage of emerging technologies. New ways of communicating with the end user are being developed quickly, and are finding their ways into applications of all types.

This chapter takes a brief look at several emerging technologies that will have a substantial impact on user-centered application development over the next several years. At present, all of these techniques are supported in some form by the latest release of Visual Basic, in at least the Professional version. You can start making use of them today, and get a jump on the rest of the century.

This chapter is not all-inclusive; there are many more new techniques available, even within the Visual Basic development environment. It is meant to be a sampling of new approaches that are starting to be incorporated both in development environments like Visual Basic, and in commercial and custom applications.

USING SOUND IN AN APPLICATION

The use of sound in software has made great strides since the days of beeps and chirps emanating from a tiny built-in speaker in the computer. While some thought these types of sounds to be cute, most users found them to be shrill and annoying. Today, however, it is possible to get 16-bit or even 32-bit sound, in stereo, that offers minimal distortion across the entire range of audio frequencies typically perceived by people. As a result, true sound is coming into more and more applications today.

Unfortunately, today's PCs require digital sound expansion cards in order to reproduce sounds saved as .WAV files. Not all PCs have these cards, although they are beginning to be installed as standard equipment in many models. The good news is that they, like most other types of computer equipment, are coming down in price and may be purchased for less than $100 today.

This means that it is not always possible to count on the end user's PC having the requisite hardware capabilities to make use of sounds in applications. That is unfortunate, because sounds can be used not only to supplement the communications within an application, but they can also be used to send and receive essential information.

In time, sound may come to represent the primary input and output mechanisms for computers. It is already very possible for a computer to communicate with the user by use of an electronic voice. While voice recognition of the human voice is a difficult technical problem, it is currently in use in specialized surroundings, and may eventually become the primary way we get information and instructions into the computer.

To use sound in an application, Visual Basic Professional provides a custom control entitled MCI.VBX (MCI is the abbreviation for Media Control Interface devices). When displayed as an instance on a form, this control looks like a typical media player, with buttons for Previous, Next, Play, Pause, Back, Step, Stop, Record, and Eject, as shown in Figure 12.1.

The control can be used to play .WAV files for sound, or to play graphic files in an animation sequence, or to play other multimedia sequences. For applications that involve using the operations provided with the MCI control on a simple .WAV file, you can use the default behaviors of the MCI control buttons without modification. For example, to load and run a .WAV file, first you initialize some of the control's properties. The best time to do this is when the form containing the control is loaded:

```
Sub Form_Load ()
        SoundControl.Notify = False
        SoundControl.Wait = True
        SoundControl.Shareable = False
        SoundControl.DeviceType = "WaveAudio"
        SoundControl.FileName = "C:\VB\SOUND\WAVTEST.WAV"
        SoundControl.Command = "Open"
End Sub
```

where SoundControl is the name I've given to the MCI control instance, and the fields represent properties of that control. Incidentally, all of the components of the MCI control, such as Play and Pause, have a Visible

■■■■■**Figure 12.1** The Visual Basic MCI custom control.

property so that you can display only those components that you need for your application.

Most of these properties deal with setting up the conditions necessary to play the .WAV file identified in the FileName property. Notify tells the control whether the next command to be issued generates a Done event. Wait tells the control whether to wait for the next command, or to return control to the application after completing the current command. Shareable designates whether more than one application can share an MCI device. Last, DeviceType signifies the device driver the control should load to perform the desired action—in this case, sound.

When closing the application, you should also close the sound device driver. You can do this with the Form Unload event:

```
Sub Form_Unload ()
      SoundControl.Command = "Close"
End Sub
```

This is all you need to play a simple sound file. You may, however, want to use sound in different ways. For example, you may want an application that *talks* to the user in an electronic voice under some circumstances. You may want sounds to reinforce user actions, or to signal the user that an application operation has been completed. As long as you are aware of the potential limitations of users' hardware, and of the ability of sound to act as a communications medium to the user, then the use of sound can open up many new possibilities for creating user-centered applications.

ANIMATING WITH VISUAL BASIC

Animation is the act of making a drawing or image appear as if it is moving on the screen. Once the purview of Saturday morning cartoons, animation is now moving into the mainstream for many types of applications. One reason for this is that more powerful computers have made it possible to present realistic animation at reasonable speeds. Another reason is that, given adequate computing power, animation is relatively easy to do. It is simply a matter of displaying multiple sequential images close enough together so that the visual effect is one of continuous motion.

Animation is clearly not useful for all types of applications. There is little need to provide animation for applications that are largely textual, such as word processors and spreadsheets. Where, then, is animation useful?

The most obvious answer is in computer games. Animated figures abound in graphical computer games, especially adventure games, and have been getting more and more realistic as computers have been getting faster. Games are often in the forefront of the adoption of new technologies, typically because many people find them compelling means of entertainment, and because their attraction makes them highly profitable.

However, animation also has a role in more general-purpose applications. For example, the emerging standard for business presentations includes animation. Many of the commercial presentation software packages, such as Microsoft's PowerPoint, include the ability to animate the transitions between slides in a slide show. These packages also let you display your presentations as movies so that there need not be any artificial breaks in the presentation of information. Increasingly more powerful computers have enabled business and entertainment applications of animation to become useful ways of communicating with users.

The MCI custom control also works with animation files. To play a simple animation file, the MCI control works in exactly the same way that it did with sound. You initialize some of the control's properties when you load the form, and once you load the desired movie file (designated with the file extension .MMM), then you are ready to play the animated movie:

```
Sub Form_Load ()
    AnimateControl.Notify = False
    AnimateControl.Wait = True
```

```
        AnimateControl.Shareable = False

        AnimateControl.DeviceType = "MMMovie"

        AnimateControl.FileName = "C:\VB\SOUND\ANITEST.MMM"

        AnimateControl.Command = "Open"

    End Sub
```

Likewise, you should also close the animation device driver when the user closes the application, or leaves that part of the application:

```
Sub Form_Unload ()

        AnimateControl.Command = "Close"

End Sub
```

MULTIMEDIA AND VISUAL BASIC

One of the truly hot emerging technologies in computers is multimedia. Multimedia involves the combination of text, graphics and images, sound, animation, and even full-motion video in a single application. Therefore, it combines some of the techniques previously described separately, and adds still more.

Multimedia is a hot technology today, with the use of CD players, sound cards, and even digital video players and editors growing far more rapidly than the computer industry as a whole. Entertainment, education, reference, and even productivity software is finding its way onto new types of media for a new approach to application use. The opportunities for creating new forms of user interaction are practically unlimited.

Before embarking on the path to multimedia application development, be warned that combining these types of media within an application usually involves the use of specialized hardware, and requires a great deal of disk space for storing multimedia files. In the most extreme example, full-motion video running in a large window on-screen can require hundreds of megabytes of disk space for only a few seconds of running time.

Another caution is that designing an application that makes effective use of multimedia is much more difficult than doing so with conventional techniques. Since there are so many possibilities for interacting with the user, it is far easier to choose a combination that is an inappropriate or confusing way of presenting information or encouraging user interaction. You should include extensive user participation and testing in any multimedia application you develop.

Visual Basic uses the same custom control, MCI.VBX, that was used in developing the preceding sound and animation applications. In addition to working with sound and animation, it also works with CD-ROM players and MIDI sequencer devices.

DATA ACCESS

One of the most talked-about buzzwords for the 1990s is the phrase *client/server computing*. In general, it refers to dividing up the computing workload between a desktop computer and a (usually) larger and more powerful remote server. The desktop system does what it is best at, usually by providing the user interface, while the remote server does what it is best at, usually crunching numbers or looking for data.

Visual Basic supports the client/server computing model by providing a graphical front end on desktop systems for running programs on older, text-oriented minicomputers and mainframes. The sample application for electronic student course registration built in Chapter 6, although designed to be a stand-alone program, can be enhanced to interact more closely with the existing student management software on the minicomputer.

There are a number of ways to perform database-type operations in Visual Basic. In addition to working with plain ASCII files, it includes facilities for working with SQL-type databases, and with Microsoft's own ODBC (Open Database Connectivity) data transfer standards. Although not specifically designed for database transfers, you can also use the Object Linking and Embedding (OLE) custom control for this same purpose.

ASCII DATA OPERATIONS

Reading from and writing to ASCII files is the most straightforward way of working with an external database, and is very flexible, since it makes the fewest assumptions about the format of the data. However, this format prevents you from taking advantage of many of the powerful features found in most commercial database managers.

There are several possible Visual Basic commands that you can use to write data from your application out to an ASCII file. These include Write, Print, and Put. In practice, there is very little difference between these commands, so you can make use of them, according to the desired structure of the resulting file. For example, Write automatically puts double quotation marks around text strings, while Print does not. These minor differences may prompt you to use one over the other if the application reading the file requires quotation marks around strings.

To write data from the student registration application to an ASCII file, I've associated a series of Write commands with the Click event-handling subroutine of the Done button (see Figure 12.2 for a reminder of the appearance of one of the application forms). This code opens an ASCII file, called DATAFILE, and writes all of the data from all of the input fields on the three forms into that file when the user clicks on the Done button. Following are a few lines of the code that does this, so you can see how it works:

```
Sub DoneCommand_Click ()
        Open "DATAFILE" For Output As 1
        Write #1, Head.StudentName.Text
        Write #1, Head.StudentAddress.Text
```

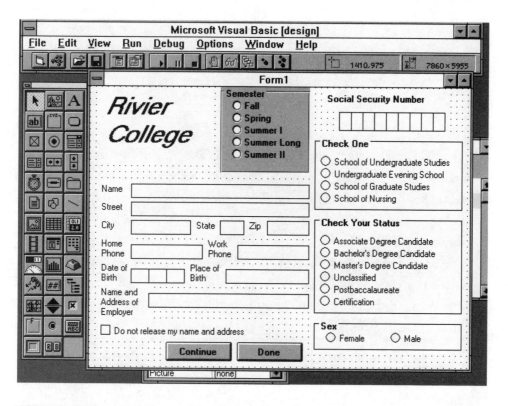

▬▬▬▬**Figure 12.2** The rapid prototype from Chapter 6.

```
Write #1, Head.StudentCity.Text

Write #1, Head.StudentState.Text

Write #1, Head.StudentZIP.Text

. . .

. . .

Write #1, Head.FallOption.Value

Write #1, Head.SpringOption.Value

Write #1, Head.SummerIOption.Value

Write #1, Head.SummerIIOption.Value

Write #1, Head.SummerLongOption.Value

Write #1, Head.SUSOption.Value

Write #1, Head.UESOption.Value
```

```
            .  .  .

            .  .  .

        Close #1


    End
    End Sub
```

The Visual Basic command Open opens the DATAFILE file for writing, and the Write commands perform the actual writing operation to the file. Note that there are many option boxes and check boxes on the form. The Value property on these controls is a Boolean type, and actually generates a value based on whether the control is selected or deselected. In this case, a selected option box and check box generates a value of –1, and a deselected box generates a value of 0. These are the values that are written to the file. Last, the End command prior to the ending of the subroutine finally exits the application.

The database application reading this ASCII file has to be ready to accept values from all of the fields in the order they are written to the file, including the option and check boxes that may never be selected. Alternatively, rather than writing the Boolean value for every option and check box, you might just want to write a single value that signifies which box in each form is enabled. You can check this by running a subroutine that examines the Value property of all of the boxes in a frame, and writing a code to the file corresponding to the enabled box.

If you want the additional features conveniently available from working with a database utilizing relational tables, you can use the database custom control object included with Visual Basic Professional. This gives you the ability to work with databases created with Microsoft Access, which is the native format for this Visual Basic custom control, or with other PC-based databases, such as FoxPro, Paradox, and dBASE. This custom control will also provide an ODBC-compliant connection to any database that follows that convention.

Another alternative for database access is the Visual Basic SQL Libraries for Microsoft's SQL Server. These libraries provide a direct programming connection between Visual Basic and SQL Server. You can use these C-based application programming interfaces to generate queries from Visual Basic and run the queries on SQL Server.

Your decision will depend to a great extent on the needs of your back-end database, and any performance considerations you have. However, there are many ways to integrate database activities with Visual Basic, so finding one that meets your data requirements should not be difficult.

VISUAL BASIC AND DESIGNING FOR THE USER

Visual Basic can be used in creative ways to adapt to different needs of the user. A single user interface design can be constructed to change itself based on the type of user, or the type of data, with which it is working. This sounds rather exotic, since applications are deterministic; that is, they do what they were programmed to do, rather than what we would like them to. However, thanks to its event-driven architecture and the ability to change properties on the controls while the application is running, it is an easy matter to change the look and feel of an application while it is being used.

One way to do this is through extensive use of hidden fields that can be displayed based on the user's interaction with the application. There are a number of ways to use hidden fields and controls so that the application appears to change with the user's actions. A few of the things you might do are described in the following section.

CREATING NEW FORMS DURING RUN TIME

For example, consider a user who may need more than just a single form of information. Using the DDE techniques discussed in Chapter 7, it is possible to create and display a new form on the fly, while the application is running. Part of the following code was shown as an example of the use of the Show method in Chapter 4. This expands the concept to actually send data to each of the newly created form instances:

```
Sub GoButton_Click ()
For i = 1 To GBLRCNT
  F(i).Caption = Trim$("RAND" + Trim$(Str$(i)))
  F(i).LinkTopic = F(i).Caption
  F(i).Text9.Text = i
  F(i).Text6.Text = GBLPROB
  F(i).Show        ' Load and display new instance

  ' Move and color new instance
  F(i).Move Left + (i * 400) + (Width \ 10), Top + (i * 400) + (Height \ 10)
  ' F.BackColor = RGB(Rnd * 256, Rnd * 256, Rnd * 256)
  DoEvents
Next i
Timer1.Enabled = False
Timer1.Interval = 100
Timer1.Enabled = True
GoButton.Caption = "Pause"
End Sub
```

This example subroutine creates new instances of the form **F(n)**, based on the value that the user enters into a text box. Since this is, in effect, an array of forms, you do have to declare the maximum number of forms to be available, using a statement such as this:

```
Global F(100) As New RAND
```

However, the new forms aren't loaded into memory and displayed until you do **F(i).Show.** You perform this action only if the user has filled up all of the data input fields (normally text boxes), or has used all of the controls on the existing form. You simply check their Value or Text properties to see if they have been modified, then use that as a conditional test to determine whether to load the new form.

The result of this example is shown in Figures 12.3a and b. The first form asks for data input from the user on the number of forms to be created, and then sends that information to the subroutine creating the new forms. Once the forms are created, they each begin generating and displaying random numbers.

Consider combining the preceding techniques to develop an application that automatically expands its available data input facilities as the user requires. If the user runs out of space on one form, the next is loaded and given the focus so that the user can continue the task without interruption.

AN ADAPTABLE USER INTERFACE

Last, the ability to show and hide different forms and controls on the user interface offers great potential to design a so-called *intelligent user interface*. One of the goals of an intelligent user interface is to make the

▐▐▐▐▐▐**Figure 12.3a** The data input form.

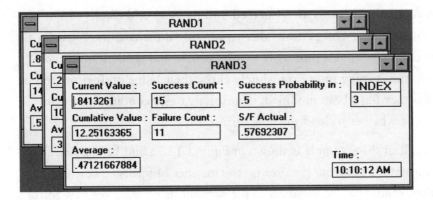

■■■■■■■■**Figure 12.3b** The multiple random number generator form.

application more accessible to the user by *learning* how a particular user works, and changing its characteristics to better accommodate that user.

The event-driven nature of Visual Basic, combined with the ability to show and hide controls, makes this easy to do, although it does require a great deal of thought on your part. One simple example of this technique is shown in the following. This example lets a user select a button to choose a Beginner, Intermediate, or Advanced mode, which determines which user interface the application presents to the user.

The three different user interfaces appear in Figures 12.4a, b, and c. The Beginner mode shows only those controls and fields necessary to accomplish basic tasks. The Intermediate mode adds more controls that let the user do more tasks with the application, while the Advanced mode provides still more features and functions, enabling the user to take the application to its fullest potential.

This sample application is a tracking mechanism for customer calls into a company's hot-line system. The hot-line staffers work at the Beginner level, and see only the parts of the application related to collecting customer information. The engineering department sees all of the information that the hot-line staffers do, as well as additional information related to

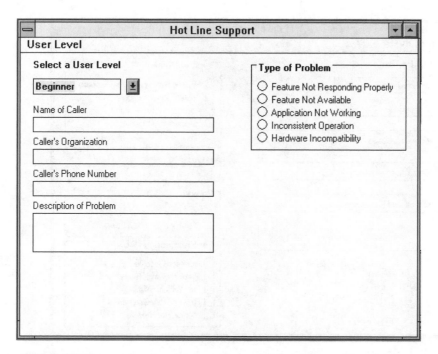

Figure 12.4a Example of a Beginner user interface.

problem priority, problem assignment, and problem status. Company management sees all of this information, and also has the ability to generate several different types of statistics on hot-line calls and problem priorities.

In this kind of application, the different user levels might be given different names, such as Support, Engineering, and Management. They might also be given a password, through the use of a modal dialog box, in order to gain access to each of the different levels.

Choosing the mode is done from a combo box, so the user need only choose the appropriate selection from those already provided. Alternatively, you can consider using a menu selection on a pull-down menu, or a set of command buttons, or even check boxes. The combo box or the menu selection are the better alternatives, however, since users can see all of the options at once and determine which is most appropriate for

━━━━━━━**Figures 12.4b** Example of an Intermediate user interface.

their skill level. While three command buttons can also serve the same purpose, such buttons are not normally used to select options, and they also take up a great deal of display space for a single purpose.

The code to implement the different user interfaces examines the user selections, and shows or hides controls based on the value of the selection. First, the combo box selections can be added at the time the form is loaded, where UserLevel is the Name property of the combo box. All of the controls that have to be hidden at the basic level of the application should also be hidden at this time. They can, of course, be hidden at application design time by setting the Visible property to False as the default, but this may interfere with subsequent users of the application, as described in the following.

```
Sub Form_Load ()
UserLevel.AddItem "Beginner"
```

▆▆▆▆▆▆▆**Figures 12.4c** Example of an Advanced user interface.

```
UserLevel.AddItem "Intermediate"
UserLevel.AddItem "Advanced"

Statistics.Visible = False
Assigned.Visible = False
AssignedName.Visible = False
Priority.Visible = False
Engineering.Visible = False
End Sub
```

In the UserLevel combo box itself, the user's selection will appear as the box's Text property. The Text property should start out either by being labeled with a user prompt, such as "Choose a User Level," or should default to one of the three available levels. You should default to a user level and include the user prompt as a Label control above the combo box.

Prompt the user in the box only if you don't have room on the form for the Label control.

The combo box utilizes a Change event that will perform actions in the application as the user chooses different alternatives. In this case, we use the Change event to make controls visible as users work their way up the different user levels, or to hide them as the users go back down the user level hierarchy. The event code only modifies the Visible property on each of the controls affected:

```
Sub UserLevel_Change ()
  Call Adapt
  If UserLevel.Text = "Beginner" Then
    Statistics.Visible = False
    Assigned.Visible = False
    AssignedName.Visible = False
    Priority.Visible = False
    Engineering.Visible = False
  ElseIf UserLevel.Text = "Intermediate" Then
    Statistics.Visible = False
    Assigned.Visible = True
    AssignedName.Visible = True
    Priority.Visible = True
    Engineering.Visible = True
  ElseIf UserLevel.Text = "Expert" Then
    Statistics.Visible = True
    Assigned.Visible = True
    AssignedName.Visible = True
    Priority.Visible = True
    Engineering.Visible = True
  End If
End Sub
```

When first used, your application should normally default to the Beginner level, since defaulting to a higher level initially may confuse or discourage novice users. After the first use, however, your application should default to the level at which it was last used. In other words, users should be able to return to the application in the same state in which they left it. This means that your application has to record the user level upon closing, and save that level to an initialization file. It can then be checked and loaded the next time your application is opened.

Note that you can achieve the same effect via a menu selection. I've added a User Level menu item to the menu bar that lets you accomplish the same thing as with the combo box. This may be preferable on applications where you need the space on the form for additional controls, or when you've established an application paradigm that depends heavily on menu selections.

You can even do this on individual menu selections, using the Visible property available in the Menu Design window. Based on user selection, you can show or hide menu items on pull-down menus. Several commercial applications offer a Short Menus or Long Menus option, giving the user control over just which menu features are available in using the application.

TOWARD AN INTELLIGENT USER INTERFACE

However, you need not require the user to choose a particular mode of operation. You can record a user's interactions with controls early on in the application, then use this information to determine how to present operations later on. For a user that seems to be using only the very simplest features in an application, you can reduce the complexities that the user has to deal with. For other users that appear to be taking full advantage of available features, you can make still more sophisticated features appear.

Intelligent user interfaces such as these are also good for translating a problem into terms that are understandable by the typical user. This enables the application to, in effect, say to the user, "you describe to me how you want to tackle this problem in your own terms; I'll worry about how to make it happen." This requires a great deal of planning on your part, but Visual Basic has the tools to let you pull it off.

WHERE TO GO FROM HERE

I hope that this book gives you some insight into how a computer user looks at a graphical user interface, and some of the information display characteristics that are important to the user's easy and correct perception of your applications.

Further, I hope it demonstrates how Visual Basic can support many of the principles of user interface design in a number of different ways:

1. Through its many predefined controls with properties that can be changed while you're designing the application, as well as when the user is interacting with it

2. Through the predefined controls, properties, and events that let you rapidly prototype a graphical user interface, show it to prospective users, receive feedback, and iteratively complete the application with the participation of those who will be making use of it

3. Through its Dynamic Data Exchange facilities that enable applications to exchange data with existing Windows applications, especially those sold commercially in the mass market, such as Word, Excel, and dBASE

4. Through the ability to call upon code written in other programming languages, to take advantage of existing programs or to improve the responsiveness of your applications

5. Through the ability to extend the development environment, to add additional controls that give you more options in designing the user interface, or that give you the tools needed to create specialized types of applications

6. Through the features that help you to create applications that make use of database, multimedia, and animation, leaving your imagination as the only limitation in designing highly capable applications with dynamite user interfaces

There are many more ways to take advantage of user-centered application design with Visual Basic than I've discussed in this book. However, this gives you ideas of how to analyze a problem from the user's point of view, and how to design a graphical user interface, as well as the operations underneath it, that make it more friendly from the user's point of view.

The strength of Visual Basic is that it encourages you to design an application from the user's point of view. You know what the application looks like before you worry about how it operates. You can also solicit user participation in this process, since the design process in Visual Basic lets both you and the users see the application in different stages of development. These are strengths that you should take advantage of as you create increasingly sophisticated applications with Visual Basic.

INDEX

A

About box, Help file, 133
Access, 306
Access keys, 121
ActiveControl property, 114
ActiveForm property, 114
Alias, Help file, 140
Animation, 300–302
Applications
    assembling, 28–36
    exchanging data across, 191–210
    user-centered, 7–19
Applications Programming Interface
  (API), 160–61, 254
    and DLLs, 228
    leveraging software with, 246
    and 32-bit applications, 290–94
ASCII character set, 286–88, 290, 292,
  294
ASCII data operations, 303–7

B

BackColor, 95–96
Baggage, 141
Basic module (.BAS) files, 205
Bitmaps, 138–40
Black boxes, 243
Bold-faced font, 74

C

Borland C++, see C language
Borland Pascal, see Pascal
Build tags, 140
Business process reengineering, 187–89

C

Call statement, 226–27
Case-sensitivity, 292
CD-ROM players, 303
Champy, James, 187
Characters, 286–88
Check boxes, 19–20, 116
    3D, 124
CheckLink function, 205
C language
    custom controls in, 262–64, 273, 277
    developing underling codes in, 217,
      218, 221–22, 225, 229
Class, definition of, 3
Client/server computing, 303–4
Codes
    in traditional development cycle, 40
    placement of, 30–31
Colors, 56, 94–98
Command buttons, 19, 116
Common User Access (CUA), 58–59,
  65–66
Component reuse, 245
Config, 140